NICHOLAS LEZARD is an English journalist and literary critic. Lezard has a weekly column, 'Down and Out', in the *New Statesman*. His book *The Nolympics: One Man's Struggle Against Sporting Hysteria* was published in 2012 by Penguin Books. Lezard's first volume of memoirs, *Bitter Experience Has Taught Me*, was published in 2013.

IT GETS WORSE

NICHOLAS LEZARD

SALT

CROMER

PUBLISHED BY SALT PUBLISHING 2019

2 4 6 8 10 9 7 5 3 1

First published in Great Britain in 2019 by
Salt Publishing Ltd
12 Norwich Road, Cromer N R27 0A X United Kingdom

www.saltpublishing.com

Salt Publishing Limited Reg. No. 5293401

A CIP catalogue record for this book is available from the British Library

ISBN 978 1 78463 210 6 (Paperback edition)
ISBN 978 1 78463 211 3 (Electronic edition)

Typeset in Neacademia by Salt Publishing

Printed and bound in Great Britain by Clays Ltd, Elcograf S.p.A

For L. S.

INTRODUCTION

T HIS IS THE second volume of columns culled from my
weekly "Down and Out" column in the *New Statesman*,
which has now, incredibly, been running for ten years or so.
The first volume, *Bitter Experience Has Taught Me* (published
by Faber and Faber; I'm pretty sure you can find a copy somewhere), told the weekly adventures of a dissolute, or let us say
under-disciplined, middle-aged man of slender means who
had been kicked out of the family home by his wife. This man
drinks far more than the recommended guidelines; he spends
somewhere between 110 and 120% of what he earns, however
much he earns; he falls in love; he gets his heart broken; he is
devoted to his children and his friends; he gets into all sorts
of scrapes, some of which, like the case of Sherlock Holmes's
Giant Rat of Sumatra, the world is still not yet prepared
for. This is more or less all you have to know, and this book
more or less picks up where the last one ended, on a note of
cautious hope.

In one sense, the title of this book is slightly dishonest:
for a large part of it, things got better, rather than worse.
This was thanks to a brief period of domestic happiness, five
or six years ago, in which my then-girlfriend moved in with
me. I was worried at first that I had become feral, or like
one of those wild children who used to get discovered in
German forests and who never really managed to fit in with
civilisation. But it turned out fine, for a while; and only when

the woman concerned got a job in another country did this period of happiness end. (Readers may be slightly confused at the off-and-on-again status of the relationship. Believe me, it was even more confusing at this end.) Since then, things have got *much* worse, and if there are subsequent volumes in this series – and there's enough material for two or three more, at least – you'll be able to see just how bad things can get. (At the moment, I am technically homeless.)

There's another aspect to this book: the pieces collected here were written in gentler times. There are contemporary references which may remind you of that. But there are rumblings, which many noticed at the time, of a new, more disgusting age to emerge: the rise of Johnson (Alexander de Pfeffel) and Farage (Nigel); and although it needed no great clairvoyance to see that they were destined to poison public life, I don't think even I could tell just how much destruction they would cause. Also, I was conscious that my brief was not to take weekly snapshots of the political life of the country: the rest of the magazine did that very well; is indeed its chief *raison d'être*.

Which leads me to thank the editor of that magazine, Jason Cowley, who invited me to start the column and who still, as I write these words, allows it to continue. Without him, nothing. (Every so often I wonder whether my writing a column about – as it says on the cover – love, loss and penury actually contributes to my chaotic existence or is simply a reflection of it. However, that is the kind of existential question which is more or less meaningless whenever I contemplate my bank balance.)

Before I get onto individuals, I'd like to thank, after my editors (as well as Mr Cowley, there is Kate Mossman, to whom I file every week, and who is as wonderful at her job as anyone I have ever met, and who only very rarely asks me to rewrite anything. When she does ask, she's always right), I'd like to bow to my readers, the vast majority of whom seem to be fine, upstanding, decent and sympathetic people. Without the editor, nothing; but also, without the reader, nothing, and I hope they don't mind my cheek in asking them to pay a second time for what they have already read – although I have added quite a few footnotes, taken out some of the more obscure references and verbal tics and infelicities (including about three thousand instances where I used the word "anyway" to begin a paragraph), and generally gone through the pieces in order to give some kind of impression of narrative coherence.

That said, I think this book is best read in small doses. A weekly column of 850 words or so has a different rhythm to two and a half pages in a longer narrative (cf. Karl Ove Knaussgard. Some readers may think my columns deal in banalities, so imagine how cross they'd be if I wrote 850 words each week on eating breakfast cereal or something. Incidentally, my standard joke about Knaussgaard when people ask me what I think about him is that I despise writers who mine their personal lives for financial gain), and I worry that if you read too much of it in one go you might feel something like a kind of literary seasickness. The ideal place for it is the bog, actually. There is no shame in this. Ten minutes at a stretch and then wait until tomorrow. Also, the bedside table, and if it slips from your fingers as you pass into sleep then I will consider at least some of my job to have been done properly.

Thanks are first due to Jen and Chris Hamilton-Emery, the good people at Salt Publishing who decided to take on this venture; and Grizelda Grizlingham, the cartoonist who I insisted draw the cover both to this and the previous book, because she gets me. I'd also like to thank my retired agent, Derek Johns, who said "yeah, that's fair enough, I suppose" when I told him how much Salt were paying me. As for the friends who helped, many of them are mentioned by name here, but of course there are some people who do not like to be mentioned in the column, for reasons which I do not understand but I do respect. Chief among the cast of characters I'd like to thank, whether they've been named or not, or never even appeared, is my Estranged Wife, Siân (yes, we are still married, at time of going to press, which is weird, I know, after twelve years of separation, but there you have it: we don't like lawyers), who has done such a good job of doing the heavy lifting when it comes to raising our astonishingly cool and clever children. Other people who have kept my heart and soul above the waterline include (in not entirely, but partly, arbitrary order) Toby Poynder, Kevin Jackson, Louise and Paul Ramsay, John Moore, Hannah Griffiths, Will Self, James Spence, Anna Prygodzicz, Saga Lynd, Alison Alexanian, Katie Ray, Louisa Young, Alison Finch, Katy Evans-Bush, Maggie Ryan, Miriam Holland, Laurie Penny (in whose flat I am now writing these words), Linda Grant, Alba Arikha, Deborah Ronane, Howard Jacobson, Richard Coles, Linda Lawton and Stephen Israel. If I've forgotten anyone, forgive an ageing brain, buy the book, waggle it angrily in my face, and I will sign it, and, if you have a plausible case and I am in funds, reimburse you.

NICHOLAS LEZARD
September 2019

IT GETS WORSE

A RK! WE HAVE a new resident at the Hovel. A fledgling seagull who has presumably fallen out of the nest
on the roof. I first find her cowering behind dead pot plant
number 7 on the terrace while having a relaxing fag and listening to the Archers. (I am the one with the fag and the stupid
radio programme, not the seagull.) Obviously she has read
last fortnight's column and knows that I have a dim view of
seagulls who venture too far inland.

Laurie, of course, is delighted. "Can we keep her can
we keep her can we keep her please please please?" (She has
decided early on that the seagull is an oppressed wimmin.
Who am I to say otherwise? I dozed all the way through my
seagull-sexing classes at school, and I have no intention of
checking her out to make sure.) She has decided to call her
"Riot Gull", which I have to admit is rather good.

"No," I say, "we can't keep her."

"Pleeeeeease!"

This exchange is repeated a few times until I give in. You
know the drill. "OK, but you have to feed her and clean up
after her, ok?" I know, from previous experience with children
and their pets, who's going to be doing the feeding and cleaning up. At first Riot Gull's parents, perhaps like Billie Piper's
when she married Chris Evans, disapproved of the arrange-
ment and speculated darkly on my fitness as a provider and the
age gap between us. Their disapproval mainly involved trying

to peck my eyes out and shitting all over the place, but I am used to the ways of in-laws and we have now reached a fairly easy *détente*. After all, I am providing free board and lodging. Laurie, who I suspect believes in the essential goodness of the entire animal kingdom, thinks Riot Gull eats grapes. She does not. She eats bread and regurgitated fish. I didn't think this was going to be part of the plan, regurgitating fish to an unfortunate seabird at my time of life. I wanted a pet; but not like this.

The vexing thing is that my gentler side has been exposed. To think that only the day before I was thinking of getting my dad's air rifle out of storage and blasting away at these pesky fowl until they got the message and moved to Thanet. Now the whole bird world knows me as a soft touch. My friend H——— was recently delegated by her flatmates, presumably because she's the comeliest, to ask the downstairs neighbour if they could use his garden this summer. He said that would be fine if she gave him a blow-job. I got hugely indignant about this for about half an hour until it occurred to me that maybe this neighbour was saying "no" in a way which didn't make him out to be simply mean-spirited (and which also carried the – admittedly faint – chance of getting a blow-job). I, however, cannot refuse to be hospitable. I don't seem to have it in me.

And so the Hovel's terrace fills up with seagull crap. As my children observe when they stay, it looks like a scoop of chocolate ice cream has been put on top of a larger scoop of vanilla ice cream and then been allowed to melt; thus putting me off both chocolate and vanilla ice cream for the rest of the summer.

She has a penetrating voice, too, does Riot Gull. You can hear it from the other side of the building. "ARK!" It means

"I'm hungry," obviously, but sometimes I think it means "I'm bored." Meanwhile her parents are swanning off, or I suppose that should be seagulling off, to various parties and barbecues while I wonder whether the next rain shower will be strong enough to sluice the poo away.

Meanwhile, I am besieged by advice, except from where I want it. The RSPB passes me on to the RSPCA. The RSPCA says all its lines are busy, but if I have a fledgling bird knocking about the place, press 1. It is, ominously, their only option. Pressing 1 results in my being told to leave the bird alone, her parents will provide. Will they hell.

So what's in it for me? I think of Kehaar, the black-headed gull who somewhat improbably helps the rabbits in *Watership Down*. Will Riot Gull and I forge a lifetime bond, resulting in her being my loyal protector, following me around like one of Philip Pullman's daemons? Or is she just going to carry on going "ARK!", eating me out of Hovel and home, and crapping everywhere? When, and come to think of it how, is she ever going to fly the nest?

※

So, there I am, strolling towards Marble Arch station from the North, passing the swanky Indian restaurant on Old Quebec Street and thinking that thanks to some extra work I've got lately, I might be able to pay off a couple of debts and still have enough left over for a mediocre Chinese meal, when I am accosted by a young Indian-looking man wearing a suit.

"Excuse me," he says, "but you have a very lucky face."

"Why, thank you," I say. (And I think: he wouldn't have said that if he'd seen me last week.)

He then informs me he's a student, and that he would just like to try something out on me. Well, I have a few minutes to spare, the weather is pleasant, this young man himself has a bright, guileless face, so why not? He then says:

"You will have three pieces of good fortune in the next few days." Well, that's always nice to hear, isn't it?

"Now, please let me try this. I am a student. Can you think of a number between one and five and the name of your favourite flower?" Feeling sunnily doltish, I opt internally for three and the rose, respectively. Is it corny of me to choose the rose? I also like the lupin, the foxglove, the forget-me-not, *Myosotis palustris*, and the one that looks like an orange bog brush and whose name I always forget; but every time I smell a rose I am transported back to my earliest memories, so the rose it is. Its furled petals also remind me of the labia, or is it the other way round? Anyway, the student, who has already asked me my name and what I do and written it down, scribbles something on a scrap of paper, folds it up tightly and then blows on it, hands it to me, asks me to blow on it, touch my forehead with it, then the back of my neck, or some such rigmarole, and then open it. Well, would you credit it, there in his spindly handwriting is the numeral 3 and the word "ROSE".

"Very impressive," I say.

At this point he asks me for some money, and I think, well, that's not a bad trick, and well worth a quid, so I put my hand in my pocket. He seems to know what I'm doing and shakes his head. "People always give paper money," he says.

Why, at this point, even though my mood suddenly darkens, because I know that the smallest denomination note I have in my wallet is a tenner, which I can ill afford to give away, do I not tell him to sod off and carry on my way? There is a salt-grain of menace, with reproach behind in it, in his bearing, but looking back at this incident I am baffled at the fact that I do, in fact, hand him over the tenner, which he invites me to place on the opened pages of his pocket-book.

He then offers me a deal: if he guesses the name of my wife, I will hand him a purple note, and if he doesn't, I get my tenner back.

"Word of a gentleman?" he asks. Of course, I say. He then goes through the same rigmarole with the paper, although this time I notice that he asks me her name before handing it over to me. The order of events I described earlier is obviously not as I recall it. Now, I am on safeish ground here, I think. My wife is technically but not de facto my wife; and, moreover, she has a name that foreigners and many English have difficulty with, as indeed my student does, who thinks I'm making it up. He asks me how to spell it. More business with the paper, and when I unfold it, there is my wife's name in uncertain lettering. The whole business, which I know you could have told me by the time I'd been told I had a lucky face, was a scam.

And yet I still do not demand my tenner back. I wag my finger at him and say he's not going to be getting any purple note, and he protests, invoking our gentleman's agreement. But I turn and go, and decide that the lost tenner is a stiff penalty for my own gullibility, a lesson learned: that there is no one so easily fooled as the person who considers himself unfoolable. Reader: take that lesson away with you.

As I approach the station, I see two idling policemen. "There's a conman operating just up there," I say, and describe him, and off they go. They won't catch him, but the sight of them might make him sweat.

Funnily enough, over the next couple of days I do, in fact, receive three pieces of good news.

※

I am driving down to Wiltshire on a Wednesday morning, listening to Radio 3, and for some reason the weather forecast presenter Siân Lloyd is invited to choose a piece of music and say why she likes it. She chooses Handel's "The Arrival of the Queen of Sheba", and the general drift of her appraisal is that it never fails to cheer her up. "All the blues just melt away," she said. Normally I would at this point snap the radio off or change channels but I think: well, let's see. I could do with some cheering up.

It doesn't work. Ms Lloyd must either have successfully banished unhappiness from her recall, or have an unusually sunny disposition. But then again, how was she to know that the reason one of her audience was at that moment failing to be cheered up by Handel was that he was driving to a friend's funeral? A couple of days later on, it occurred to me that as that person was a musician, and quite a few of the people driving to Wiltshire to remember him were also musicians, some of them may well have been listening to the same programme, and being not cheered up by it too.

Robert never expressed an opinion about Handel to me – but I have a feeling he would have considered him beneath even his contempt. As a rule, he didn't like German composers at all, although I once sprung a recording of a Haydn piano sonata (Hob. XVI no. 50, in case you're interested), and he admitted to liking it. The novelist David Flusfeder once wrote a piece for this very magazine in which he got Robert to explain why Mozart wasn't necessarily the sublime genius he is generally assumed to be. ("The sweet sound of piddling on flannel", 26 July 2010.) Robert, a musician of extraordinary gifts – he was given a half-fellowship at Oxford at the age of 17 – made a good case against Mozart, but the comment of his that struck me on rereading the piece was that Mozart's structures "appeal to people who like their lives to be highly ordered". It made me smile then, and I smile again now.

Robert did not like his life to be highly ordered. Most 16-year-olds at Oxford, I would imagine, would be pretty intimidated and knuckle under; but Robert was given his half-fellowship in spite of never getting up before noon, pissing in the sink so often it had to be replaced, and then pissing out of the window thereafter. He then spent the rest of his life being brilliant at music and scandalising people. He never quite managed to scandalise me; I existed on the same continuum, albeit far, far behind; Robert Lite. I've never had the balls not to care tuppence about what people think about me. I certainly envied him his success with women, for despite his being an astoundingly heavy drinker who would often have more than one cigarette on the go at a time, and strikingly lax in his personal hygiene, women were drawn to him. I remember a dinner party where most of the guests were women, and conversation had drifted towards him, as it often did. "Hang on," I said, as I realised where the talk was converging. "Hands up everyone round this table who's slept with Robert." All the women bar two put up their hands. One of them was my wife; and the other one came up to me later and said she would have put her hand up, but her husband was sitting next to her. I don't think my wife slept with him because he kept asking her, usually in front of me, to do so; it got to the point where if he didn't, I'd feel faintly insulted, or wonder whether he was ill.

And he did get ill; very ill, first with an alcohol-induced coma which would have killed or unbrained most people, and which left him unable to walk except very slowly, with two sticks; and then with throat cancer which obliged surgeons to remove his jaw and tongue. After the former but before the latter, when he became more reclusive, he was one of the most assiduous of my friends in cheering me up, rather better than Handel has ever managed, after my marriage went phut; he never even pressed me for the £150 I lost to him at backgammon one day.

I learned at the funeral that to be beaten soundly by Robert at backgammon was a rare distinction. Last night, sleepless, I felt slightly embarrassed by my tears on the day; for there were others who knew him better and for longer than I who were keeping it together. (Although I've never seen so many crying people in a church at one time.) The portrait I have drawn may make some of you wonder what on earth there was to like about this man. I assure you there was plenty. And to love.

⁂

An email from one of the editors at the *New Statesman*. (I imagine them, with ultimate power over my life and fate, as grave and puissant as the High Council of the Time Lords in *Doctor Who*.) Craig Raine has asked for my email address, and the editor, seeing this as an innocent request, has passed it on. This discomforts me, for I infer the intent behind the request: Raine has noticed that in a recent piece for the *Guardian*, I have described his novel/poem *History: the Home Movie* as "ballsaching". (I so rarely get the chance to be mean about books that when the most fleeting opportunity to do so arises, I let rip.) There is nothing like being stood up to to make the bully nervous, and I am duly unnerved. I reply to Raine with a kind of grovel, adding the text of my original review (which is much less nasty). Raine graciously replies that he perfectly understands the need to "enliven" one's journalism. I then say that as I am going to Oxford for the weekend with the Significant Other (hereinafter referred to as the Divine H——, or the Best Girlfriend Ever), why don't we meet up for a drink? He can have one free hit, but not the face, ha ha.

I must say, I am looking forward to seeing Oxford again. I used to go there at least once a term decades ago, from 1980 to 1983, visiting my friends Andy and Matthew and P-J and Nick and others at Balliol; as splendid a bunch of people as you could hope to meet, fine upstanding lefties the lot of them, and connoisseurs of tea, Twiglets, beer and speed, and indulgent to an impecunious young pup like me. I went there so often and so regularly that I was plausibly co-opted into the Balliol pool team when one of its players was unable to make his match. Unfortunately, as I never drew a sober breath there except on the walk from the train station to the college bar, my memories of the place, while gilded with unalloyed pleasure, are hazy in the extreme, and they need to be resubstantiated.

"What's that college?" I ask the Divine H——. "Balliol," she replies. (Later, when approaching the place from another angle, I ask "and what's that college?" "Balliol, you fool." "Oh, ah.")

It is beginning to snow, which makes us both rather excited. We begin to hope strongly that it snows hard enough for our return to London to be delayed indefinitely; we are staying in guests rooms in Christ Church ("what an adorable little court," I say on seeing Tom Quad, in order to tease her), in a room with a balcony overlooking the Meadows, and it has become very clear that we are going to have a terrific time.

But the impending encounter with Craig Raine is beginning to weigh on me. We go into Blackwell's (which seems to have moved to the other side of the street since my day) and I go to the poetry section to buy Geoffrey Hill's *A Treatise of Civil Power* and *Clavics*. The latter was recently described by Lachlan Mackinnon as "sheerest twaddle", which I consider – thinking what I think about Mackinnon – the highest recommendation. I then recall a conversation at a *TLS* party when, in conversation with Raine and the poet Hugo Williams, I brought up Hill's name, and there was a sharp intake of breath, as if I had said a Bad Word. I wonder, mischievously, if I should leave the books out on the table in the pub.

We are meeting at the King's Arms. On the outside, it looks like an ordinarily pleasant provincial Georgian hotel; inside, it is paradise, like so many Oxford pubs. A curved wooden settle at the back of one of the bars gives us a commanding view, and the Young's London Porter has survived the trip down the M4 and is Heaven, in a pint. We are early, and I nip out for a fag. Should Mr Raine arrive early, I attempt a description. As he is now looming large in my fears, my mind's eye exaggerates him. He is now about six foot tall, with flowing locks and a majestic beard that would, were he unclothed, cover both his nipples. I might as well add that he will be arriving on a green horse with an enormous axe with which he will invite me to behead him, after which he will pick it up, tell me to meet him at his castle in a year, and ride off.

Outside, in the snow, I see a mild-looking gentleman with

a neat, trimmed beard locking up his bike. Ah. I dash in before any damage is done. "Hide the Hill!" I say. "Hide the Hill!"

And then we all have a very affable chat. Strangely enough, though, he is the one to bring Hill up first, after about five minutes.

⁂

An email arrives from the CEO of a magazine which went bust last year, owing me £750. Well, it has been weighing upon me. It is the kind of sum which Boris Johnson* earns every time he writes 0.012 of one of his columns – but then he's 83.3 recurring times a better writer than I am. (This column has taken rather longer to write than usual because of (a) the hard sums I've been having to do and (b) I had to spend a lot of time weeping with pity at how he can survive on the mere £250,000 he earns a year from his opinion pieces alone – £50,000 a year of which he has been obliged to give away to charity, ever since saying, in one of those moments of light-hearted banter which have made him the best-loved politician in the history of the planet, that the former figure was "chicken-feed".)

Anyway, where was I? Oh yes, this matter of £750. As I say, for some people this is loose change. For me, it is hugely significant; and if you have the extremely tight margins of the freelance journalist with three children to help maintain, life-changing. It means, in short, the difference between having to humiliatingly borrow money from friends towards the end of the month, and not.

So every time I thought of this sum, which repeated calls

---

* As the reader will note, I have been enraged and disgusted by this lying, amoral and vicious buffoon for some time.

to the receivers had confirmed was lost for ever, I felt a hollow pain within me, and although the list of creditors sent to me by the Insolvency Practitioners dealing with the case cheered me up a bit – there were people and institutions who were owed both far more than me, and also, touchingly, far less (why did the £7.00 owed to one person affect me so much?) – there remained within me a deep, ineradicable sense of loss, which only extreme fortitude and the knowledge that we cannot take it with us when we die did anything to mitigate.

Still, I thought of it every time I walked past that excellent, unpretentious family owned-and-run Italian restaurant, the Casa Becci on Paddington Street, because they'd stuck an adoring article of mine about them from the magazine in its window. (I once took a lady there and they were so pleased to see me they gave me absolutely heaps of food, which was unfortunate because we were splitting up, for complex reasons, with great sadness, and neither of us felt like eating much.) I had become resigned to this, hoping that one day I too, might be so wealthy as to consider a quarter of a million pounds, let alone one one-thousand-and-thirty-third of a million, as chicken-feed.

Having not quite reached that point, despite my hard work and unflinching devotion to the economic theories and practices of the Coalition government (gosh, isn't it just plain weird that shoving half the country into penury isn't helping the economy? Why won't the economy just see sense?), it came as a pleasant surprise when the said CEO asked for my bank details and then just popped the money in, like that. It is a piece of remarkably good fortune.

The question now arises what to do with this money. I toy briefly with the idea of sending it to Boris Johnson or whatever group of steely-eyed wonks is in charge of his re-election campaign. (As someone recently pointed out, if he loses the mayoral race, he'll go for Prime Minister, and that, I think, would be the greater evil.*) The general rule these days seems to be that only the already wealthy should have money, as giving it to the poor is an affront to the natural order. But in the end I decide that, ok, there's only one thing to do with it, and that's to help plug the sucking chest wound that is my bank account. Which in turn will benefit the estranged wife and children, who very nearly had to forego their annual skiing trip, things were so tight. (It has now been so long since I've had a holiday – you know, a couple of summer weeks in Italy somewhere near a venerable city and a swimming pool – that I actually think I have forgotten how to do it. Still, as I write, whole families in my borough are being kicked out of their homes by the council for the crime of being on benefits, so I really had better not grumble.)

But before I do that, I think I will have a slap-up meal for two at Casa Becci, and I know just whom to invite. This time we will be able to stuff ourselves. There are some stories that have a happy ending, and I really do recommend their calamari, which are among the finest I have ever eaten in my life.

⚜

Mousey is back. Or should that be micey? One steps into the kitchen and sees a little grey flash scuttling guiltily away. Over the chopping board. This distresses me, for in a kitchen where space is so much at a premium that having a microwave

---

* And look where we are now.

would reduce the available surface area by about thirty per cent, the chopping board also serves as a kind of plate. And call me some kind of weirdo clean freak if you want, but I really don't like the idea of eating food that has rested where mice have trod. (If you wonder why I have food out in the first place when there is this wonderful new invention called "the fridge", I suggest you look at my fridge.)

I suppose having mice around the place doesn't automatically qualify a household for Hovel status any more; they're on the increase everywhere. And I like mice elsewhere: on the underground, for instance. (I tell my children they are the stunted descendants of the miniature ponies that were used to haul the first tube trains.) But the Hovel is a place that was made for mice, with its loose floorboards, its crumbs all over the chopping board, its crumbs behind the backs of immovable things, its crumbs everywhere, come to think of it. The children alone are quite capable of covering the entire living room with crumbs when they stay, as if they had pulverised the contents of a tube of Pringles and then wafted it about like the "shake" part of a Shake n' Vac ad, but without the vaccing. I used to compare them to locusts to evoke the level of devastation they can cause simply by sitting down and watching an episode of *Black Books*; but locusts strip things bare, I realised, and so could at least be said to have left things tidier than when they arrived.

I thought that if I turned the top of the washing machine into some kind of chef's station then this would at least keep the food safe from mousey; but then one evening I came into the kitchen and there one was, as bold as brass, having a leisurely stroll over the top of it, during the spin cycle of all things, as if it were on some kind of funfair ride, or about to press its little groin into the corner and give itself a mousey orgasm. (I hear doing this is popular in certain parts of suburbia, and not just among mice.) Now all outside edibles are huddled on top of the fridge, as if flooded out, or besieged.

The first thing I noticed was that this rodent had got me saying things like "bold as brass". I nearly said "without so much as a by-your-leave." When disruptions like this make one's language slip back half a century or more, then you know you're in trouble. The problem is that when language reverts, so does the thinking, and so the only mousetrap I consider aesthetically possible to use is the classic "Little Nipper", whose coy name conceals a very vicious reality: a tightly-coiled spring that can propel the hammer – this being the correct technical term even though it doesn't look like one – with such force that it all but bisects the mouse, and forces a little turd halfway out of its bottom for good measure.

I have no problem with this. Then again, neither does Mousey. One of his forebears got done by the Little Nipper about three years ago, and since then they have set up whatever the mouse equivalent of the DVLA is, whose teaching in its entirety consists of what a mousetrap looks like, and to avoid it. Even if I put mouse cocaine, or "peanut butter" as it is more commonly known, on the catch (technical term: thank you, the internet), they're not interested. Indeed, the only thing the mousetrap has caught recently is my index finger; another resident, I know not who, had placed a trap by the light socket in the living room and when I went to plug a light in without bothering to see if there was a fucking mousetrap by the fucking plug, I brushed against it and – well, it's a miracle they didn't have to amputate. And my children learnt some new swear-words, or combinations thereof, and they thought they'd heard everything.

Which means it's off to the hardware shop to buy the kind of trap that has a very sticky surface and basically glues the mouse into a position where one can be Blofeld to its Bond, gloating over its demise. It is not a situation I relish, having to dispose of a live rather than a dead mouse (see David Mitchell's soapbox rant about this on YouTube; just google David Mitchell soapbox mouse. It's most amusing), so this is the only way I will be able to deal with it. "I look forward to watching you try and get out of zis one." The only snag is that it probably will.

I am wandering around the Hovel, looking for a book. This would be fine if it were a simple matter of finding any old book, just some reading matter in the form of a book to pass the time; but it is not any old book I want, it is a very specific book, i.e. the one I agreed to review last week which I have not yet picked up, and which – because I am old-fashioned like this – I think it would be a good idea to read before passing judgement on it.

Well, where does one hide a leaf? In a forest. (Although why anyone would want to hide a leaf in the first place is beyond me. They are of scant value.) And where does one hide a book? In the Hovel. Despite increasingly frequent clear-outs, the books continue to multiply; indeed, rather as shaving more often is said to increase the vigour and purpose of one's stubble, so hauling off boxes to Oxfam seems to make more of them come through the letterbox. And about twice a week, the postman, whose sad eyes carry a message of eloquent rebuke about them, rings the bell and hands over a heaving sack of the things.

So the book I want nestles under any one of about two dozen tottering Matterhorns of books, and what I will have to do is ring either the publisher, or the newspaper, to send me a replacement copy, and then, shortly after it arrives, I will find the original, usually in plain view, in a place which I could have sworn I'd searched several times already. This is the kind of thing which makes me suspect that books have finally achieved sentience, and can actually hide themselves, snickering quietly like kids playing hide-and-seek, while I thrash around the place in my underpants, going increasingly crazy until I find myself actually calling out for them by name. A Kindle, someone suggests. No: the books would gang up, and eat it.

This, though, is what happens when one is left to one's own devices. There has been an interregnum since Laurie's departure for New York, and during the day I am the Hovel's sole occupant. I am accountable to no one but myself. The key word in the last paragraph, you will have noticed, is "underpants". What is the point, I ask myself, of wearing out a perfectly good pair of trousers when one can saunter freely about the place in one's gunties? (I could, I suppose, take this to its logical conclusion and go around completely in the nip, but I don't put the heating on during the day and there are, after all, neighbours to consider, and one can still get a rather stiff sentence for indecent exposure, even these days.)

I suppose I am, more than four and a half years on from my ejection from the family home, quietly proud that I have not actually got much worse, in terms of orderliness and hygiene. There's a minor but interesting character in Antál Szerb's wonderful novel *Journey by Moonlight* whose study gets so unusably messy that it becomes impossible to tidy, so he simply rents out another room and repeats the process; what happened to me was, essentially, more or less the same. My old study became a nightmare of books and papers; I used to have to walk on books to get to my desk. This is not an exaggeration: and I used to dream about it being cleared out by the wife, and although in the dream I was alarmed at all sorts of guilty secrets being unearthed, I was in the end relieved that something had been done.

Well, that problem has long since resolved itself, and things have never got as bad since; but there is still the matter of my innate reluctance to tidy things up. I am not made for domestic matters. The washing in the machine, if it is of the boring, non-essential sort like sheets and tea-towels, can sit there for almost a week; I just put it through a quick rinse cycle every day so it doesn't get smelly. (How long, I asked on Facebook the other day, can one go on doing this before it becomes clear that one is insane? About three days, was the general consensus.)

Anyway, in a few days' time there will be another inhabitant of the Hovel, keeping Laurie's room warm until she returns. An old friend, as it happens. The only problem is that, by virtue of this, she will not put up with any nonsense. I suppose I am going to have to clean up my act, and start at least pretending to act like a responsible adult. The washing will come out of the machine today, I promise. In the meantime, though, where the hell has that sodding book got to? And, come to think of it, what on earth has happened to my trousers?

Sober, blameless, virtuous even, for I am doing the washing-up – and another glass breaks. Down to four now – which is still acceptable, just. I don't really like having more than two guests in the Hovel at a time, and not only for reasons of space, although that is an important consideration. (I took the *Guardian's* "are you an introvert?" quiz the other day and discovered that I am apparently about as sociable as a paranoid dormouse, which is odd, as I consider myself the life and soul. Yet when was a quiz in a newspaper ever wrong?)

But the main thing is the glasses. By "glasses" I mean, of course, wine glasses. What else are glasses for? Whisky, I suppose; and a wine glass, once rinsed clean, works perfectly well for a fine malt, on the two or three occasions a year I have enough cash to buy a bottle.

There are now few other glasses in the Hovel. There are a couple of pint glasses; you just need these. There are some ancient glasses which are good for holding shots of frozen vodka and not much else, some disgusting artisanish blue wine glasses which I just don't use, on principle, and one remaining highball glass, which is either the last of a set that Razors bought a couple of years ago, or one I nicked off the Duke, I can't remember, which is pretty useful for, well, highballs. Also, it just occurs to me, for the kids.

I think they have given up on the idea of my going down the road to John Lewis and getting some more of these. For a few months they nagged me about this. It would be tedious to repeat the dialogue. I just ignored them, which I have always considered a perfectly good technique, applicable to an enormous number of situations, for making a problem go away. So now they have their lemonade from an assortment of mugs, the solitary highball glass, a Bonne Maman jam jar that has since been pressed into service as a glass – and, of course, wine glasses. How better to teach them familiarity with the shape and heft of a laden glass, so that by the time they're actually old enough to drink wine, they can do so without making fools of themselves?

But there is still the matter of their breaking. Once or twice it's been the kids' fault – but breakages committed by children who are, for instance, doing the washing-up are counted as natural wear and tear, and you don't shout at a child who is doing the washing-up even if he or she breaks every damn glass in the sink, because a child doing the washing-up is a beautiful thing to behold, like a butterfly landing on your arm, and just as easily spooked. I have also learned that shouting at children for breaking things through mere clumsiness doesn't really get anyone anywhere; the thing broken is not restored, the child's co-ordination is not improved, neither is his or her opinion of you as a just and reasonable father, and, of course, it doesn't stop them from doing it again. Could even be said to increase the chances.

It wouldn't be so bad if you could expect some kind of order or pattern in their breaking – say, one every three weeks or so. No, you can go for ages, sloshing the wine around in gay abandon, with impunity. And then, tinkle tinkle tinkle, three go in a week. Four glasses, as I say, is borderline acceptable. What's not so acceptable is that this is down from an all-time high of seven, achieved a couple of months ago when I bought six from the local Majestic to keep my last, lonely, shivering wine glass company. Seven glasses! I felt like I'd joined the 1%.

That was then. The good people at the Sediment wine blog

(motto: "I've Bought It So I'll Drink It") recommend Duralex glasses but for me they are too redolent of schooldays, and people look at you funny when you give them wine in such glasses. Ah, vanity, saith the preacher, all is vanity; and every breakage is another erosion of our foothold in the universe. You tend to take these things personally, like bad omens. I know that things fall apart and the centre cannot hold, I'm not thick, but still, this is getting ridiculous. I know, I know. Delta is greater than zero, or $\Delta > 0$, an equation even more beautiful to my mind than the majestic $e^{i\pi} + 1 = 0$, because it actually tells us something useful: the second law of thermodynamics, which from its innocuous-sounding proposition – that heat cannot pass from a colder to a warmer body – we get entropy, or the idea that everything eventually falls apart in your hands. And not just wine glasses. Regular readers of this column with long memories and for whom time hangs heavy may remember that one of the recurrent problems of my life is my inability to do accounts, send invoices, keep receipts and, er, pay taxes on time. I am not proud of this. It is a problem many writers have but I seem to have it worse than anyone else I know. Even my great friend the Moose, who will do anything, up to and including writing long narrative poems in rhyming couplets in order to put off doing his taxes, keeps his affairs in better order than I do.

It's the tax bit that bugs me the most. I do not like tax-dodgers, believing that tax is the price one pays for living in a civilised society, but when the question arises in conversation, I mumble a bit and then start to pretend to play with my phone or something until the subject is exhausted. For I feel I am not one to point the finger, even though I wouldn't know, even if it was explained to me in words of one syllable, how to set myself up as a business or whatever, to line my pockets, or at least keep them better-lined than otherwise.

But you know how it is. You shudder at the sight of the first brown envelope from HMRC. This is the mistake. For then you shudder even more at the arrival of the next one, for your shudder incorporates the one that the previous brown envelope occasioned. By the time you are on your fifth or sixth brown envelope, you are such a nervous wreck when you catch sight of them that you might well require hospitalisation. And you know that with each brown envelope you are deeper in the shit than you were before. My ex-housemate, the sorely-missed Razors, once offered to open one of them up, after I'd had a stiff drink. He did so, and there was a silence.

"Well?" I asked.

Razors gave a long, low whistle.

"Have another drink," he said, and we never spoke of it again.

A couple of years ago the tax people sent someone round to pick the money up in person, took one look at me, and at the entrance to the Hovel, and realised, correctly, that the repo men were going to have a hard time extracting anything more valuable than the machine I use to earn what we shall loosely call my living.

Then someone at HMRC had a brainwave. "Why not send him his demand in a WHITE envelope? And maybe not put 'HMRC' on the front of it? It's worth a shot." And that's what they did.

What they don't know is that after years of experience, and mysterious, rigorous tuition from a Zen master of an arcane sect at a secret location in Grays, Thurrock, I am now able to intuit with astonishing precision the contents of an envelope simply by looking at it. So I guessed, from its radioactive hum, that there was something iffy within.

And indeed there was: a note, from a debt collection agency, informing me that my repayment offer of [four-figure sum of money] payable weekly ("weekly" in bold; a nice touch, I thought) had been accepted. Well, if someone offered to pay me a four-figure sum every week, I'd accept it too; only no such offer had been made. What had happened was that someone representing the tax man had called and asked for a large sum of money, and I said I could actually pay some of it back now, but I'm busy, can you ring tomorrow around 4? Which they never did. Fair enough – in their shoes, I'd forget to call back too. Again, I can hardly wag the finger.

So for the last few days this letter has been sitting, as attractive as the putrefying rabbit in Polanski's *Repulsion*, on the table in the Hovel, and, like Catherine Deneuve in that film, I have been gradually losing my mind. In the end I decide to call the number given for those who, in their words, have any queries. The first query that springs to mind is: will I be going to an open prison, or the Scrubs?

Those of you who have had experience of debt collection agencies may well be feeling for me at this point. But funnily enough, things seem to have turned out ok. I get put through to the person who made the original assumption about my capacity for repayment; she acts, and treats me, like a human being; I make a somewhat reduced if still crippling offer for repayment; and she accepts it. It turns out to be as simple as that. And in a few months' time I'll be able to look any tax-dodger you care to mention in the eye.

"A big day tomorrow," I say to the Beloved as we stir our cocoa and retire to bed. As she well knows that I have to do a week's work in two days in order to deliver a manuscript in time, she is somewhat surprised when I add, by way of explanation, "eye test."

But I do have an eye test: and they're important, I gather. I tend to skimp on these, counting contact lenses as an expenditure bordering on the frivolous, for they are more a matter of vanity than utility, as I have a pair of perfectly good glasses, and another emergency pair; and I now have to wear reading glasses if I'm wearing lenses, thus defeating the whole object of not wearing glasses in the first place. But the sun has come out, and I want to wear my spiffingly good sunglasses, which cost only a fiver, and are probably for women, but look as though they cost a lot more. The contacts also make my eyes hurt, which is probably bad. (Although having them in is an infallible prophylactic against tears when chopping onions. I pass that tip on gratis.)

I am also mindful of the various other things that are going wrong with my body, all part of the ageing process, whose relentless march I am doing little to prevent, and, touch wood, nothing serious, or at least so far, although I would really like to find out what's going on with my hands, and anyway the old lenses are beginning to bug me, so off I go, having negotiated a lunchtime appointment.

I am met at Reception by a young woman whom I would place roughly in her mid-twenties, and of what seems to be, on casual inspection, astonishing pulchritude. And she also speaks with what sounds very much like a Russian accent, which is, for various reasons upon which I need not elaborate, one of the world's sexiest. Oh dear, I thought, shame on you,

Specsavers, for reserving your eye candy for the reception of your clients. I have been having my eyes tested since before the Beatles broke up, and she does not fit the mould of Eye Inspector I have become accustomed to.

But she is not eye candy. She is, in fact, as it turns out, my Eye Inspector. This alarms me slightly, and not just because I now recall her rather stern manner when I gave her overly careless answers to the questions of whether I drove, and which doctor I was registered with. For an eye examination is one of the more intimate non-invasive encounters one can have with a professional dedicated to your health. One is leant into; one's eyes are probed deeply by another's; it is all about eye contact. Or, to put it another way, as William Empson's lines from "Courage Means Running" have it: "It is the two/ Most exquisite surfaces of knowledge/Can get clap (the other is the eye)." The examination proceeds. With her face close enough for me to feel her breath on my neck, she passes the little lorgnette over and then away from the trial frames. "Is better vid . . . or vidout?" "Vid," I say, in a strangled voice. Her clipboard presses into my thigh. I cross my legs like a terrified debutante.

This goes on for an hour and a half – there is a lot of ground to make up. Because of my insouciant lens habits, the exquisite surfaces of knowledge that are my eyeballs are all scratched up. "You hef been very naughty," she says. Oh Christ, I murmur to myself, think of my Beloved, and change the subject. "How long does it take to train as an, er, ophthal-molmolmologist?" I ask suavely. "I wish. I am an optometrist. If I was an ophthalmologist I would be performing surgery on eyes and cutting them open." Even this, frighteningly, is not quite as much of a cock-crinkler as it might look on the page.

"And four years." Then she tries to invert my eyelid, but that, I decide, is going Too Far. "Normally I'm quite brave, ha ha," I say. "No, you're not," she replies.

In the end, feeling like Gawain, I manage to get away without making a huge fool of myself. (Having a girlfriend like the Beloved, whose only fault is a tendency to value the works of Handel over those of Haydn, is a great help, and after this I really should build a shrine to her.)

I mention this all to my friend The Moose, who funnily enough says he too was examined by an improbably beautiful optometrist, at Boot's in Cambridge. How did he cope? I asked. "I invented a seven foot tall, 300 pound boyfriend with a pathologically jealous streak. That just about got me through the final minutes, and stopped me from howling." I was glad to discover that I am not the only one suffering out there.

Anyway, she's Iranian.

❧

So, I've finally done it. I've bought a bottle of l'Oréal Elvive conditioner because it said "age-defying" on the front. My excuse? I thought it was a bottle of l'Oréal Elvive shampoo with "age-defying" on the front. I'm always doing this: mistaking conditioner for shampoo. The bottles, you see, are similar in design. And once you've squirted some conditioner onto your hair and discovered that it's not lathering, it's too late for you to go back to the chemist and exchange the conditioner – one of the great cons of the age, in my experience – for something that actually cleans your hair. Even if your chemist is the wonderful Meacher, Higgins and Thomas, which has been around for 198 years so far. Round the corner from me, along a small stretch of Gloucester Place, are plaques advertising the fact that, at various addresses, lived Elizabeth Barrett Browning, Anthony Trollope, and Wilkie Collins. Did they all live there at the same time, I wonder? And did they all pop in to Meacher, Higgins and Thomas for their laudanum, or maybe to try and exchange a bottle of conditioner for a bottle of the shampoo they'd wanted to buy in the first place? We shall never know. But I like to think they did.

All of which rather obscures, intentionally, from the initial admission: that what I'd wanted was something "age-defying". One of the things men used to do when they saw a beauty product for women advertised on the telly – it's usually for a product made by l'Oréal – with lots of sleekly-animated ping-pong balls wheeling and clustering to the rescue of a magnified human hair, or skin pore, suffering the ravages of neglect or time, is to laugh it, and those gullible enough to believe in such nonsense, to scorn. The implicit suggestion is that men would never fall for it. Oh no. We just want something manly to clean our hair with. We'd do it with bars of soap, or Fairy liquid, or our own urine, if it worked.

And then, as we all know, something happened to men. No one knows why, although I favour some kind of alien invasion, in the manner imagined by John Wyndham in his excellent sci-fi novels, but with only risible consequences. (So far.) Men started "grooming". They started putting "product"on their hair and on their skin. As it happens, I do not groom myself in this way. Women, who already groom themselves like crazy because the patriarchy demands it of them, had only one place to go when affected by this alien menace: they stopped buying soap in bars and started buying it in dispensers, even though they contribute to landfill and are umpteen times the price. What the hell is all that about?

But something, in my case, had to give, and what gave was my robust indifference to shampoo. True, a significant part of my decision about which shampoo to buy still resides in how much it looks like it will stand up on its end without leaking so that you don't have to wait five minutes before the last bits come out of the nozzle; but I have also started looking a bit more carefully at what claims are being made for each bottle.

As it happens, in the Hovel, where two men and two women regularly shower, though not together, there are about twelve bottles of hair things ranged around the bathtub. I shall, for purposes of space, restrict myself to the l'Oréal Elvice products. The nutri-gloss shine shampoo contains, we are told, "the secret to glossy shine". Full Restore, although now mostly full of water, is for "weak, limp, damaged hair". (I bought this one and I think my hair got a bit offended, and then depressed, by the description.) Then there is Colour Protect conditioner, "Caring Conditioner", but that rather suggests that other conditioners are uncaring, does it not? They give your hair a rushed, distracted condition and then piss off, leaving your hair feeling cheap and used.

Then there's the age-defying conditioner, already mentioned, which buys your hair a sports car and gets it a younger girlfriend. Finally, the "Damage Care" shampoo, which was the only one on the rack at the chemist's which looked like it had any common ground at all with the age-defying conditioner. It's got to this point: that I've now started worrying whether my conditioner and my shampoo will get on with each other. (My daughter, marvelling at the array of different kinds of shampoo for different hair types in Waitrose the other day, asked, "don't they make any shampoo for dirty hair?") And is my hair any better? No - but I suspect that's because, paralyzed by choice, I haven't washed it for two days now. I suppose what I should be doing is thanking my lucky stars that I've still got any hair - damaged, weak, old, limp, and grey though it is - to put shampoo on in the first place.

☙

Time, once again, for the annual bacchanalia, that violent and sordid spectacle of excess and debauchery, that powder-keg of social unrest and insurrection that is the Marylebone Summer Fayre. This is my fourth now, since being exiled to this neck of the woods, and I am becoming familiarised as to its ways. Bitter experience has taught me that one has to be prepared for this event, and the best way, once one has dusted off the trusty stab vest, is to come with lots and lots of money.

Regular readers of this column will appreciate this is easier said than done. However, the other day the good people at NatWest decided, in the teeth of a veritable gale of expert economic opinion, to give me a credit card with an unfeasibly high limit. I've managed to live without one for five years, which I'm actually quite proud of, but a perfect storm of underpayment and overspending has contrived to make the new Mastercard a necessity rather than a luxury. As for the final reckoning, I'll cross that bridge when I come to it. It is this healthy and responsible attitude to finance that has made the neo-liberal financial model the success story it is today. (Besides, if the world economy collapses, I'd be looking pretty stupid if I was actually in credit, wouldn't I?)

Anyway, Marylebone Street Fayre. I think that spelling of

"fayre" says it all, no? For a start, anyone using "fayre" as a way of advertising, say, their pub's food, should be sent to a particularly stern re-education camp. (There's a pub off the A3 somewhere which used to have a sign which said "great beer, lousy food", whose candour deserves some kind of award, I think.) "Fare" is bad enough, but it at least is a word. Anyone using "fayre" when they mean "fair" deserves to be sent to a particularly stern re-education camp and then shot anyway, particularly if they are using the word to publicise an event whose roots go all the way back to 2004.

Still, as I said a couple of weeks ago, I love a street party, and also like getting the kids away from their screens (as the wonderful film writer David Thomson has observed, the word "screen" is reverting to its original meaning: not so much something upon which something is displayed, as something which hides), and besides, it's Fathers' Day, so I get to drag them along without them moaning too much.

Now, the great thing about a street party is that it allows people to eat good street food at cheap prices. Sorry: I mean good street food at extortionate prices. Three beefburgers set me back the very best part of fifteen quid, the Pimm's comes in at 6 quid a pop, the amount of Pimm's within barely making the lemonade blush, and there is a stall selling oysters at £2.60 EACH. Even the normal weekend market, whose motto must be, like the Harry Enfield character's catchphrase, "we saw you coming", only has the brass neck to charge £1 for each shucked bivalve. And anything that is actually worth it – the seafood paella stands, for example – have queues which go halfway down the High Street.

My favourite parts, though, are the stalls which do not sell food but reflect the local concerns. So there is a stall which promises to tell you how to recharge your Qi energy (I actually offer the daughter a fiver to go up to them and ask them to recharge her phone, but she assures me that this will not be as amusing as I think), a kabbala tent (saints preserve us) and various right-on stalls advertising good intentions but with nothing for sale anyone with eyesight would want to buy. (Things are not looking good, for instance, for the orphans in Peru, if the jumpers being displayed are anything to go by.) As for the other knick-knacks available for purchase, the phrase that springs to mind is from Tamsin Greig's Fran Katzenjammer in *Black Books*: "I don't half sell an awful lot of *wank*." Then there is "a music stage featuring some of the most exciting up-and-coming acts in the country", which always means a unaccountably unembarrassed singer-songwriter with an acoustic guitar and nothing else you might want, e.g. talent.

All of which would be hilarious. But the day before I discovered that the framing and print shop down the road from me is closing down: the landlord has asked for a shocking rent rise, so the nice Italian guy who listens to Resonance FM and actually knows who the hell I am has got to pack up and go. And so the shittier parts of London get shittier and shittier, and the swanky parts get swankier and swankier, but those who find themselves in the grip of spiritual crisis, or enervated by these developments, can seek solace with the Kabbala or recharge their batteries at the local Qi centre.

༄

Coming up to the fifth anniversary of the eviction from the family home, and I am beginning to wonder whether it is even a good idea to remember the anniversary, let alone mark it. Not of course that there aren't continual reminders of the condition, which start at the moment I wake up and go on until I fall asleep (with occasional further reminders, sometimes surreally twisted, popping up from the id from time to time during the night).

And, of course, not being the kind of father who skips the country and/or refuses to do anything to contribute to the upkeep, spiritual and financial, of his offspring, I pop in to visit them so I can take them to cricket training sessions, deal with the occasional crisis (eg cat fallen out of window) and generally do those things that a freelancer not shackled to an office can do. I remember once, long, long ago, hearing with an appalled thrill the words of the newly-separated Bill Drummond relayed to me via a mutual friend: being divorced meant you still had to do the chores, the difference being that this time around you had absolutely no sex as a reward (as opposed, presumably, to the scant and resentful sex that categorises relationships nearing the very end of their tethers). Wow, I thought, that sounds like the worst of all possible worlds, and resolved, for all the fat lot of good such a resolution eventually made, not to make the same mistake.

As it turned out, Mr Drummond's main mistake, as I interpret the chain of events, was to set up his post-marital home more or less across the road from the family one. This, clearly, was the move of a mug, or at least one more item of evidence that suggests he is a starry-eyed idealist rather than one capable of a clear assessment of where his own best interests might lie. (He has form on this. My friend and I speculated what our own wives might say if, when we got in the front door and were asked how our day was, we'd replied "brilliant, I took that million pounds I earned from that song

and burned it on a Scottish Island as a work of conceptual art."
We doubted, somehow, that they would applaud the gesture.)
To move across the road is simply to beg for exploitation. For
what reasonable father can say no, when duty calls, if only a
few feet of tarmac separate him from it?

Anyway, I made sure I did not fall into this trap by re-
locating about five miles away, or a 40-minute tube journey,
door-to-door. Close enough to be able to get there in a real
emergency, far enough away to say "not my problem" when
something footling turns up, like running out of milk. But
sometimes this distance means that I am asked to stay the
night while the children's mother goes gallivanting off somewhere with whichever moustache-twirling Lothario has her
in his clutches this time. (I jest. Her beau is in fact a man of
great probity, and sincere, if to me puzzling, religious beliefs,
and is – the important thing – Good With The Kids.)

So last Friday I pocketed the toothbrush and set off for
my one-time demesne with instructions to look after the boys
while the eldest daughter celebrated one of her best friends'
17th birthday. This was going to take place in the house over
the road, so it was felt that it might be a good idea if I was
around should some kind of outrage take place. (Not the most
unlikely of events. I am very fond of N——, the friend concerned, but I sleep easier in my bed knowing she is not my
responsibility.)

It's odd, though, going back to the former home. The cat,
who either has a very bad memory or a very good one, still
assumes I have full visiting rights, or at least suspects I know
how to open the tin of Whiskas, so I get a proper welcome
from her; there might be a new kitchen and a new loft con-
version, but the basic layout of the place is unchanged and I

can stumble in the dark down the corridor for a pee without forgetting where the steps are.

But it is not my Home. There being no spare beds in the house, I sleep on the sofa in the living room: to sleep on either side of the vacant marital bed would make me uneasy. It is not a sofa that induces sleep easily, though, and the bedding is perforce rudimentary. So I lie in lonely vigil for my daughter's bacchanalia to end, listening to the whoops and shrieks from over the road. In the end I go over after lunch the next day and find that she and her friend haven't even been to bed yet. She confesses to being a little spaced out. "Welcome to my world," I say.

These are times that try men's souls. And women's, obviously. This week the *New Statesman* is celebrating London but I am finding it hard to fall into line as I am actually beginning to get sick even of the very word "London". If I write "London 2012" here, could the Olympic Branding Police come round to the Hovel and take me off to a nice prison somewhere up North, please? Somewhere without a telly? Seriously, a city which has got large, well-populated sections of it that are accessible only by train or buses with letters as well as numbers on the front has got to be seriously screwed up when it starts bragging about itself as a world contender. I am think-ing, precisely, of Clapham Junction, but I am sure you can nominate your own south London contender, what with only 10% of tube stations even now being south of the river. The Beloved hails from these regions and often mocks me for the anxiety that strikes me the moment I travel across or under the Thames, but even she concedes that there is something wrong about buses with letters on them as well as numbers. But not nearly as wrong as the prerecorded announcements being made at train stations. While dashing to catch a train to Clapham J. the other day, I suddenly heard the voice of London's mayor, Boris Johnson, urging me, as far as I could tell through the haze of my own urgency and nausea, not to take a train during the Olympics. What fresh hell, I murmured to myself, is this? Are we now living in North Korea? I have before, in this very column, borrowed the term "gestapo khazi" from Peter Cook in order to describe this country's push towards stupid authoritarianism, but this new intrusion into our public life, both farcical and sinister, is a New Low. Last week, when I said that an Olympic travel-related fiasco on a grand scale would finish "Jackanapes" Johnson's re-election chances for good, I was, I feared, being a little optimistic; but now I have heard his voice on the platforms, and those murmured "fuck off, Boris"s that raise a little cheer from other commuters, I begin to think that he really might have gone too far. Of course, if there's one thing that Johnson incarnates, it is that toxic mixture of greed and ambition that has done so much to enhance the reputation of the Conservative party in recent years, and – more relevantly – the widening wealth gap visible in this city. This is really beginning to get me down. Go into the centre of town and you risk being run over by some bell-end in a Ferrari who thinks it's fun to do 60mph in town. Go to Shepherd's Bush and you risk being run over by someone in an electric wheelchair who thinks it's fun to do 15mph on a crowded pavement. I jumped over the wealth divide the other day. The Beloved and I were invited to a dinner in Islington, mwah mwah. Actually I do not want to be too rude about this as one of the hosts is an old friend, and his girlfriend, who owns the flat I went to, is delightful, but still there are Things to be said. The first is, well, Islington. Have you seen it lately? I'm old enough to remember when it was run down. This is the kind of thing that can really age one. But that's not the real problem. That would be the venue. Do you get the idea if I say there was a lift from street level to the living room itself? I didn't see this until the end of the evening, and when we went down I suggested we all move to the edges. I mean, only supervillains have private lifts, right? With floors that open to plunge you into a pool of sharks. But I was anxious to escape because one of the guests was one of those people you wish never to see again in your life, but who always shows up. The last time I met this pustule, whom I shall call "Damian", it was at the last dinner party I went to, which was about fifteen years ago. Having endured him at both big and little schools for over a decade I had wearied of him before he started becoming The Person Who Pops Up Every Few Years and Makes You Think You're Living in a Novel Sequence by Anthony Powell. Fate has a nasty sense of humour sometimes. But my big problem, the one that has been keeping me awake for days now, was with the bookshelves. The flat, as tall as the Sistine Chapel, was well-stocked with books. But, as a design statement perhaps, all the spines had been turned to the wall. And when this happens – books as pure decor – we can truly be said to have come to civilisation's end.*

My girlfriend, who didn't know him from a hole in the

---

* I hate dinner parties, but this was the worst ever. What I didn't say at the time that one of the things that made it so was the presence of Toby Young, the bumptious, idiotic right-wing "contrarian". At the time he was busy setting up schools, or "academies", under the impression that he was contributing to the public good.

ground (this is a good quality, and I took great amusement when she was introduced to Dave Gilmour from Pink Floyd and asked him what he did. He had the grace to smile and reply that he was "in the music business". Later on, he revenged himself by eating the last of her cheese. Long story) kept interrupting him with why and how he was wrong when he was talking about music education for school children. She knows a lot about this subject; he thought he did. I have never been Prouder of a human being who was not my own offspring. I cadged a lift off him on the way back and spent the whole journey being rude to him.

⚘

To ——, a non-Oxbridge university in England, with the Daughter, for its open day. To think this was the girl whose first spoken word was "fuck". (She would pick up a book, drop it on the floor, and then say the word. Where on earth did she learn such behaviour?) She has come so far. But a gruelling encounter with a Latin A Level paper has made her change her preferred university course from Classics to Philosophy. Also, because her state school does not teach Latin at A level, she has been obliged to take these lessons at a well-known public school – there's a long-standing connection between the two – she has developed serious misgivings about the products of the private education system. Which pleases me, for even though (or rather, because) I am such a product myself, I have identical misgivings, and consider such a system both the symptom and the cause of the most pressing problems this country faces.

Yet although she is certainly more intelligent than I was at her age, and very possibly more intelligent than I am now, just

41

not as well-read (but, as it happens, even more of a grammar Nazi than I am), her state-school education, excellent though it was, means an Oxbridge place is far from a foregone conclusion, so other universities must be considered. She is mindful, though, of my own outrageous snobbery when it comes to tertiary education, and makes me promise that I will not be sniffy about ——. Well, what can one say? I begin to question these days the value of a university education *tout court*, given the amount of debt young people are saddled with by the end of it, and the rather rotten future that awaits them when they leave it. Can't she just form a band?

Anyway, we turn up at ——, and go to the philosophy display. In a room about the size of an ordinary living room, there are a few display boards up with pictures of various philosophers (Wittgenstein, Descartes, Nietzsche), brief accounts of the lecturers and professors' careers, and so on. It is a warm day, and the town of —— is hilly, and I am unfit, and wearing clothes for colder weather, so am sweating freely. There is a lone lecturer standing in the middle of the room fielding questions from those who care to ask them. They look so young! After a gander at the display, I shove my daughter towards him and suggest she asks some questions about the course. It's not an idle interest – I gave her Daniel Dennett's *Consciousness Explained* a couple of years ago, and wrangling with the mind-body question has kept her awake more nights than it even probably has Daniel Dennett.

The lecturer lists some of the great thinkers they cover. He mentions someone whose name he pronounces "day CAR." Oh Christ, I think, and start to sweat some more. While my circulatory system makes a noise like a kettle coming to the boil, I wonder whether I should Say Something. Eventually

I crack. "Sorry, did you say 'day CAR'?" "Yes," he says, "is the name familiar to you? Do you have vague memories of him?" Okay, gloves off. "I think you'll find it's pronounced 'day CART'." "Oh, do you know how the pronounciation [*sic*] of medieval French?" "Yes I do, as it happens, and anyway he's not medieval, he's at least early modern period, you *berk*." (I don't say the last two words. But perhaps they hang in the air.) Afterwards, I apologize to the Daughter, but she says she, too, was dismayed at his pronunciation, and added that she also knew that "pronounciation" is not a word. We have a thoughtful pub lunch before going to the philosophy lecture – which, as it turns out, is really good, almost thrilling, and makes me wish I was studying the subject myself. (In reply to a later text from her mother, I reply "your question is philosophically meaningless." Philosophy can be fun.)

Later, there is the big room with All The Stands, and we cram our pockets with bumf. As we are about to go, we are beckoned over by a stand which turns out to be the one devoted to students' health and well-being. "Could you take part in a survey?" we're asked. "Just write down the thing you're most worried about when starting university and stick it on that board over there." The Daughter gives that blank look I know so well: it's when she is confronted by idiocy.

I have a look at what's already on the board. "Not fitting in." "Being lonly [*sic*] :(". And many variations thereof. There is some shocking handwriting on display, too. I beckon the Daughter over and invite her to contribute. "I refuse to participate in this tomfoolery," she says quietly. "Well, I know what I was most frightened of when I went to university," I say, so I write "not getting laid" on a Post-it note, and stick it on the board.

The first time you brush your teeth with shaving cream instead of toothpaste, it takes a while for your taste buds to believe their own evidence. You have, after all, albeit without paying due care and attention, squeezed something with roughly the consistency of toothpaste, from something roughly the same size and shape as a tube of toothpaste, that lives on the same side of the sink as the toothpaste, onto the brush. It takes a while, then, for the taste-buds to recognize the inappropriate mouth feel, the unusual, to put it mildly, flavour, and to scream out the message that you are doing something fundamentally at odds with the laws of God and Man.

The second time you do it, you go through the same experience, with the added refinement of feeling like a stupid clot, and "clot" is not the first word that springs to mind. You also start worrying. Is this the mind going? Has it finally started, the descent into senescence? "What a terrible thing to have lost one's mind. Or not to have a mind at all," as Dan Quayle once put it; or, if you prefer, "let me not be mad, not mad, sweet heaven."

I am painfully conscious of my age these days – I tend, what with one thing and another, to be surrounded by the nimble in body and mind, and while the general effect is rejuvenating there is no gainsaying the terrible depredations of age, before you even consider the damage I inflict upon my own grey matter due to my louche and intemperate habits.

So I went down for a late breakfast in pensive mood. (What, you may ask, was I doing going down for breakfast after brushing my teeth? Well, you try brushing them with shaving cream and see if you don't need something like strong black coffee to get rid of the taste. It is disgusting.) When I got down there was conversation going on that had been picked up from the night before: one of my friends there had recently been diagnosed with Attention Deficit Disorder, and he was talking about all the hoops he had to jump through in order to get his low-dose Ritalin. Because, as doctors and psychiatrists were at pains to tell him, people with ADD tend not to have PhDs. Or be, manifestly, and by some degree, the most intelligent and amusing person in the room – you know, the kind of person everyone is sort of waiting for to speak, the person you feed the lines to because you know he's going to make the best joke out of them. Witty in himself, and the cause of wit in others, but without Falstaff's less endearing traits of cowardice and grossness.

However: these characteristics can be just the kind of accompaniment to ADD. Quick thinking means, by definition, that you don't have to spend time on it. I think of the oddities that separate me from the majority of my fellow human beings and gradually begin to see that it is all adding up. Inability to concentrate on mundane tasks? I will offer, as evidence, my stack of unopened envelopes from Her Majesty's Revenue and Customs, spanning five years. Contract for a book signed in 1997, book named in contract yet to appear? Check. Vast tottering piles of books, papers, newspapers, magazines and god knows what else in every room I inhabit? Check. Complete unemployability in normal world of work? Checkitty check, with knobs on. Tendency to wait until the last minute to do things? Ask the editor who has been drumming her fingers on the desk waiting for this to come in. Vagueness of mind sufficient to make one brush one's teeth with shaving cream, which after all comes in a green tube, instead of toothpaste, which comes in a white one? ("Deep Clean WOW Sensation", it says on the tube, but "wow" is not the word that I used. The Beloved thought I'd seen a frog come out of the tap.) Checkmate.

I am mistrustful of a culture that seeks to validate individual shortcomings by giving them fancy-sounding names. And I am mindful of the old Freak Brothers cartoon in which Fat Freddy simulates the symptoms in order to get hold of a scrip for what is, in effect, cheap speed. But my friend's life has, he says, been transformed, and it would be fascinating if just one small pill would help me become a better-functioning adult. So I will make an appointment with the doctor. If I can – you saw this coming, didn't you? – be arsed.

⁂

That'll teach me to go around quoting from King Lear. Last week I thought I was losing my mind so said "let me not be mad, not mad, sweet heaven" and heaven took the hint and is now assaulting my vile jelly, ie my eyes. Or rather the left one. At the suggestion of the dizzyingly attractive Iranian optometrist at Specsavers who examined me about three months ago, I started using daily contact lenses instead of the monthly ones, whose working life I would usually extend to about a year. I was assured that not only was this naughty but that it was very bad for my eyes. Being told you are naughty by a gorgeous woman who is so close to you you can feel her breath on your eyelashes is not, I admit, the most painful experience a man can undergo – in fact, some men will pay good money for the privilege – but I do take advice, eventually, where my eyes are concerned.

For, as the optician's poster reminds us, we only get one

pair. (Looking at posters in optician's can be quite rewarding. Prolonged examination of one taught me that there is a part of the eyeball called the Zonules of Zinn, which sounds like one of the lost bands from Liverpool of the late 1970s, cf. The Teardrop Explodes and Echo and the Bunnymen. I once asked, in the pub quiz, where the Zonules of Zinn were, and was, as always happens when I set the pub quiz, roundly and fluently abused for my efforts.)

Anyway, I duly got a three-month supply of dailies, and although there was a part of me that felt I was somehow being wasteful, and contributing to a culture of disposability that I strongly disapprove of, I relished my new freedom from having to put them away in a little pot every night, and suspend them in a lotion so expensive it might have been composed largely of unicorns' tears.

There was one thing I really didn't like, though, and that was that sometimes, at the end of the evening, after a night of convivial chat and smoking and drinking my head off, they would tend to get rather difficult to remove. Something in certain kinds of roll-ups conspires to make the surface of the eyeball more adhesive than it normally is, or dries it out, perhaps, and this combined with the small but perceptible decline in dexterity that can afflict one after a bottle and a bit of Shiraz can make for a frustrating pre-bedtime experience. But with disposables it's even worse: they're flimsier than the normal kind of lens, and now I can be in the bathroom, fossicking around the cornea for ages and ages, while the Beloved waits for me, and then dozes off.

This time I was at least on my own but it was worse than usual – the damned thing just wouldn't come out. And then something went wrong, and all I could think of by way of explanation was that my fiddling about had pushed the lens round the back, behind the eyelid, if not, at least, into the very Zonules of Zinn themselves, but somewhere deep and inaccessible.

When I first met the Beloved, one of her best friends had only one question about me to ask of her (well, I imagine she had several, but this was the first): "is he good in a crisis?" I remember, when this was reported to me, breathing a large sigh of relief. There are all sorts of questions she could have asked which would have resulted in a much more negative or equivocal response, like, is he good with money, is he tidy, is he fundamentally a decent human being, does he lust after optometrists, etc, etc. But crises I am kind of ok with – for a start, I've learned that a surprising number of them go away, or resolve themselves, if you don't do anything about them.

This wasn't one of those crises, though, but there was little I could do about it at 2 in the morning, so went to bed; and anyway, maybe it would resolve itself – I recalled something about the eye being very good at expelling foreign objects. But the next morning – a Sunday, when Specsavers is shut – I saw a tiny little square of transparent blue in the sink, which I could immediately tell was about one-third to one-half of a daily contact lens, which could only mean that one-half to two-thirds of a daily contact lens was lodged somewhere in my eye.

So there we go: a culture of disposability leads to suffering one way or the other. You would have thought that someone might have worked out that you don't make contact lenses with the fragility of rice paper just in case this kind of thing happens, but no. And I didn't even get the gorgeous optometrist when I went to get the eye checked out.

Something strange and unwelcome is happening to me: I am turning into a non-party person. Whereas once I would turn up, as the saying goes, to the opening of an envelope, last week saw me staying at home first, on Friday, for the launch of an Extremely Famous Author's book (name removed in order to protect your ears from the harsh clang of a Name being dropped) and then, the next day, for the annual party of an old colleague and friend, which I haven't been able to go to for the last umpteen years, simply due to diary clashes and/or child-care duties. This was different to a big literary party: this was going to be a shindig which was going to be attended by many people I love and have known for years and years (and yet still love them). There were two snags, though: (1) it was being held South of the river, in Lewisham, and (2) I was feeling lousy. That kind of non-specific exhaustion lousy, where the eyes feel weighted in their sockets, like those of a creepy doll in a horror film, and there is a marked disinclination to travel to parts of London in which either a train journey or a ruinously expensive minicab journey is involved. (You know civilisation has taken some kind of wrong turn somewhere when you discover that you can now fly to an airport roughly near Venice for less than the cost of a taxi ride within London.) So I get out my large-scale map of London and, with the Hovel as the centre, draw a circle indicating the furthest border at which this party, which I really have been looking forward to going to, would have to be in order for me to haul my carcase out there. The circle's boundaries are around Swiss Cottage to the north, and Soho to the south. Still, I reckon that maybe a spruce-up will help, and I am anyway disgusted with myself for such feebleness, so shower and shave and dress reasonably smartly . . . but no. I find that it is not enough to wash the tiredness from my bones. So I try that old wheeze where you say to yourself something like "it is much better to have done something and regretted it than not done something and then wondered for the rest of your life blah blah blah". You know what? That saying is a crock, and anyone who believes it, or worse, lives their life by it, is operating under profound self-delusion. I can think of any number of things I should not have done but have, and very few things I have not done that I should have. Even the unambiguous pass made at me decades ago by a multimillionaire's daughter – on whom, moreover, I had the most enormous crush – I was right to turn down. Even more relevantly, I can think of many parties I have gone to which I have deeply wished I hadn't.

So, the clock ticks, the half-hourly trains to Ladywell trundle away from Charing Cross, and the window of opportunity slowly closes, and besides, *Doctor Who* is on, and I am alone in the Hovel . . .

It is that last that is the clincher, and, I suddenly suspect, the real underlying reason why I am so reluctant to leave. For it is all very well living in fun Bohemia in central London, but the downside of that is that I have to share accommodation. Yet this evening I have the run of the place to myself. You know what? When you're going to be 50 next year, living in shared accommodation, even with the most delightful companions, isn't fun or something to be particularly proud of. There are only four people on earth I would really like to live with, and three of them are my children. One of the basic definitions of acceptable shared living arrangements is this: that you live with people who could, without their asking, use your toothpaste without your minding in the slightest.

And I have been trying to pretend that this place is more my own these days: buying things to hang on the wall, tidying up, etc, etc. It is a mockery, a simulacrum of domesticity. As the autumn approaches not only of the year but of my life, I start worrying about where I can really cosy up in without fear. (It's the prospect of new life that brings out the nesting instinct in women; it's the prospect of death that brings it out in men.) So what with one thing and another, I decide to stay at home, if an expression of humiliating inertia can be dignified with the word "decide", and spend an evening in, enjoying that exquisitely bitter cocktail of emotions: remorse, regret, and self-pity, and by the time I realise I really ought to have gone to the party it is too late. Still, *Doctor Who* was good, wasn't it?

❧

Could you all please be a little quieter? Razors has been here, and I am feeling a little delicate this morning. Thank you. The Aymara of Peru and Bolivia have a very good word to describe the condition of a hangover: umjayanipxitütuwa – "they must have made me drink". (I love that: it encapsulates the feeling of helplessness, of compromised personal agency, and memory blanks.)

For those who have come in late to this column, Razors was my old housemate, as well as being a friend of old. Our marriages effectively terminated, we found ourselves together in the Hovel and had many a pleasant evening, playing Mahjong, comparing needlepoint techniques, and composing elegiac verse in Latin. Once every so often - say, every six months or so – we would open a bottle of sherry, and, in the course of about four or five evenings, work our way through its contents. Happy days! Luckily, my work does not involve arrival at an office at a predetermined time of day, so I could recover from these bacchanalia in bed, at a gentle pace. Poor Razors, though, would have to drudge off to commute to a Well Known Broadcasting Organisation, muttering curses as he went. I was always shocked and disgusted by his language on these occasions. One day he took the pledge and flew to America to earn an obscene sum of money and since then life has never been quite the same. Still, every six months or so he comes back to taunt me and throw things around the Hovel after one or two of his teeny-weeny sherries. In days gone by he favoured the empty wine bottles which multiplied unaccountably around the place (do they breed? Do the mice have an account at Majestic?); yesterday evening, he was much taken by the cricket ball, and kept throwing it at the wall until I confiscated it. ("Why isn't it bouncing properly?" "It's a sodding cricket ball, you maniac.")

This morning I awoke to . . . sorry, I'll start that again. This afternoon, I awoke to find a can of Ronson Universal Gas Lighter Refill hiding in the lining of my coat pocket. What the hell was that doing there? Had we, crazed by sherry, and in the grip of the kind of feral social behaviour that so excites columnists on the *Daily Mail*, taken to solvent abuse to add to all our other crimes? I'm not given to carrying cans of lighter fluid about my person, and have never really cared for the stuff except insofar as it is really useful when it comes to filling up gas lighters.

It then occurred to me that Razors had decided, after maybe another insy-wincy little amontillado, to play with this. "Look at this, this is great," I have a dim memory of him saying, before squirting a pool of the stuff all over the table and then setting light to it. He then tried it on a door, covered with a weird papery artex which looks like one of the most flammable substances ever invented, and I had to grab the can off him before he did some serious damage. I soothe him with some Virgil. "Tityre, tu patulae recubans sub tegmine fagi . . ." I begin encouragingly, with hand gestures. Eventually the next line comes to him – "silvestrum tenui Musam meditaris avena", he murmurs, sleepily (it's actually "sylvestrem", but I let it go, as he has done so well considering his state) – and he allows me to gently prise the cylinder from his hand, while he starts reminiscing about a sordid encounter with a girl on the top deck of a Routemaster when he was 20. ("But only after we'd finished did we notice the mirror which the driver uses to see everything.")

The rest of the evening is a bit of a blur. We synchronise our watches and agree to see how we're doing at around noon to see if we want to go to, or can face, our traditional post-Saturnalian full English breakfast. At around 1 p.m., as I try to fulfil one of the three horrible deadlines looming over me, I start worrying about the fact that I have heard nothing from him. Is he dead? This is a real fear, for we are both getting on, and I barely feel in the land of the living. I'm getting on a plane the next morning, and if his corpse, rather than his inert yet still living body, is what awaits me on the sofa, then this is really going to screw up my plans. Of course I will miss him and all that, but I still have my own pain to deal with.

Luckily for both of us, he still lives, and we stagger along for our Full English. Generously, I place him in a seat opposite a pretty woman, so he can play with his sausages and upset her dining experience. It's hard on her, but sometimes you have to do the right thing for an old friend.

❧

Lunch with the Moose. It is our custom, when this happens, to start at the French House for a little sharpener, and then eventually peel off towards Chinatown for our favoured dim sum establishment, the name of which always escapes us but as we know exactly where it is this is never a hindrance.

I am always haunted by feelings and memories I had thought long dead, but were only dormant, when in the French. For those who do not know of it, this is a long-established Soho pub which – as its name suggests – is sympathetic to all things trans-Channel. Or sous-Manche, or something. You can get Lillet there, which is not what you probably think it is but is in fact the vermouth favoured by James Bond for his Martinis. I do not drink this, but instead opt for a kir, which they do nicely there. I believe, along with Ford Madox Ford, that the chief responsibility of a wine is to be red, yet even I can't really drink red wine for breakfast (technically; I am on an empty stomach, for a prior deadline has obliged me to miss out on anything solid) but the cassis makes the white wine blush a bit, so that's all right. Inside, there are memorials to its various louche regulars, old and new, and its splendidly-mustachioed former proprietor, Gaston Berlemont, who once invited me (when the drink was still illegal in this country) to a sampling of a pre-World War 1 absinthe, but which I turned down because I would have then missed out on a chance of getting laid. I once met Francis Bacon there, and was introduced to him by a girlfriend who had never even heard of him, and we spent the whole night being fed Champagne by him while he discoursed on life, and how happy he was. He was charm itself, and I found myself wondering: if I let him fuck me, would I get a painting out of it?

But it is the sliding open of the bolts as the Moose and I wait outside, just before noon, that really takes me back. It is a long time since I have heard that noise. It is one thing, with Falstaff, to hear the chimes at midnight; it is another to hear the chimes of noon, and to be panting outside licensed premises as one does so. In this one experiences the true, old Soho, where noon – or, at the Coach and Horses, 11 a.m. – would find any number of well-worn alcoholics trembling outside the premises, their habit vindicated by the company they kept, their own veneer of high opinion of themselves, and their deep fund of anecdote about the area, dating back to the days, in some cases, of Dylan Thomas. So, what with one thing and another, there is often a grace-note of melancholy to our conversation when in the French, although it is really only heard by me. Over an enormous amount of dim sum, though, the talk falls to the encroaching barbarity. I am told three anecdotes about the children or the pupils of friends who are at universities.

1. Subject being studied: English literature. Student: "And we're meant to be reading someone called . . . O'Grady?" Moose (guessing wildly): "Do you mean Thomas Hardy?" Student: "Yes! That's the one!" Moose, helpfully: "Then, er, obviously, of course you should read *Tess of the d'Urbervilles*, *Far From the Madding Crowd* and *Under the Greenwood Tree* . . ." Student: "Hey, hang on! I've only got a year."

2. Subject: Philosophy. Student – no, recent graduate in philosophy (on being asked which philosophers have been

studied): "well, we didn't study any individual ones, really, but we read lots of articles. Like, on euthanasia." (NB May not have been euthanasia, but something similar. Was too busy howling to be sure.)

3. Subject: English lit. again. A class of students announces that it refuses to continue discussing, or perhaps reading, *Emma* because "it's boring and nothing happens in it". And so on.

Much of the talk between any two writers these days is spent either on this kind of thing or about which literary editor has lost his or her job recently, and where it is all heading. And meanwhile a gang of crazed twerps and hypocrites with transparently vested interests is seriously arguing that the BBC should be closed down because it never sacked Jimmy Savile. A vile, vile, man, one of the vilest, but shut down the Beeb because of him? Really? So forgive me if, every once in a while, I drown myself in drink and dim sum.

❦

I am lying in bed in the afternoon reading a fascinating article in the *TLS* – a very good review of the film *Amour* by Adam Mars-Jones, if you want to know – when I hear two loud bangs from downstairs, in quick succession. A nasty smell climbs up the stairs and the smoke alarm goes off. Those things never make a pleasant noise, do they? Why does no one have the wit to make them emit the stirring sound of the red-alert noise in *Star Trek*, or – for even older customers, to really give them the heebie-jeebies, a World War II air-raid siren?

Anyway, all this is by the by, as it is clear grievous disaster has stricken the Hovel, and I am going to die horribly. Death by fire has always struck me as a particularly nasty way to go, although neither am I a fan of its wetter counterpart, drowning, or its crunchier one, being eaten by a shark. Reports of shark attacks on humans always affect me strongly, and it may well have been reading of a recent one in California that made me take to my bed in the first place.

I suppose I've had a good run in the Hovel – five years or so of not being nagged by anyone and not tidying up unless I really feel like it. True, I now have mice, and piles of books that, were the roof to be removed, would be visible from space, but I also have peace of mind, of a sort, and it is in this frame of mind that I prepare to meet my maker, if such an entity exists. I do not have time, I reflect, to put my affairs in order – that would take about a year, entirely devoted to putting my affairs in order, allowing for a maximum of five hours' sleep a night and only one main meal per day – or even to call my great friend John Moore and tell him that, yes, he can come round and have my red 12-string 1967 Baldwin semi-acoustic after all. I mean, I could call him and tell him that, but it wouldn't be in such a great state by the time he found it. (John has been much on my mind lately, what with the Jimmy Savile affair: it is a subject that seems tailor-made to justify a reunion of his band, Black Box Recorder, and the writing of a really creepy and disturbing song. After all, his song-writing partner, Luke Haines, managed the same, to great effect, on the subject of Gary Glitter on a solo album a few years ago.)

In the end, though, I decide that while death may be, in the words of J. M. Barrie, an awfully big adventure, it would also be massively tiresome and inconvenient, so I decide to stir myself and see what's going on downstairs. The smoke is really getting quite thick, and the stench is becoming insupportable.

For some reason – and this is a detail that only occurs to me long afterwards – I do not take one of the little fire extinguishers with me, and all I am wearing is my dressing gown. I suppose I am giddy with bravado. I am also, above all, curious as to what could have happened. It turns out that there is a very simple explanation: I have been feather-headed. I always used to laugh at the warning on certain items of soft furnishing: "carelessness causes fire". One of my little comedy routines, which I flatter myself to think were found amusing, was to muse on this aloud and then go through a pantomime of a boy scout tutorial whereby the scoutmaster, instead of having to go through all sorts of business with bits of wood and string in order to teach his charges how to make fire in the wild, would simply have to walk into a tree, or drop something from his pocket instead. It is not a joke I will make any longer. It turns out that I have, about an hour earlier, put a pan of water on with two eggs in it, so that I might have, later, a teatime hard-boiled egg sandwich as a special treat. However, a combination of incipient senility and an unusually engrossing edition of the *Times Literary Supplement* conspired to make me forget all about this. The bang, the smoke, and the stench, were caused by the eggs exploding. I reset the alarm and then put it in a drawer so it doesn't start going off again. (I'd put it outside on the terrace but it looks like rain.)

I do worry, though. I've never done this before, unless I've been pissed or stoned. Now, it turns out, I can contrive my own end even without being intoxicated. It is, I feel, a turning point. But later on, when I recover the scattered bits of egg, the whites turn out to be, if tough, perfectly edible.

A brief spell of financial viability, boredom, and a clear schedule conspire, towards the end of October, to propel me on one of my occasional little benders, and I awake on November 1st with an erased memory and only some enigmatic clues as to what I've been up to around me – an empty bottle of baby oil, a memory stick with the words "property of GCHQ" neatly embossed on it, and a crude tattoo on my left forearm; you know, the usual stuff – but also with, and this is the crucial thing, three days' growth of stubble on my face. I grasp the great implication of this straight away: it means I have a head start on Movember. Movember, for those who do not know, is the annual month-long event in which men who are too idle or unfit to run anywhere, or too cowardly to do anything risky, or too dignified to do anything involving bathfuls of baked beans, contribute to charity simply by growing a moustache. Hence – do you see what they did there? – Movember.*

I have to admit that my reasons for wanting to participate in this event are not entirely altruistic. This stunt has fluttered about the periphery of my consciousness for a couple of years now. In 2010 I thought the idea a silly one; in 2011, as I contemplated a poster advertising the event in the gents of the Barley Mow off Baker Street, I felt a distinct pang that I had missed any chance of getting meaningfully involved – it was now getting to the end of the month, and I was clean-shaven. For, if I may admit it, one of the questions which has nagged at me since I've been old enough to shave was this: what would I look like with a moustache? I would furtively take myself off to the passport photo booth at East Finchley tube station and then, in the privacy of my bedroom, experiment on the strip

* As of 2019, Movember is more or less history. Which is a good thing, assuming the charity concerned has found a way to make up the shortfall.

of snaps with an assortment of styles: the Inspector Clouseau, the Zapata, the caddish Terry-Thomas, and even, to my own horror, the Chaplin/Hitler. I think it was after I saw what that looked like that this period of experimentation drew to a close.

The thing is, I always remained deeply ambivalent about the idea of facial hair. It was all, I knew perfectly well at the time, about the desire to become a man: the achievement of a proper moustache, as opposed to the vague thistledown on my upper lip, was a metaphor, simply, for that moment when, in the stirring jargon of the analyst, I would achieve full gen-itality, or, to put it another way, finally Do It with a woman. Growing a moustache was, in other words, my equivalent of the cargo cultists' building of a plausible-looking airstrip in the vain hope that it would compel aeroplanes to land there and disgorge their bounty.

I knew, too, that they were also about disguise and vanity. A line, or rather half a line, from a children's book stays with me to this day: in it, a child and his father have been abducted by a criminal gang, and sticking-plaster has been fixed across their mouths to effect silence. When this is finally torn off, we are told that it is a mercy that the boy's father had not been vain enough to grow a moustache, for otherwise this would have hurt tenfold (I don't remember anything else about the book except that it was deservedly recommended by the Puffin Book Club).

However, I also knew, from my collection of Beatles' LPs, that you could grow a moustache on a whim, as it were, to ring the changes in one's personal journey, to signal that the composer of "Penny Lane" was not the same man who wrote "I Saw Her Standing There"; that one had acquired a certain hard-won wisdom, and an appreciation of backward tape loops. And also, I could not forget the military moustache, as worn by Nicholas Courtenay in his unimprovable portrayal of Brigadier Lethbridge-Stewart in *Doctor Who*.

So, as I write this on the 5th, I find myself with a surprisingly robust 'tache, which I must admit is dividing the audience. The Beloved, who has made a very good argument for its removal – propriety obliges me to be vague about the details, you will have to work them out for yourself – looks on it with a kind of glazed horror. The ex-wife all but threw up into a bucket. The daughter – cruellest of all – says I look like one of the Chuckle Brothers, although she is unsure which. My sons, though, think it is a scream. Which is as good a reaction as I am going to get. Everyone else may as well be Jeeves confronted by one of Bertie Wooster's ill-advised efforts. Well, nuts to you all, I'm doing this for charity. Which excuses everything.

꧁

Readers of last week's paper edition of this magazine may have noticed that the illustration accompanying this column was enhanced by the addition of a moustache: of a style made famous, I am afraid, by Adolf Hitler. I suppose I asked for it. The idea was that over the course of the month readers could follow the progress of my moustache, and I suppose that as the shading of degrees of stubble was beyond the reproduction process, we're going to pretend that moustaches actually grow outwards from the centre. I just hope that this week's issue sees me looking a little less . . . Nazi.

Anyway, that's enough unpleasantness. The point about growing this sodding moustache is that it is meant to raise awareness of – i.e., in effect, raise money for an organisation that raises awareness of – men's health issues in general, and testicular and prostate cancer in particular. As my arch-feminist friend Zoe, who has, I note, made a donation, says, there is no fun in chopping men's balls off if they're dropping away of their own accord.

Still, there is this worry niggling away at the back of my mind about the concept of good works, for this is the first time I have got into this thing since I was a schoolboy, and would go from door to door holding out a blue NSPCC papier-mâché egg and looking like a spokesperson for abused children (not that, in those days, I had any real idea what atrocities really lurked beneath the phrase. We were being used, I suppose, but at least the cause was a good one, and we got to earn increasingly covetable badges the more we collected. I can see them now: denoters of achievement and rank as visible as the rings on an RAF pilot's sleeves. I assumed at the time that these signified diligence, and never suspected that their wealthy parents may have contributed to the NSPCC's egg boxes.)

One of my very favourite biblical injunctions is the bit about charity, which is to be done secretly: "let not thy left hand know what thy right hand doeth". The problem with charity these days is that this is very far from the way people now go about it. It is often, in fact, a way of pushing one's own virtue up the public nose, even if one is not, privately, virtuous at all. (There was a bloke, very famous in the seventies, did a lot of marathons and stuff for charity, his face everywhere, and if you didn't sign up to one of his causes you always felt that someone might actually think that you were in favour of children dying of leukemia or whatever. From

Yorkshire, long white hair, always wore a track suit, smoked cigars, you know the one I mean.)

Anyway, the thing about this bloody moustache is that it is indeed very much in your face. I suppose it is a more ambiguous gesture than, say, wearing a pink ribbon – you can always say that you're just growing the thing for your own pleasure – but in my case, each public appearance has to be prefaced by an announcement on my part that this is in fact all for good works rather than a personal lifestyle choice and fashion statement. For the thing is, that apart from the itchiness, and the really quite surprising way that it registers at the lower edge of the peripheral vision, but really mainly the itchiness, it is more your problem than mine. In this I have something in common with Guy de Maupassant, who loathed the Eiffel Tower but was often to be found dining in its restaurant, on the grounds that it was the only place in Paris where he couldn't see the damned thing. (Incidentally, de Maupassant had an incredibly impressive moustache, although he did spoil its magnificent purity, in my opinion, by having one of those little sprouts of growth bang underneath his upper lip as well.) But it is a lonely business, at times, fraught with peril; the journalist Nick Cohen, who knows a thing or two about speaking fearlessly, told me that he lacked the courage to grow a moustache; he might just possibly have been joking, but what's bothering me right now is that I am due, in a week or so, to be meeting the Beloved's mother for the first time. I have, for the previous year and a half, been skulking on the sidelines, waiting for my moment, but when she finally claps eyes on me in the flesh she's going to be seeing facial hair that has been nearly a month in the growing. And whatever I say or do to explain afterwards, her first appalled thought will be: "my daughter is going out with a man who grows a moustache". I could, of course, get her daughter to warn her beforehand; but there is a mischievous and self-destructive prankster within me that wonders whether it might be more fun if she did not.*

꼭

I always find this time of year particularly fraught. It is the season of cold and damp, the three-year-old grime on the windows of the Hovel so effectively blocking the light that even during the day people without the sharp eyesight of youth are obliged to carry torches, and the realisation that that really is it, there isn't going to be any sunny warmth for five months at the very least. As I might have remarked here before, my favourite Hungarian novelist, Antál Szerb, once noted that November in London wasn't a month, it was a state of mind; he wrote that before the Second World War and it's still true. But it is also the season of profound personal disorganisation. "What am I doing?" is no longer an existential question, but a practical one.

Like many people, I start the year with the good intention of keeping a diary. I don't mean a Dear-Diary-today-Binkie-was-beastly-to-me-at-lunch-and-no-one-understands-me kind of diary, I mean one which says things like "2.30 dentist" (I am a poor keeper of dentists' appointments, but it is surprising how many of them actually *are* at 2.30) on a given date, in my

* I wanted to write about moustache the following week, but my editor – and by this I mean the generalissimo, Jason Cowley, and not the person I send my copy to – ordered me never to mention it again. Well, I did, as you will see, but at least I knew where he stood on the pro- or anti-moustache divide.

own handwriting, so that I can turn up to the dentist with a clean conscience and that inner peace which comes from having remembered something arranged a long time ago. In this case, that of buying a diary I mean, my incompetence works in my favour because by the time I remember to get one it is February and even though most of the decent ones have gone, you can still pick one up at a considerable discount. The next few days are spent in a frenzy of putting dates in the diary and marvelling at how organised one is being.

No they're not. They're spent waiting to find something to put in the diary, but no one's inviting anyone to anything, either because it's February and too cold, or it is in a year after 2008 and no one has any money to hold a party. After a couple of weeks of this you get an email from the Moldovan *chargé d'affaires* inviting you to a reading and reception in celebration of Mihail Pushofscu's searing new novel, *The Landlocked Seagull*, and you think, what the heck, this beats staying at the Hovel for the 150th night in a row, maybe they'll be handing out glasses of splrtz, the famous Moldovan firewater, and you hunt for the diary to put in the date, and either (a) you can't find it and have to go out to Ryman's to buy another, even nastier, discounted diary, and the only ones they've got left have bunnies on them, or perhaps cats if you're lucky, or (b) you contemplate the pages and pages of blank space on either side of the orgy at the Moldovan embassy and think: Is this it?

But of course by the spring things pick up again, except by this time you've given up buying diaries altogether, and I don't know about you – you probably have one of those phones with a lower-case I in front of them that does everything for you except blow your nose – but what I do is give up on the whole idea of planned socialising and rely on a system of hunches, bells being faintly rung, and chance remarks by friends about parties they're going to that I have a vague memory of having been invited to myself. Hardly anyone sends out proper invitations any more, and in my inbox they just fester away along with all the other invitations to ogle schoolgirls, lose my belly fat and get a degree from the University of Pinner. I have now taken to telling the Beloved when I'm doing things; she puts them in her phone beginning with a lower-case I, and then tells me when something is happening. If I remember to tell her in the first place. Except by the end of November people start thinking: we haven't had a party/book launch/excruciating literary event for ages now, let's fit about 80 of them into the last six weeks of the year – and it gets very hard to keep track.

So it was nice to see, last week, that it is not only freelance writers like myself (by the way, the 23rd of November was National Freelancers Day: I plan to have celebrated it by staying in bed till 4, as usual) who are rushed and disorganised: accountants are, too. I received a fascinating peek inside the mind of one the other day when I asked an editor if it could be possible to chase up payment. (I hasten to point out that the editor is a kindly one, and that the magazine is most certainly not this one.) The accountant replied, and accidentally copied me into the mailing list, with the immortal line: "I just dont [sic] have time to go around making payments". Well, as I now know his name and the company he works for, I know what I can get this person for Christmas. A lovely new diary!

"*Alles in der Welt lässt sich ertragen,*" wrote Goethe, "*nur nicht eine Reihe von schönen Tagen.*" It is a hard one to translate as mellifluously as it runs in the original, but roughly, it means: "you can put up with everything on earth, except for a succession of wonderful days." Well, as Bertie Wooster says whenever Jeeves throws a line from one of the Stoics at him – I think it's usually Marcus Aurelius – the next time you see Goethe you can tell him he's a silly ass. (I don't really, of course, think this about Goethe. But for comic purposes, right now, I do.) I have found that you can put up with pretty much everything fate throws at you except, it turns out, a moustache. Even my sainted editor wearied of this topic barely two weeks into Movember, instructing me to write about anything else, anything. I took a grim amusement, incidentally, into how easily and immediately I caved into editorial pressure. Who needs Leveson when you have lickspittles like me around? Anyway, having laid off the subject for two weeks, and checked with one of his deputies, I think I can touch on the subject for one last time. And how could I not? I've hardly been able to think about anything else for a whole month. It's all been about the 'tache.

The thing is, that whereas at the very beginning only other people were upset by it, it didn't take too long for me to get upset by it, too. You actually can see it yourself, as I said, floating at the bottom edge of the peripheral vision, like something from a nightmare. It is, after all, a growth; in the least pleasant sense of the term. And also, as I said, it itches. It itches like mad, and in a way that is not improved by scratching it. For some reason, that only makes it worse. So one ends up in a spiral of itching and scratching, and one finds oneself obsessively touching it, hoping, at some point, to find just the right kind of motion that will make you able to pretend it's gone away. But you never achieve this, and all that happens is that you just can't stop fidgeting with it, and everyone looking at you thinks you're the kind of self-fascinated berk who thinks stroking his moustache makes him look important and wise.* I imagine that my occasional next-door neighbour in the *New Statesman*, Hunter Davies, passed this phase a long time ago, and, to rephrase Jeeves's delicately-phrased *aperçu* about David Niven's soup-strainer, his moustache is very becoming to Mr Davies. And I also suppose that he long ago passed the existential phase of facial hair ownership, which involves asking oneself, in the still watches of the night: "what is it doing there?"

Only charity and a desire not to be known as a quitter kept mine there, but it was a trial. There are many out there who think that growing one is not exactly swimming the Hellespont or bungee-jumping off the Chrysler Building. That is, there is no effort or risk involved. To which I say: balderdash. There is effort involved in not shaving the thing off and ending the unpleasantness. Just as the exquisite sadism of the Chinese water torture resided in its apparent innocuousness, so the itchiness of the upper lip was made all the more unendurable by the way so many people seem not to be bothered by their own. I would look about me when in public – when I could bear to venture outdoors (and as fate would have it, November involved an unusually large number of shindigs and events where I had to give some kind of reading or public performance on a dais) – and look at the men with facial hair and ask myself: "how can they put up with this? And do they not know the root of the word 'rebarbative'?" I suppose I

---

* Five years on from these events, and I am still deeply relieved that I have a moustache no longer. I do not think I would grow one again, even if I needed one as a disguise to evade capture.

should salute the tireless work of Keith Flett, founder of the Beard Liberation Front, and I think the world would be a sadder and smaller place if the BLF did not exist, but I don't think I'm going to be joining it any time soon.

The worst thing of all is the way it commanded so much attention. Those who know me as a smooth rather than an hairy man would, on my entering a room, immediately stop talking, laugh, and then make cracks about Clement Attlee/Borat/squadron leaders/pimps of various nationalities. (Everyone had a different joke. Gosh, what witty friends I have. The best one was "exhausted Cypriot restauranteur".) Very often the reason for holding the event to which we had all been invited was forgotten completely. I'm just glad that I didn't have to go to any funerals in November. Well, the money has been raised, the health awareness achieved, the Beloved may now kiss me on the lips again. But remember, next time you see a moustache, try and think of the poor man suffering behind it.

Half past eleven at night, and I am thinking of turning in early for once when the phone rings. I am jumpy enough when the phone rings during the day so at this time of night it is positively nerve-jangling. But the name displayed on the screen is that of F——, an ex-girlfriend of so long ago – we're talking the first Thatcher administration here – that we can't even agree on which of us gave the other one the boot, so even though we disagree radically on just about everything from whether the *Daily Mail* is a newspaper or not to fun ways to spend a weekend, there is a residual sentiment there which makes us very fond of each other. I'd last got a communication from her late in the evening about a week before; she'd asked me to be on standby while she participated in the village pub quiz. I sternly told her that I do not approve of cheating in pub quizzes, which must have given her the hump, for some time after closing I got a rather garbled text which said sarcastic thanks, and also that she'd been beaten up. Shit, seriously? I asked. No, she replied, mortified, she meant beaten – in the quiz. Incident closed, I thought. So when I answered her call and said that she'd had a row with her – can you call a man in his fifties this? – boyfriend, and could she come over, I said Yes, of course.

I have heard much of this man over the last year and a half or so. None of it is good, and I assure you this is not the proprietorial air of a man who thinks that his exes are worthy of no one but him. No, it's because he sounds like a bullying, mean shit who disappears off to "do business", of an unexplained nature, in Russia more often than looks good. Never mind, though, that's not my business. And, after all, I tend to get called more when things are going badly than when they are going well. I only hear about the bad times.

What became my business, though, is that during the course of the debriefing session with F——— when she arrived half an hour later, was that it turns out he has, on about four or five occasions, maybe more, beaten her up. Her slip of the fingers in her text message from the week before was no accident.

At which point I will leave the details obscure, except to say that the violence, as described, sounded frenzied and dangerous, with her at one point fearing for her life. She showed me her forehead where he had slammed her head against the door a week earlier; the bump was still palpable.* How long, do you know, does it take for a bump to go down? I would have thought that one that lasted a week must have been rather impressive to begin with.

I must say, I really don't get it, this woman-hitting business. F—— was so impressed by the quality and strength of the violence against her that she wondered whether he'd had professional training of some sort, but I assured her that she would be amazed by the intuitive manner in which men can become masters of savagery against someone of the opposite gender who is much, much smaller than them. However, I only know this at one remove. There are only two people I can think of who deserve a thrashing which I would be happy to administer, but they are both men and live in nos. 10 and 11 Downing Street, London SW1. Even then it would be done more in sorrow than anger. Hit a woman, though? I can only imagine that for the men who do it, their very weakness must be some kind of provocation. This might be one reason they do it again and again.

So I went through my spiel, honed after listening to the experience of another good friend who had suffered the same, that she must never go back to him under any circumstances, for otherwise it will happen again, and the next time the consequences may be worse than a bump on the head. She assured me she'd do this. But please, she said, don't mention this to anyone. She was "embarrassed".

I suppose I am breaching a trust by writing about it here, even though she is unidentifiable. But she now tells me she has

---

* Not the float of the door, i.e. what you push to close it, but the narrow bit that's at ninety degrees to it. If I showed you where it was – this description might be unclear – on any door, you would go "Jesus".

gone back to him, and I brace myself for further worse news. It is the shame that women feel when evil has been done to them that I find the most perplexing, yet at the same time one of the reasons the violence persists, the men get away with it. I hear that one in four women suffer from violence at some point. Which must mean that one in four men are perpetrating it. Sometimes you just want to throw up.

⚜

And now there is yet another resident at the Hovel. He is looking at me reproachfully as I write. A stuffed fox cub, called Cuthbert, apparently. He sits on a plywood plinth, head bowed, his ears not the typically perky vulpine sensory organs, but looking dishevelled and somehow contingent, as if they are some kind of afterthought. I suppose it isn't easy to stuff ears. Also, as I discovered since taking him home on the bus, his tail keeps falling off.

I must say, I had been looking forward to more of a reaction from my fellow-passengers when I took Cuthbert to his new home. I had certainly been expecting one, ever since my friend Z——, whose gift this was, had suggested that I might prefer to take a taxi back from her place rather than expose my present – she was at the time only giving me hints and riddles as to what it might be – to the outside world, and its probable censure. (I'd pretty much worked out it was going to be something dead and stuffed from the animal world – Z—— had said "it's taxidermy for everyone this year" – I just didn't know what.)

I wouldn't blame the outside world for censuring me. I am not the kind of person who spits on women's fur coats (I

72

harbour a suspicion that the kind of people who do so are at least as interested in spitting on the woman as they are on the coat), and indeed anyone who has looked after chickens looks upon the fox with a jaundiced and bitter eye, even if, like me, you think *The Cunning Little Vixen* is one of the greatest works of art, never mind operas, ever conceived, but there are sensibilities to be considered from time to time. Taxidermy is not to everyone's taste.

Back in the Hovel, I notice something sinister at work. I would like to think that I am pretty robust about things that make others uneasy, but I discover, to my great surprise, that the damned thing is freaking me out. For a start, it seems sentient. And it seems to shift position as I catch a glimpse of it from the corner of my eye. This need not, on the whole, be a bad thing. I have run out of ideas about how to deal with Mousie (although one reader's suggestion that I use peppermint oil might have some mileage in it, although I have no idea at all as to where I might buy such a product, assuming it exists and I'm not being toyed with – I mean, come on, peppermint oil, you'll be trying to sell me Essence of Maynard's Sours next), and for all I know a stuffed fox might be just the thing to put the willies up him. I put him on the floor of the kitchen last evening and I have to report that Mouse Activity was considerably down on what it has been in recent weeks. Whether this is coincidence or really down to Cuthbert I don't know. But I do wish he wouldn't move about like that. I mean, either move or stay still. Don't do that out-of-the-corner-of-my-eye thing. I am reminded, suddenly and horribly, of the WW Jacobs story "The Monkey's Paw", in which a stuffed simian hand grants its possessor three wishes, but always at a horrible cost. I cast my mind back to see if I have been making rash wishes. Well, Max Clifford* was arrested, but what is the possible downside to that? I see none. That leaves me with two. However, I have, since Cuthbert's acquisition, been struck down by infections in both the right lower jaw and the right lung. A cheque I have been waiting for very badly has not yet appeared, even though the relevant accounts department swear blind that they sent it. (I believe them, incidentally. After a quarter of a century in this game you get to know when Accounts Payable are telling the truth or not.) My parents' cat is going to have to be put down, in the absence of any religious busybodies telling us that only the Almighty can determine the hour of her departure from this vale of tears.

And now this just in: my mother has fallen on an icy pavement and broken her arm and shoulder. These are not, I gather, trivial breaks, insofar as they can ever be. In fact, this last news is both so terrible and fresh that I am quite unable to digest it. Nor can I seriously attribute this to Cuthbert. Can I? Like all supposedly rational people who go on about their rationality, I am, deep down, horribly prone to superstition and the worst kind of animism. I don't know how one appeases the unquiet soul of a fox cub untimely dispatched, but if anyone out there does, I would be keen to learn. Maybe peppermint oil might do the trick.

To the Royal Opera House for a performance of the *Nutcracker Suite*. What, the writer of a column called "Down

---

* Someone else settling deservedly under the rubbish in history's dustbin. Google him if you have to, but it is not edifying.

74

and Out" going to the ROH? Let me reassure you that, as far as being in the soup financially goes, I am still up to the eyebrows in the stuff, with extra fear and nausea for next year thrown in, and my lower right hand molars are in such a state that putting anything harder than soup into my mouth makes eating a thrilling adventure. But if you know how to attune yourself to the music of the cosmos in a rudimentary fashion, sometimes little pieces of luck fall into your lap. It also happens that I am close to someone with professional connections there, and so it is that on Epiphany, the Beloved, my children, the Estranged Wife and I find ourselves in the Director's Box.

You may care to cast your eyes again over that cast list, in case you thought they were deceiving you the first time round. Yes, that's right: quite the blended family are we now, as I believe the contemporary phrasing goes. As it was, when the freebie landed in my lap, it was the Beloved herself who suggested that the first Mrs Lezard came along too, and I thought, Hell, why not? Readers who have occasionally expressed concern that I have not treated the ex with perfect gentlemanly reticence or respect will be pleased to hear that such animosity or bitterness as once existed between us seems to have evaporated. We have other, and bigger, fish to fry. Of course, there are always going to be irreconcilable differences – I noticed that she has changed the settings on the car stereo so that it now tunes to something called Absolute, which as far as I can gather is a radio station whose sole purpose is to play U2's entire back catalogue – but it is nice that, when I float the idea of going to watch the ballet with the kids past her, she not only jumps at the chance but tells the children this is a three-line-whip event.

I must say that I had entertained misgivings about how to put this to the children. The boys – hey, they're boys aged 15 and 12, they're going to have massive problems with anything that isn't prefixed by a lower case "I", let alone with ballet – but I recall that even the girl has form on this, for we all recall the time she trashed the props box of her ballet school at the age of three, an age traditionally held to be the one where tutus and whatnots hold maximal appeal to the female child. Not in her case. That was at the very beginning of her second lesson, and we decided instantly that this was a battle we were happy to lose.

It is, seen from a distance, quite amusing to monitor the degrees of contempt and boredom displayed by adolescent boys when confronted by ballet. Did you know it was possible to lean back and stare aggressively at the ceiling? The 12-year-old managed it, despite my whispering fiercely into his ear just before curtain-up that any disciplinary failures on his or his elder brother's part would be met with punishments whose severity it was beyond even my scope to imagine.

I can, alas, sympathise with the notion of antipathy to ballet. It is, as an art form – and there's a large part of me that questions whether it is an art form, rather than a highly sophisticated form of exercise – completely nuts. All art forms require some degree of stylisation, but here it has evolved into something utterly removed from my idea of human experience. (To use Paul McCartney's words, I may be a lover but I ain't no dancer.) I try to think if Tchaikovsky was trying to smuggle any subversive ideas about Russian imperialism into his battle between the soldiers and the mice, or whether he is trying to enact an almost parodic distillation of the essence of the Russian imagination. Or is it just people in tights prancing about to really good music? (An EP containing excerpts from the Suite was one of only about four records I possessed when a child, and so every note has been burned into my brain, and will be among the last things to go.) The Beloved explains it to me later: it's all about sex, duh: "a creepy uncle figure gives a girl a nutcracker – *a nutcracker* – and she has a reverie in which she has her first sexual experience." Ah.

I notice, in the second act, that the boys seem properly attentive, although they seem to be scanning the audience rather than the stage. Afterwards, I congratulate them on their patience. "We played 'spot the black person'," they said, which is not racist, but their way of marking occasions they suspect of cultural homogeneity. "We found four." Which is a start, I suppose.

❦

Well, we love the snow but to have snow it must be cold, and if it is cold then there must be central heating, but if one is freaking out at the gas bill then there cannot be central heating on all through the day. This is where things get problematic. There is an obvious and easy solution to the problem of a chilly Hovel: one stays in bed. This is very much an option for the freelance writer – in fact, it is one of the main reasons we decided to become freelance writers in the first place. However, it comes at a price.

The thing about staying in bed is that it is cosy and nice. When the place is still relatively warm at 8.30 am, it is even cosier. Why, asks the cosy freelance writer, should I bother getting out of bed to start the day with a cup of tea when I could stay in it and just have forty more winks? I am my own boss, and my boss seems intensely relaxed about my staying in bed for a bit longer. So the cosy freelance writer snuggles back under the covers and has forty more winks, and what with the wink being a very elastic unit of time, one then wakes up about two hours later, in a complete fug, also driven half-mad by the crazy dreams that happen in late-morning sleep, completely unable now to distinguish between them and reality for about half an hour, but still perfectly well aware that the temperature has dropped now the heating's gone off, and it is too cold to get out of bed to make a cup of tea, and then the freelance remembers, with a feeling like that of being trapped in a free-falling lift, the almost grotesque bravado with which various editors were assured on Friday afternoon that their copy would be waiting for them in their inboxes by the time they got into work on Monday morning.

It is at times like this that I miss, or almost miss, the discipline forced upon one by living in the same house as one's children. They are now all perfectly capable of getting their own breakfasts, but it is poor form to stay upstairs in bed on a school day while they fight over the Crunchy Nut Corn Flakes. One could, of course, have gone back to bed after they'd been packed off to school and the wife had gone to work, but that involved a level of selfish laziness that even I am incapable of. Most of the time. So now I feel I am getting flabby, spoiled. I am wasting away to becoming little more than an intelligence, if that is the word, barely encumbered by physical reality. The philosophical question of whether we are all brains in jars pretending to experience the outside world (you would be astonished at how *The Matrix* reinvigorated philosophy departments. Every smart kid who saw him- or herself as Neo or Trinity got the bug) now becomes more charged: for all practical purposes, and especially on those days when I don't have to take my mother for her physio at the Royal Free, I have become a brain in a jar, well, a brain in my bed. (I use the word "brain" in its loosest sense.) Only the grosser physical needs can get me out of it. The internet can take some of the blame: I don't even have to get out of bed to buy and read the *Guardian* any more.

It is, though, not a morally sound way to live. There is such a thing as toughening oneself up; there is also such a thing as becoming unhealthily detached from reality. I remember when I was at school we had a – very good – history teacher who would stand up just before we tucked into our meals on Fish Finger Day (i.e. the only day the food was in any way pleasant) and remind us of the latest part of Africa to be suffering from appalling famine. We rolled our eyes but managed to soak up the message. In the same spirit I am now haunted not only by the vastly increased number of *Big Issue* sellers I see about the place, but also by the figure of the man in the underpass at Baker Street station, swaddled in blankets against the deep chill, too cold or dispirited or proud to ask for money, just staring ahead, as if he were trying to imagine a television on the wall opposite him. Here is my, and our, *memento mori*, or not so much a reminder of our death, but a reminder of where any of us could end up, should those people in charge of the state decide that it is no longer the state's job to pick up the pieces. Enjoy the snow.

※

Time for a showdown at the Marylebone Farmers Market. It is not normally, you would think, the kind of place one walks to on a Sunday morning with "Do Not Forsake Me Oh My Darling" playing on the internal soundtrack, is it? So let me explain. First, the market. This was billed as one of the chief attractions of the area when I landed in it. I accepted this billing: I am a sucker for artisanal produce, dancing cheeses, chickens so free-range they have to be tracked down with detectives, bread that breaks paving stones if a loaf slips from your hands. Then again, I am not a fan of paying the kind of prices that these people demand. I know that there are economies of scale enjoyed by supermarkets but unavailable to the smallholder, but still . . . paying a fiver for a small bag of stalky spinach is not for me, I'm afraid. However, there was one attraction that kept me going back week after week: the Maldon Oyster stall. There, for £1 a bivalve, or £5 for six, a jolly bearded fisherman right out of central casting would open oysters for you until either he ran out or you burst. I may be horribly broke all the time but a little luxury on a Sunday is acceptable, I think. It became a ritual: I would go down there with my children, and after a while the two eldest would join in. Imagine: a ten-year-old English boy eating oysters! My heart swelled with pride. (I should add that this oyster-eating business represents a personal triumph. I used to get very sick indeed, after a bad oyster experience, every time I tried them again: but a wise woman advised me to wait seven years. This advice, which sounds like something out of a fairy tale, actually worked, and, touch wood, I have never had a queasy moment since. But it meant my late twenties and early thirties were oyster-free.)

Anyway, one day Beardy Oyster Man decided that doing two London markets every weekend was too much, and he decided to drop the Marylebone one and stick with the one off

Sloane Square on a Saturday. That's too much like the suburbs for me, but I wish him well. (Free advertising alert: Maldon Oysters really are great.) The slack at Marylebone was taken up by the fish stall on the other side of the car park: smaller, and run by a man of sinister mien and pronounced surliness, as opposed to the Cap'n Birdseye warmth of the former. The new oyster man took to his duties with all the bad grace of someone who actually resents earning an extra 500 quid from upper-middle-class ponces and tourists between the hours of 10 am and 2 pm on a Sunday. He has a high turnover of assistants, for some reason, and often, when serving alone, will not open your oysters for you. I once asked to borrow his knife and do it myself, for I craved some on the spot, and, with the absolute minimum conceivable degree of grace short of outright abuse, said "no". Internally, I christened him Bunty Oyster Man, or something very like that. (Shift a letter along somewhere.)

Last week it snowed, and the idea of eating a freezing oyster as the flakes fell on it seemed almost unbearably attractive. Bunty Oyster Man had an assistant; the queue was small; the oysters were there; but the condiments, I noticed, were stashed under the table. The assistant, though, was happy to retrieve them; but Bunty Oyster Man said no, no one was to be served shucked oysters. I offered to do it myself again. No, said Bunty Oyster Man. That evening I resolved, next Sunday, to go along prepared, like the Walrus and the Carpenter, with my own knife, vinegar and pepper. If he was going to be a bunt about opening my oysters, I'd do it in front of him.

This was an idea which had a lot more mileage in it after a bottle of Shiraz than when considered in total sobriety on a Sunday morning, especially as Bunty Oyster Man looks like the kind of man who beats his fish up if they don't behave themselves. But I was determined, and with the Beloved, set off for the market prepared to do my own shucking, if he couldn't be shucked to do mine. We timed our arrival for high noon (hence the soundtrack mentioned above).

You can guess the rest. He opened the oysters with no more than his usual ill-temper – they were quite delicious, and I even said so – and honour all round was saved. But he will have to be on his guard. I can quite understand how a stallholder can have contempt for his customers, but there are limits. One day, there will be a reckoning. The Marylebone Farmers Market will be renamed Hadleyville, and I will afterwards also answer to the name of Gary Cooper.

⚜

Last night I dreamed that I got paid again. Say it in the cadences of the opening line of *Rebecca*. It's a nice dream, one of my favourites, but sometimes I wonder: is it better to have a horrible dream which you are relieved, on waking, to discover was only a dream; or a pleasant one to which reality is an insulting and uncouth rebuke? Anyway, the long-standing non-payment of a significant sum of money is having serious and worrying side-effects. There was a letter in last week's magazine which suggested that I was not literally Down and Out, which is technically true – I'm not shivering under a blanket or selling the *Big Issue* by Baker Street station – but when I head along to the cashpoint, as one does, it tells me that my account has insufficient funds for the transaction I'd suggested. I'd wanted to take out £30. Well, I thought, that's happened a little earlier in the month than I'm accustomed to. Much earlier, in fact. So that was the end of my evening out. And when you find that you cannot even afford to buy a copy of the *Big Issue* you think: just how substantial is the difference between the vendor and yourself? Not as much as you'd like, is the answer – which is itself not a helpful or healthy thought.

Where does the money go? You'd have thought the whores would have dropped their prices in a recession, and I suppose decent cocaine is always going to be a little pricey, and if you can find a drinkable claret for under fifty quid a bottle I will accuse you of poor taste or sharp practice . . . but no, this is not where or how the Lezard money goes. Money has its own gravity, as anyone who has ever played Monopoly knows: when it accrues, nothing can stop it from accruing further, just as the way that when enough rocks in space have smashed together, nothing can stop them from becoming a planet; but when money disappears, it takes everything with it, and scrimping and saving just doesn't seem to have any effect. This is a phenomenon to which I think the economists have not paid sufficient attention, and may account at least in part for the continuing, mystifying immiseration of this country despite its government's manifestly sensible policies.* Another interesting facet of this phenomenon is that when the absence of money is caused by the tap-dancing and delaying tactics of a company who really ought to behave better, the effect is still the same: virtuous poverty has much the same effect as the kind caused by fecklessness or extravagance. The debts accumulate, and you end up having to earn twice as much

* At the time the Coalition government was implementing a policy called "austerity", which doubtless you remember. By the time this book comes out, you will recall it as, comparatively, a soothing back rub compared to what is going on now.

just to get yourself out of the hole the late payment put you in in the first place. And I have been as busy as a bee lately: it is all most vexing.

The worst thing is the humiliation. You may not feel, as I don't, that financial health equates to moral wealth, but it doesn't mean you don't feel like a lowly spotted thing when times are hard. You can't buy your girlfriend that lovely thing you saw, you can't pay in full the money you owe to people who are themselves blameless, and the whole business becomes a continuous background noise affecting everything, like tinnitus, which doesn't even manage to drown out other worries but somehow only contrives to bring them into even sharper relief. When in the company of others who are at least comfortably off, you start playing a kind of Poverty Bingo: when they mention a holiday they've had, you think, "can't afford that", when they talk about a nice restaurant they've been to, you think, "be a while before I can afford that", and you even start wondering whether the latest cool film will still be in the cinemas before you can go and see it yourself so you can see what all the fuss is about. When one is locked into a consumer society, as people of my class and upbringing are, however much one affects to despise consumerism and avoid its seductions, this drip-drip of anxiety leads to shame. I am particularly dismayed about my parents' reaction to this column when it comes out. So I would like to be able to say that, by the time it appears in print, the company responsible for the status quo in the Lezard coffers will have ceased to drag their feet, and I will have some good news at last.

Welcome to my world of pain. I woke up with what I imagine is a trapped nerve in my left leg, making any movement at all with its involvement really rather painful. The Beloved told me the story of an Australian nurse who told a friend of hers suffering from Man Flu, "what you need is a six-pack of toughen the fuck up" (it works really well if you do the accent), but really she was sympathetic, particularly as I had to go in this morning to have the various shards of my splintered rear molar pulled out. It is nice, if "nice" is really the word I'm groping for, to have a dentist within walking distance, but if you're going "ow" every time you move your left leg what would have been an otherwise jaunty and insouciant stroll towards a thoroughly enjoyable extraction, as these things so often are, turned out to be like something from Napoleon's retreat from Moscow.

"Cold enough for you?" asked my local *Big Issue* vendor, the nice guy whose pitch is outside Waitrose. I assured him it was, and was glad he wasn't carrying any magazines, as I had only a tenner in my pocket, and indeed the world, and needed to buy tea, bread, butter, and orange juice on the way back. As I sat in the waiting room I took out my *TLS* and read a very interesting article on the British Secret Service's use of torture from the Second World War on. I suppose that the reviewer didn't go into any precise details about the techniques employed was some kind of relief. Then again, the imagination was left free to roam. On reflection, I think it is safe to say that if you are an arm of the intelligence services of this power or any other, it would be unwise of you to entrust me with any particularly sensitive information that you would prefer me to keep to myself.

Do you know that brief but memorable sequence when

Homer Simpson goes to the dentist? You can find it on YouTube, but it goes roughly like this: in a dentist's waiting room, we hear Homer screaming and calling the dentist "you butcher!" A mother reassures her spooked child: "I'm sure that man has a special tooth problem." We then hear Homer screaming: "I don't even have a special tooth problem! This is just a routine check-up!" and the child dives out of the window. That's what I'm like when I have a scrape and a polish. I suppose it would help if I didn't leave an average of two and a half years between check-ups, for the plaque build-up apparently leaves my teeth in the condition of a kettle that has been in constant service, in a hard water area, since the Coronation, but then that's the way I roll. Take it or leave it. It is also a noble family tradition, inherited down the male line. My dentist, of whom I am actually rather fond, is also the family dentist, and my mother once asked him how good a patient my father was. "It's all I can do to get him in the chair," was his reply. I am, perversely, proud; for my father has always been very grown-up and stoic, and it is comforting to know that he, after all, has his weaknesses. Anyway, even with three injections, there was a lot of my saying things like "no, stop", and "can't we just leave that bit in?" and, to be honest, the nurse holding my hand. I was interested to note that you really do break into a cold sweat in situations like this. I also only thought much later of saying something funny like "you know, if you want my bank account details and PIN number, we really don't have to go through this rigmarole."

After a lot of yanking and fossicking about he finally got the bastard out. I looked at it – or rather, its shards – in the little tray next to me. They looked ancient, degraded, like something an archaeologist could plausibly claim dated from the Cretaceous. Jesus, I thought, are all the others like that? I also wondered why the pink water they give you to swill your mouth out – so coloured, I always thought, to disguise any blood – was in this instance replaced by clear water; for now the blood was plain to see. And the *coup de grâce*? I'm allowed no more than one glass of wine this evening, for alcohol is a vasodilator, and it would start the hole bleeding all over again. "Don't they know who you are?" asked my friend Tig when I whined about it on Facebook afterwards. "It's an outrage!" I wonder whether a little bleeding is such a bad thing. Oh, and I forgot the bread and the butter at Waitrose. Can't wait for the mile-and-a-half limp there and back.

I am still thinking about an article that appeared in the *Guardian* last week – and, judging by the way it hung about in the "most read" chart for so long, I'm not the only one. It was by one Philippa Ferry, who I gather is a psychotherapist, and what she said was, if I summarise correctly, that people who lie about their alcohol consumption do so because they want to project a favourable self-image; that they are, in short, narcissists. Which is all well and good, and shows that she has learned how to use the word "narcissist", which is the insult *du jour* when you want to tell someone you disapprove of their behaviour and want to sound clever while doing so. A few years ago the word was "entitlement" but ever since we got a government whose cabinet members stink of self-entitlement so much the smell is unsupportable as far away as Lerwick, the potency seems to have gone out of that rebuke.

Anyway, does it make me any less of a narcissist when I

am flat-out honest about my own alcohol consumption to the health authorities? I doubt it. People lie to their doctors because they're tired of being told off all the time. I am inured to this now so I like looking at doctors' faces when I say "oh, a bottle, a bottle and a half of wine a night, on rare occasions two". The dose varies because sometimes I've been told to lay off the sauce (or can't afford it). After I'd had my tooth pulled the dentist said if I had more than one glass that evening I'd bleed like a stuck pig from the hole, so I only had the one bottle and everything was fine. I know someone who assumes a straight face and tells her doctor she drinks one bottle of wine a week, which I suspect is something of an underestimate, but there's something I like about that, too: if you're going to fib, make it outrageous. I can't remember the last time I tried bare-faced cheek like that to someone I wasn't married to.

I was toying with the idea of the self-aggrandizing lie the other day. Having finally had some funds pushed into the bank account, I had felt brave enough to open the door when the bell rang, and it was a man asking if I wanted the windows cleaned. As it happens, believe it or not, the living room windows in the Hovel have about three years'-worth of grime on them and you can't tell when it's day or night any more, so I said "yes". While I was making him a cup of tea he started asking me how long I'd lived here, and various nosy questions like that. I very nearly replied that I was merely caretaking the place for a friend who was doing ten to fifteen for murder, and that he'd given me the keys because I was the only honest man he knew. But you never know where these conversations can end. He was the kind of person who looks around a place where the books are piled, everywhere, in their thousands, and asks "do you read books?" When I replied, without resorting to sarcasm, that indeed I did, he fished into the bag where he kept his bucket and chamois and handed me a little volume by the Reverend Moon whose title suggested within a recipe for world peace. Maybe I should have read it.

I tried to lie again on Sunday, but not for narcissistic reasons. I was trying to get an oyster off the grumpy oyster man in the market I wrote about a few weeks ago, but someone had shown him the article, or he's an NS reader himself, and he refused to serve me. I really can't say I blame him. Withdrawal of service is the only potent weapon the worker still has, and if I was fool enough to think I could get away with such rudeness then serve me right. I still asked him why, so that I could then claim a case of mistaken identity ("I'm always getting mistaken for that twat, it's beginning to get me down"), but no opportunity was offered, so I had to go away, feeling wretched (Oyster Man: if you're reading this, I apologise), and endure a lecture from my 15-year-old son, who reminded me that actions have consequences, and that it's not all just me in my own little world. It is one of the stations in life, getting a legitimate telling-off from one's offspring. He'll also be taller than me in a couple of months, the way things are going. I suppose, in his way, and without using the word, thank god, he was calling me a narcissist. For, as I implied earlier, to use the word "narcissist" is in itself rather narcissistic; so what does it mean when you say it of yourself?

⁂

And so it gets worse. Another pair of boots has bitten the dust. I was crossing Paddington Street during the cold snap and felt a draught in the side of my foot. I am used to feeling draughts in unusual or unwelcome places, and they are invariably signs of what are in some circles described as wardrobe malfunctions. Normally they strike me in the area which cricket commentators coyly refer to as "amidships" and are the result of a faulty fly-button. My children are vexed and confused by me for many reasons but the one which drives them up the wall the most is my predilection for fly buttons rather than zips. What can I say? The Levi's 501 black jean, which is the only trouser I wear during the winter months (they are modestly stylish, unassuming, are the right shape, and are hard-wearing) does not come with a zip fly, ok? Unfortunately the middle buttonhole of the fly degrades over time and opens at the slightest pretext, or on no pretext at all. The last time this happened when I was with the kids, the *Big Issue* seller at the market had to point it out to me. While my offspring died several deaths from embarrassment, the BI seller made light of the incident, reminding us of what Churchill had said when someone pointed out that he was flying low: "dead birds don't fall out of their nests", which amused me but didn't make the kids feel any better at all for some reason.

But I digress. This was the boot, one of a pair I had bought about 13 months before, from the expensive manufacturers, and had been so excited about – I'd never spent so much on footwear – I put it in one of these columns. (http://www.newstatesman. com/2012/01/feet-boots-gout-pair-evening). The idea was that by investing in a pair of expensive boots whose makers have a royal charter – I am, I assure you, very much a republican, but even I suspect that Her Maj and co. don't put any old shit on their feet – I would have something that would outlast me. My children, their past shame-making experiences with my fly buttons now forgotten, or recalled with a wry, indulgent smile, would find my Loakes boots, bought in 2011, many years hence while going through my effects. "He loved those boots," they would explain to their own children. "He looked after them, and they lasted him until the end of his days. I hope one day you, too, come to appreciate the hard work that went into his seemingly effortless style."

Anyway, the bastards more or less exploded while crossing the road at my usual leisurely pace. I showed them to the shoe shop-cum-repair-shop – which only sells that brand – which supplied me in the first place.

"Never seen that before," they said. "You must do an awful lot of walking."

"I'm a writer," I explained. "I don't even get out of bed if I can help it. And I don't wear them during the summer." (Which I concede means that, last year, they only got about a week's rest, so awful was the weather.) The idea, of course, was that they would get on to Loakes, who, realising the value of good publicity, even in this column, would supply me with a new, guaranteed pair at an extremely advantageous rate, and we would all proceed happily. But we examined them – the three people behind the bar tending the machines, myself, and a couple of customers who had happened to pop in. I must say the boots did not look as they belonged to a gentleman with a sedentary lifestyle. They had gone from something the Royal Family's matriarch considered worthy of clicking the "Like" button for to something that both Vladimir and Estragon would have rejected as being *infra dignitatem*. I was reminded of the twist on the old saying: "you cannot judge a man until you have walked a mile in his moccasins; for not only are you a mile away from him, you also have his moccasins." It was if someone had been walking miles in my moccasins and then returning them to me when I slept.

This has been bothering me for a week now. Does this mean that I will never trust the royal warrant again? Or that I should maybe try not to think too hard about what goes on the ends of my legs? And is this fannying around with foot-wear simply a displacement activity, something I am using to distract myself from the ongoing catastrophe that is the rest of my life? (As the tailor says to the customer who complains it took God less time to make the world than him to make his trousers: "but just look at the world . . . and now look . . . (he beams proudly) . . . at my *trousers*." The joke is used in Samuel Beckett's *Endgame*, to excellent effect.) Anyway, I bought another pair of the damn things. If ER uses them to boot her son up the jacksy they can't be all bad.

❧

In a few week's time, I'm going to be fifty. Fifty! There was a time when I thought I wouldn't make it, or that it would be a fine time to call it a day, but that was . . . oh, forty years ago. Still, it's a time to take stock of one's own achievements to date. This doesn't take long. One only has to rattle the box labelled "one's own achievements to date" to discover that it is empty, apart from "having three amusing children", "can still fit into old trousers, just", and an old Malteser, which turns out not to be my achievement at all. I'd like to have a big party for the day, but how am I going to be able to afford one? And by "big" I mean "have some funds behind the bar so not all of my friends have to buy their own drinks all night long".

Of course, this begs the question of why I should be having a 50th party at all. It is a milestone that is only an arbitrary numerical curiosity. Meanwhile, down the road, I notice that a new Swanky Shop is Opening Soon. This is not the kind of news I like. Ever since the picture-framer's shop closed simply because the landlord saw an opportunity for screwing more rent out of a tenant (with the result that the premises have now remained empty for months) I have been uneasily aware that the pleasant quality of my own little pocket of London – a place in which one does not have to be a millionaire in order to feel relatively comfortable – is very much under threat. (The Islamic bookshop has also closed down too, I note. I was never going to be a patron of it for all sorts of reasons, but at least it ticked the boxes marked "diversity" and "not an estate agent".)

I look up the name of the Swanky Shop Opening Soon on the net. It turns out that it is a purveyor of hugely expensive wank for people who, as the late Alan Clarke noted of the likes of counter-jumpers like the Heseltines, are so unclassy that they have to buy their own furniture. And yet have oodles to throw around, and scant reserves of taste. Later on in the evening, the Beloved comes round and I show her some of the wares on sale. There is a drinks cabinet on sale for £15,000. That's right, fifteen grand for somewhere to stash your Britvic. A four-foot by two-foot by two-foot chest comes in at £11,300. "Travel to a universe of pirates and treasure your adventures in this chest," advises the rubric somewhat bafflingly, explaining the high price thus: "this piece is layered in varying angled cuts of highly polished brass dipped in gold" which have been "individually applied to the frame by the jeweller". (It's also lined in "green copper ultrasuede", the last word of which should surely have been the name of a particularly awful progressive rock group from the 1970s, and for all I know actually was.)

The Beloved and I go through the site, marvelling at the prices they are asking. I then see that they're selling some particularly grotesque Champagne glasses, the kind you would pour the fizz into if you were the most loathsome dictator in the world trying to impress the most expensive prostitute in the world, only the price is listed on the page as £0.00. Now some of you may say that's a glitch in the system, but I see that it still costs £4 postage and packing, so, after having had a good look at the terms and conditions, as they suggest, and rather egged on, I have to admit, by the bewitching woman sitting next to me, I order 1,000 of the objects. If I can knock 'em off for a tenner each I'll be well in pocket.

Later, to see where I fit in the great chain of being that is this country's class system, for I am beginning to get quite confused by now, I take the BBC's "Great British Class Calculator" quiz. You've all done this, right? Then you'll know what a crock it is. Like many such polls, it takes scant account of nuance or allowance for flexibility or what these days we are all being encouraged to call "wiggle room". And also, with only five questions to answer, it seems like a hopelessly blunt instrument for something that claims to expand the traditional number of British classes from three to seven.

The first time I take it, it says I am an "emergent service worker". What on earth is one of those? It says I'm 34 years old. I try it again, factoring in a share of the home the estranged Wife lives in. I'm now "traditional working class", and aged 66. I see another category, a new word: "Precariat". That has a ring to it. At least my ages average out ok.

My editor communicated a heartfelt request that this column be a Thatcher-free zone,* but she needn't have worried: I have heavier matters on my heart. Namely: Oyster Man. Regular readers who have not been deprogrammed will recall that a couple of months ago (see p. 80), I wrote a column in which I expressed grievances at this tradesman's way with his customers, which stopped well short of libel but perhaps not, if you were the offended party, offence. I was intending to be amusing but, with some justification, the actual cause of the amusement failed to be amused. My folly lay in imagining that the circumstances of being a fishmonger, which is hard enough work as it is, precluded members of that fine trade from such effete bourgeois pursuits as reading the *New Statesman*.

Well, either he was an unusual fishmonger and had a subscription, or one of you lot sneaked on me, but the next time I went for my Sunday morning oysters – which are my one real luxury, a family tradition, and are moreover shared with my eldest son – he refused to serve me.

Now if I were a cheerleader for the free market I would have shrugged this off and taken my custom elsewhere. But I'm not. I wouldn't be happy in these pages if I were, would I? Also, his oysters really are very good, and he shucks them for

* In this week the former PM died. A few days before the funeral a group of friends, all writers, decided to meet up at the Academy and have a splendid lunch, to avoid all coverage and the general mawkishness that would ensue. Unsympathetic, to put it mildly, towards her policies, we called ourselves the Margaret Thatcher Funeral Lunch, and I wore a red shirt that had been sent to me by a reader. Several years on, this tradition survives, with one minor adjustment: I no longer even pretend to be able to pay for myself, and find myself quoting Christopher Hitchens's great line, "whose turn is it to buy me lunch today?"

you. I can shuck them myself but it is a much more time-consuming business when I do. It is also freighted with peril, and the memory of peril. Should you ever get the chance to inspect the ball of Will Self's left thumb, you will notice the rather impressive scar left in a shucking accident in my kitchen in the spring of, I think, 1996. Believe me, it was even more impressive when it happened. It was like something out of a gonzo production of Macbeth. Even the cat fainted.

Anyway, I wrote a column in which I apologised to Oyster Man (see page 89) and when it was printed, circled the relevant paragraph and left it on his table when he wasn't looking and then ran away. (This wasn't my first plan. My first plan was to get my son to leave it at his table, but he refused, on the reasonable grounds that the child should not atone for the sins of the father. "You have to realise that actions have consequences," he told me sternly.) I am normally good at facing up to unpleasant duties* but a face-to-face confrontation with Oyster Man doesn't appeal. His oyster knife looks sharper than mine, for a start. But what is the etiquette here? I asked my children, but all they said, with some asperity, was that they bet other people's children didn't have these kind of problems with their parents.

I did try the local posh supermarket. I had noticed that there hadn't been any oysters there for a couple of weeks (it's that posh), but assumed that this was because they'd sold out before I got there. After an exchange which confirmed that my eyes were not deceiving me and there were no oysters there, the following colloquy occurred: Me (affably): So when are you getting them back in?

Fishmonger: Out of stock – anyway, they're out of season.

* This is a lie. I do not know how I had the gall to claim as much.

Me: What, in April? FM: That's right, there's an R in the month, they're not in season then. Me: But that's exactly when they *are* in season. FM (patiently): No, it's when there's an R in the month that they're out of season. Me (making sure I eliminate all traces possible of sarcasm from my reply): You mean, like in December, or January, or (affable smile as I emphasise the Rs) Feb-ru-are-ree? FM (with a slight jolt, as if coming out from hypnosis): Yes, there is that.

We cleared up the confusion (I put his down to one of those kind of moments of mental collapse we have all had, such as when we fail to remember the name of a lover right under us (long story), or some other such moment of crazy aporia - or a desire to try and cover up for his ultimate bosses, who for reasons undivulged have decided that for the posh supermarket, oyster season ended in March, which I gather is actually the case) and he recommended I go to Selfridges, but I haven't been able to set foot in their food hall ever since I found out what they charge for Marmite.

So that's it. Oysters are now off for me. To think that this is because of my own recklessness and not because I ate a mottled one. I still wonder whether it was one of you who passed the offending column onto Oyster Man. I was brought up under an ethos which frowns upon tale-bearing, but I shall forgive you this once. Although much pain would have been spared all round had you been around and murmured caution into my ear while I was writing it in the first place. Anyway, the season's almost over, although Oyster Man looks like the kind of man whose memories last long and vivid, and he probably won't serve me next time I roll round in September. I shall have to find a new tradesperson to offend unthinkingly.

I gather that a fairly common dream involves discovering a multitude of hitherto hidden rooms in your place of abode. What these dreams represent or say of your own state of mind it is not for me to say. Personally, I always awake from these dreams a bit miffed to find that the Hovel is not actually like the Tardis, with a multitude of exotic chambers hidden within the folds of space-time. "Welcome to the Hovel," I say to new visitors. "It's smaller on the inside."

Except that I have discovered it isn't. For an interesting reason I'll get on to in a minute, there has been a lot of clearing-out going on here, and in the course of this I have discovered a whole extra room. Not a big one: but what I thought was nothing more than a glorified cupboard used for storing three-quarter-empty tins of solidified paint actually turns out to be a toilet. Not in the sense that [insert your least favourite town in Britain here] is a toilet, but a real one: you know, the kind you . . . sit on. There is also a sink opposite it, and – this is the detail I find most charming – an ashtray screwed to the wall between the two. We lost something, I think, when we stopped equipping lavatories with ashtrays. Contrary to what the publicity would have us believe, air freshener doesn't smell better than cigarette smoke, or, if you find that a hard one to swallow, work better than cigarette smoke at disguising nasty odours. Of course, this loo is of marginal utility at best. In fact, as it's no longer plumbed in, and thank goodness I didn't have to find that out the hard way, it's actually worse than useless, and makes the room's new purpose – for shoving all the things that were cluttering up the cupboard at the end of my room into – somewhat compromised. Still, you don't half find a lot of interesting stuff when you're sorting out. My stuff, of course, is all essential, for it was all I could take with me (apart from the seventeen boxes of books now pressing down on the loft beams of my parents' house) upon ejection from the family home. I had already pared myself down to the minimum. How, for instance, could I have thrown away the Leaving Card from my first job, in-house copywriter for The Folio Society? The running gags on that one, which dates I think from 1988, are that I am not very tidy and invariably late with my copy. These days I am not much tidier but I now file more promptly. Some editors I know may raise a hollow laugh at that one but believe me, the situation beforehand was much, much worse. I look at the signatures on the card. Four of the people who signed it are now dead, one of whom I still miss very much indeed, and another I miss even more, for his death was untimely. One of them is the mother of my children (our affair was a clandestine one). One or two others I am still friends with. Another, when I bumped into her in the street the other day, has now forgotten we were ever colleagues and accounts for her vague recollection of me by thinking I went to school with her. This was particularly galling because she once made what was almost certainly a pass at me, which I found terribly exciting because (a) I had a huge crush on her and (b) she was the daughter of a multimillionaire. But I was Spoken For – by another colleague, as it happened – and I had to pretend I hadn't noticed. I sometimes wonder how my life would have turned out if I had taken her up on the offer.

I also find a bank statement from those years. Now that was an eye-opener. I gather that The Folio Society (they always prissily insist on that upper case "T", like *The Times*, but no one outside the company bothers with it) now sponsors a major literary prize. A look at my bank statement will give you a clue as to how it is that a publisher is able to be so lavish: they saved their money over the years by paying me no more than £442 a month, after tax. True, this is more than twice the sum that Conservative ministers regularly claim they need to live on, but it didn't stretch that far even then, especially when, as I note with some alarm, my overdraft was, as ever, in the four-figure range, and the first figure wasn't a "1". (Still, as I may have suggested, the pay might have been lousy, but the fringe benefits were considerable.)

The reason that I was doing all this shifting of stuff from one place to another is to make room for the Beloved, who is moving in despite the fact that I am a perpetually broke slob who can't throw anything away. This is very, very good news. Sometimes it – the general scheme of things – gets better.

Walking to the tube, I fall into step with Tony, the barber. Tony ticks all the right boxes when it comes to the men to whom I entrust my thinning, grizzled locks. He is very close by. He is not ruinously expensive. £14 a go is all right, isn't it? It's half the price in Shepherd's Bush, true, but then I don't live there any more, and going nine stops on the Hammersmith and City Line to save a few quid would just be silly. He is nude of pate. I only trust bald or balding barbers. Experience has taught me that barbers who have lost or are losing their own hair are tenderer in their concerns for others' than are their full-headed colleagues. And he is called Tony. I do not know why all barbers should be called Tony, but there it is, just as all dentists should be Jewish. We are talking an ideal world here. I am prepared to admit the existence within the professions of non-Tony barbers and non-Jewish dentists, but such barbers and dentists are for people with more flexible standards than mine.

Tony, though Lebanese and strong of accent, is otherwise as British as barbers can come. Maybe there is an international sodality of barbers whose members are taught, from earliest apprenticeship, the arts of mild banter, professional pessimism, preference for the *Daily Mail* or local equivalent, and implausible claim. The customer forgives all these things while at the same time remembering the oldest joke in the world that still has something funny clinging to it: "How would sir like his hair cut today?" "In silence." But you don't want silence, not really, not forever. The implausible claims are either of the my-local-council-is-so-crazily-left-wing-it-banned-cheese variety, or the Yeah,-Elton-John's-a-regular-here variety. My Tony falls into the latter category. I cannot recall precisely which unlikely celebrities I have failed to see in my five-and-two-thirds years' experience of sitting in his chair or waiting to, but they are along the lines of Daniel Craig, The Artist Formerly Known as Prince, and the late Neil Armstrong, who popped in for a haircut during a lecture tour in 1978 and was so delighted by the experience that he kept returning. However, I remain sceptical.

"Why don't you write about me?" he asks from time to time. I am, Tony, I am. I may tease but I hope it is clear that I like him. He is about my age, and has three children about the same ages as mine. I have followed their progresses. He drives a moped in from Ealing every morning, rain or shine, and works hard, unless the punters are failing to turn up. And every time I ask him how business is, he will without fail tell me it is dreadful. Sometimes I have asked this after a half-hour wait while he clips away at several people in front of me. The first time he told me business was dreadful was in 2007. Since then he has assured me it has been getting even worse than the last time I had my Usual. (Another good thing about Tony, which I suppose I should have mentioned rather earlier, is that he does my hair Just Right. Some would say that this is an even more desirable attribute in a barber than being called Tony. I am not sure, but I concede such people may have a point.)

Where was I? Oh yes, falling into step with Tony. Now that we are not on his premises our conversation has less of the ritual about it. Even when he embarks on the usual Jeremiad, there is something keener, more felt, about it. And it is perhaps by coincidence that as we pass the shop selling Expensive Wank that he says "the area's changing." His tone of voice suggests that it is not changing in a way he would like.

"Too many people with too much money?" I venture. Yes, he says. Exactly. Something very bad is happening to a country, or a city, or a neighbourhood, in which the kind of small businessman who takes the *Daily Mail* and not only talks the talk but walks the walk when it comes to working hard in an honest job complains that there is now too much money coming into an area rather than too little. And I have seen too many small businesses close down round here to be sanguine about the future. But the local cheap barber really is the canary in the coal mine when it comes to the toxic effects of too much money. I look again at the shop selling Expensive Wank and reflect that while it may be all very well to have, as an expression of your taste and personality, a mounted zebra head on your wall (actually, it is not all very well in the slightest), such an artefact is not going to get your hair cut, or do anyone, human or animal, any good at all.

⚜

All book reviewers know by heart George Orwell's essay "Confessions of a Book Reviewer." Find one now, go on, and watch his or her lips move in unison with yours as you read out the opening lines: "In a cold but stuffy bed-sitting room littered with cigarette ends and half-empty cups of tea, a man in a moth-eaten dressing-grown sits at a rickety table, trying to find room for his typewriter among the piles of dusty papers that surround it." The typewriter is now a laptop, but the principle still applies. It's probably Orwell's funniest piece of writing, if you are not a book reviewer. If you are, then it may all be a little too painfully close to home, even if the book reviewer has since discovered that you now don't need to find a surface: you can take your laptop to bed and work from there, which was never really something you could comfortably do with a typewriter. Ah, progress.

The salient point for our purposes today is the term "dressing-gown". Writers of a certain bent tend not to bother with the whole Getting Dressed Thing until around four o'clock, when they remember they have run out of milk and need to go to the shops. In my wild youth I would occasionally trot round the corner in my dressing gown, because what I looked like then, or so I fancy, was a young devil-may-care man unafraid of defying convention. It may not have been Gerard de Nerval walking the streets of Paris with a lobster on a leash, but it was good enough.

Approach the autumn of one's life, though, and this

becomes an option that gets firmly closed off. Cross the road in a dressing gown at my age and not only will people think you are an escapee from an institution for the demented, they may well try to reinstate you there, and I suspect that the more hotly you try to persuade them that what they are doing is actually instating you, the more securely do they tie you up before dropping you off.

The problem with the Not Getting Dressed Thing, then, is that a residual shame clings to it. The books arrive, for that is the job of their respective publicity departments. Or rather, some of them arrive. "How do you decide which books to review?" I am often asked. The full answer, which I do not give, should really begin with the words "well, first they have to get through the door." After all, there has to be some winnowing process if I am being sent forty books a week and can only do one of them, and sheer chance may as well be one of the factors as anything else. If the package is too large for the letterbox, the postman rings the bell. (Sometimes the packages are small but someone has bound them together with a rubber band which he is reluctant to remove.) It is usually around eleven o'clock. But I am still in my dressing gown. And ashamed to face someone who has been up since 6 in the morning and pounding the streets with an enormous trolley weighed down mainly by books addressed to me.

So I cower in bed. I have also probably been further dispirited by making the mistake of reading comments below the line of an article I have recently written. "Mr Lezard is a literary critic, one of the most useless of all occupations," said one recent fan. In fact, he or she elaborated on the point in reply to another reader's comment, feeling that he or she had not gone far enough the first time around: "He is a literary critic, so his work is inevitably incomprehensible, unreadable and pointless."

Anyway, eventually I take a handful of the while-you-were-out cards they sometimes drop through the slot, and go to the collection office. The following exchange invariably happens.

Me: "here I am, here is my passport and an official letter with my name on it, and here are some 'while-you-were-out' cards." Post Official: "yes, we've got loads of stuff for you." (He goes off and returns with an enormous pile of jiffy bags, and starts going through the cards.)

"I'm sorry, the cards you've given me don't correspond to the parcels here."

Me: "What?" PO: "I can't give you these parcels." Me: "But this is me! Look! Here's my picture in a passport! Here's an official letter I would in fact rather have not received!"

The last time this happened, last Saturday actually, I even tried crying a little bit, as I was sure I had the correct cards this time. Still no dice. I turned to the man behind me, as if to apologise for being ahead of him in the queue, but also, perhaps, in entreaty. "This country is awesome," he said, deadpan. Quite so. And I thought to myself: wow. We've finally done it. We've created a dystopia not even Orwell foresaw, because it's silly.

❧

An email from The Shop Selling Expensive Wank down the road. Readers of this column whose minds are capable of retaining items of debatable nutritional worth will recall that a few weeks ago (see page 93), in a bid to bankrupt it, I ordered 1,000 of their revolting champagne glasses because I had noticed that their website was selling them for £0.00, plus £4 postage and packing for each order. Four quid for 1,000 glasses, however vulgar, seemed like a good deal to me, and would give whoever runs their online catalogue good cause to reflect upon the importance of proofreading even electronic documents.

The email is succinct and professional. It points out that the price of £0.00 was "a glitch", that the actual cost of each glass, which is handmade, is £180, but that should I still wish to proceed with the order they would be delighted to offer a discount. They have also refunded the £4 p&p. I contemplate briefly a scenario in which I have to explain to the Estranged Wife that I now owe a Shop Selling Expensive Wank £180,000, and so would appreciate it if she could sell the family home. As reveries go, it is not one of the more soothing ones. You wouldn't, for instance, use it to help you drop off to sleep if you were suffering from a spot of insomnia. Round One to the SSEW.

As it is, I find myself having trouble raising funds for a forthcoming Big Birthday Party, let alone 1,000 champagne glasses of unparalleled tackiness. We're only talking a few cases of plonk here, not a roomful of Veuve Clicquot. Having in the past few years just packed everyone off to the Duke and told them to buy their own drinks, this time I think it would be nice to actually splash out on some booze myself for a change. Unfortunately, the bank balance has sustained some torpedo damage in the last few weeks, largely self-inflicted for a change: the provider of my main source of income paid me two weeks early last month so as not to inconvenience its payees during a system changeover, which was incredibly thoughtful of them but lulled me into a false sense of financial security. That this very magazine seems to have paid me twice in the same month – although I may have got this wrong – added to this sense, and so I spent a large part of the last month thinking I was far wealthier than I actually was, and splurging like someone demob-happy.

So to cut a long story short I was saved by a parental birthday cheque and a fraternal last-minute loan. ("Am I going to get this back?" he asked with pardonable suspicion as I snatched the cash from him at the Marylebone Station cashpoint and made to sprint away. Of course you'll get it back, Tony.) That, and the great generosity of my friends, who, having worked out that if there's one thing I like, it's wine, brought me so much wine that I think I may even be ahead on the deal. (It would appear that Majestic accepts returns, of full bottles at least, and all they ask of you when you rent their wineglasses is a £1 deposit each, so, if broken, 1/180th the price of a glass from which even Liberace in his pomp would have thought twice about sipping.)

But the rest of the month is going to be spent in lock-down mode. The Beloved, who earns even less than me, gave me a present that must have reduced her to beggary, and certainly reduced me to tears when I opened it. (A Hogarth print that may well have been handled by the great man himself, if you're wondering.) We are going to be eating a lot of pasta and baked potatoes, the Beloved and I, until a boat, whose smoke I cannot quite see over the horizon yet, comes in. I have discovered that you can make quite a lot of rillettes from a leftover fowl. This helps. I once asked the Fromagerie – a local shop selling extremely expensive artisanal produce from, mainly, France – how much one of their tiny pots of duck rillettes costed and the next thing I knew I was being revived by the paramedics. So now I have an enormous bowl of rillettes which I can use for my daily protein allowance in the comfortable knowledge that I obtained it, in effect, for free. Against this one has to place the knowledge, which experience has taught me, that after about a week of eating rillettes one kind of wearies of rillettes. One even wearies of the word "rillettes". I bet you have now, too.

⚜

One of the interesting side-effects of separation from the family environment is that I find myself mixing with a rather younger age group from the one to which I was hitherto confined. A few years ago it was just I and my contemporaries, sliding in-eluctably, like balls rolling very boringly downhill, into middle age. Conversation began to confine itself to little more than swapping the symptoms of gradual senescence. Oh, my back. Oh, my teeth. Oh, my thinning hair. Oh, my bank balance. But now I find myself often among the young, or the younger, more than I would have expected to half a decade ago. I also seem to be going to a lot more weddings. My generation are normally past that stage. But now it is hard, among the two suits I possess, to find one whose pockets do not contain, among the bits of fluff and tobacco that line the pockets, dried lavender petals or bits of paper in the shape of horseshoes. This is all very pleasant, and I have also become quite a connoisseur of the nuptial celebration, and can now time the church service to the nearest five minutes simply by glancing at the order of service as it's handed to me on the porch. But I like a wedding, even if mine didn't turn out in the approved manner, and while I don't share Larkin's misgivings in "The Whitsun Weddings", the lines always, especially at this time of year, come back to me: "fathers had never known/Success so huge and wholly farcical; The women shared/The secret like a happy funeral . . ."

The only downside is that these days by odd coincidence the post-dinner dancing seems to involve a lot of folk dancing, and however many times I bellow in protest the line that everything should be tried once with the exception of that and incest, I end up at some point having to dance the Gay Gordons or some other reel or hoe-down or something. I was given a quick tutorial in the first of these a few months ago after the service, and I thought, bloody hell, if I can't even begin to grasp the technicalities when stone cold sober, what hope is there for me, or anyone in my immediate vicinity, after a bottle each of Champagne, Sauvignon Blanc and Côtes du Rhone? The first time I had a go I ended up running away before the end, leaving the Beloved partnerless and understandably miffed, and with my reputation as a party spirit ready for anything somewhat dented. But I had sensed disaster coming, and felt that it was better to lose face and endure months of sporadic teasing than break someone's toe, or wrench an arm, possibly mine, out of its socket.

Last weekend I didn't bail out. I made sure this time that I drank enough to obliterate all traces of self-consciousness. I very nearly obliterated all traces of consciousness too, but then I had also earlier in the day made the tricky re-acquaintance of Chris Skidmore MP, about whom I had been rather scathing in this very slot last August. http://www.newstatesman.com/lifestyle/lifestyle/2012/08/there%E2%80%99s-nowayi%E2%80%99ll-be-jamming-small-hours-tory-mp-again Cleverly, as well as graciously, he made no allusion to the piece, and was in fact politeness and charm itself, damn it. I was further rattled by being seated next to his girlfriend for the dinner, and, she, too, acted as if entirely innocent of the offending article. I ended up inviting them both to my book launch in July. Was that an apology? No; more a sidestepping of the issue. And if I didn't say sorry for not being a Gay Gordon in April, I shouldn't say so for a slightly lesser offence nine months ago.

The next day, suffering hangovers that bring us to the verge of tears, the Beloved and I meet her big sister and co. in Alnwick. I am mildly anxious, for while the Big Sister is still younger than me, Big Sisters are still Big Sisters, and their word is Law. I am encouraged that the rendezvous is in Barter Books, a legendary second-hand bookstore which has taken over the old railway station. All traces of pain and metaphysical unease vanish as I walk into this most excellent emporium. There are more books in it than you can imagine. I start hyperventilating a bit, becoming as excited as a three-year-old let loose in a free amusement park. It is, quite simply, the best place I have ever seen. I scamper up and down the aisles like a laboratory rat on Modafinil. Eventually I choose an armful of orange Penguins in excellent condition, including a first edition Lady Chatterley's Lover for £2.60 and a rare collection of early Wodehouse for 60p. Later on, in the latter, I read: "It is a good rule in life never to apologize. The right sort of people do not want apologies, and the wrong sort take a mean advantage of them."

Back from New York* and I discover that, once again, summer

* A long story, too tedious to go into, even for me, and if you're asking

has failed to materialise. It had all been so tantalising on the way out: the trees on the A312 , which links the A40 and the M4, were alive with birdsong, and that's a phrase I never thought I'd be writing in my lifetime. And I arrived in a chilly New York just an hour away from taking a battering from a rainstorm so vicious it was even given a name. The return journey was the opposite: from a glorious summer New York, not too hot or muggy, and with brilliant sunshine, to a cold, grey London. I looked out at the houses on the North Circular and wondered whether they were the most unloved houses in the world. If looking at them makes you feel like killing yourself, what must living in them be like? (For connoisseurs of depressing housing, I recommend the stretch, about three miles long, centred on Neasden.)

As those of you living in London know, the sun has returned, in a tentative way, like a guest who is not really sure whether he wants to be at the party or not, and is in fact quite conscious that there is a better one down the road, but feels an obligation to drop in just for a bit. We have noticed your reluctance, o Ra, and frankly, we are a little disappointed. At least it was pleasant enough for Charles Saatchi to be able to sit outside and half-strangle his wife without suffering a chill or getting rained on.

There. I made it right down to the end of the second paragraph before mentioning THAT incident. For although I have a hunch others in this magazine will be commenting on it, and that mine, therefore, may well be surplus to requirements,

yourself what someone who claims continual poverty was doing in New York, the answer is that his mother paid for his ticket, so he could help her on the journey with luggage and her own occasional demands. The journey was . . . trying. Suffice to say that on the outward journey, I had to hit the duty-free Scotch in the plane's lavatory.

I am afraid I am helpless: I have become obsessed with it. The pictures, once seen, cannot be unseen, and the distance between the face of Nigella we all know from the telly and the frightened, weeping face from the paparazzo shots is immense and terrifying. Not even Hitchcock, in art, managed to un-settle so much.

And I find myself unable to think of anything else. I have friends who have suffered violence at the hands of the men they love; in one case, it was very nearly fatal, and the doctors who examined her expressed relief that she had not been beaten for a second longer than she already had, so close had she come to death. I believe a grip around the throat can also be rather dangerous unless you know what you're doing. I wonder whether this is Mr Saatchi's first-ever experience as a playful gripper of women's necks. It is always rather charming when the elderly discover a new hobby, of course, but I think it might have been better if he had taken up skydiving, or, if he feels more sedentary, bridge, instead. I have, as it happens, met Ms Lawson myself, some years ago, just as her fame was beginning to crest; we talked briefly, discussing childcare of all things, and I was struck at the time by how un-famous she was acting. A little of that goes a long way when you're talking to people far, far down the pecking order, and ever since then I have refused to hear a word against her. So now one of the men at whose feet we can lay some of the blame for Thatcher's victory in 1979 has revealed something of himself; at best, his idea of play. Or "intense debate". That "Labour isn't working" poster was a masterpiece of dissembling; his statement explaining away the photographs rather less of one. You can see how threadbare the material is from too far off. And once again, we find ourselves avoiding the key question of violence against women: if the man had done that to a stranger in the street, would he have been allowed to get on with his business, with only a caution at the end of the road?

I am afraid that I do not know the workings of Charles Saatchi's mind, never having had the time or the inclination to read his book. Perhaps he may think, on reflection, that he could have chosen a title other than "Be The Worst You can Be". Its subtitle – "life's too long for patience and virtue" – may also be one he may want to revise should there ever be another edition. Not, of course, that I am implying anything about Mr Saatchi himself. For all we know, he was being playful, and all this Be The Worst You can Be Stuff is just a blind concealing a sweet and considerate nature, and that when he says he'd rather eat Dairylea on toast than anything his wife cooks, he's actually concealing a deep and private reverence for and appreciation of her art. But you know what? Somehow I doubt it.*

So it is now about two months since the Beloved moved into the Hovel, but who's counting? Bar an unfortunate interrgenum of my own misguided advising, we have been stepping out for more than two and a half years, and our time together has, as is always the case with couples, been punctuated by arguments. The first argument we had concerned the relative

---

* I was going to delete this episode from the book, but in the end decided that though the events it describes are old news, violence against women remains as bad a problem as it ever was. Also, I despise Charles Saatchi, and Nigella Lawson was so lovely to me. She even gave me her address and told me to come round with the kid so we could all go to the park together. I never did, on the grounds that I wanted to keep my marriage together. Fat lot of good that resolution did me.

merits of Haydn and Handel as composers. I am on the record as someone with little time for Handel, considering him as I do, in a phrase I lift from Martin Rowson regarding someone else entirely, a professional brown-noser to the aristocracy; at least Haydn, when employed by the backwoods Hungarian count, wrote a symphony – the "Farewell" – whose final and entire point was to remind him of his obligations to pay him and his musicians on time. That takes some balls. The other argument we have had neither of us can recall. She is against fish, so would rather I never again put anchovies, which are like fish squared, into a roast lamb ever again, but as we have compromised on capers this doesn't really count as an argument.

When she told her friends that she was moving in most of them held her hand and said something along the lines of "you're so brave", and many of my friends have used the identical adjective to describe her, but, really, what is there to be brave about? Unless you are scared of either mice or piles of books, or floors several degrees out of true, the Hovel is nothing to be scared of, and neither am I. The only domestic violence that I have ever been involved in has involved me at the receiving end, and even if I concede it was not entirely unjustified, it was never that bad. The only physical danger I represent is maybe rolling over in my sleep and hurting her, but I do not carry enough avoirdupois for that to bear a threat to anything larger than a kitten.

The only problem that might significantly obtain is my untidiness, for, like most women, the Beloved is a woman of neatness, and although she says she has only cried a couple of times at the mess, every Saturday Marta the Romanian cleaning lady, who comes with the Hovel, pops round to make everything better.

But the Hovel exercises its own benign influence, and a certain forgiving, lackadaisical attitude creeps in, and so it is only last weekend that the Beloved gets round to unpacking the last three boxes of her belongings. So as I am lathering the physiognomy during the late-Saturday-afternoon shave, she comes into the bathroom and shows to me a carving in soapstone, about the size of a heavyweight boxer's fist, and asks me, "what am I going to do with THIS?"

The emphasis she places on the word "this", and indeed her general tone of voice, invites me to speculate that I am being encouraged to offer my disdain, and although to my eye there is nothing particularly objectionable about the carving at all, I decide to give my negatively critical vocabulary a rare trot around the park. After all, I spend every week being happily nice about a book in the *Guardian*, even though, for some unfathomable reason, everyone still thinks I am one of the nastiest reviewers around. "It looks," I say, "like a woman undergoing severe abdominal pains. Or perhaps," I add, "she has been caught in private while trying to pass a particularly obdurate stool." I warm to my theme. As I say, the piece is actually quite good, but once the Scathing Vocab. has been unleashed, it is hard to contain the flow. I get a giddy pleasure from it, as the virtuous might get when lured off-guard into a den of vice. I will spare you the rest; but you get the idea.

I pause, eventually, for breath. Into that pause the Beloved says: "that's interesting, because I carved this myself when I did a stone-carving course. I didn't know what to do, and the teacher said 'the stone itself will tell you what to carve.'"

A period of backtracking on my part follows. It is more, I say, now I come to think of it, redolent of the primal power and beauty of the Venus of Willendorf, or of the tribal carvings which so inspired Picasso, Modigliani, T. S. Eliot and the bravest Modernists. Stravinsky himself would have composed the Rite had he seen it, on the spot.

It is no good. The Beloved says she will put it, for now, in the cupboard for Crap She Can't Quite Bear To Throw Away, and I reflect that although I love all women in general and this one in particular, I will never open my gob to reply to anything they say without first thinking about it for a week, and then making sure that only something nice comes out of it when I do.

⊰⊱

A *recherché* little launch for a book, itself of no great import, but it is the party season, which is good news for the thirsty freelance hack on a tight budget. It is also within walking distance of the Hovel, and this becomes an ever-more important consideration as I get older. Anyway, I am wondering how much longer I can take of this – it's in a jewellery shop, and I find that book launches held in either jewellery or, say, perfume shops do not attract people whom one could readily identify as bookish – when I notice a face from the distant past: the Empress of Charn.

She's not really the Empress of Charn. The E. of C. was, you may recall, Jadis, the rather overbearing witch-figure in C. S. Lewis's *The Magician's Nephew*. She could snap the iron bar off a lamppost as easily as if it were a stick of celery and in spite of, or probably because of, her imperious nature and scorn for the conventions, hugely impressed the weak and foolish Uncle Andrew. "A dem fine woman," he would call her in fond remembrance. Her latter-day avatar was not by any means the evil Empress of a doomed empire, later to become the White Witch and keep Narnia frozen in pre-Christmas winter for centuries.

But she did have a way of persuading those around her to do unwise things, and my friend S——— christened her the Empress after one particular exploit, whose details it is best not to repeat here. She was simply very hard to say "no" to; and she also found it hard to say "no" herself. Her appetite for drink and the uglier corners of the pharmacopoeia could land her in the most alarming situations.

This was all a long time ago: decades, in fact. I occasionally wondered what had happened to her, and learned a while back that she had cleaned her act up and was now properly and totally sober. I used, even longer ago, to be scornful of friends who went on the wagon, even if only for brief periods; at that age, I had not yet experienced the devastation that a self-destructive drink habit can cause. For the destruction is not confined to the self: it is centred on it, but has a wide radius. Now when someone gives up the sauce I congratulate them and wish them luck, if they are still in circulation. (For some reason friends who have stopped drinking tend not to see as much of me as they used to.)

Anyway, it is pleasant to see the Empress again, but the first thing she says to me, after announcing that she is sober these days, is to apologise for her past behaviour. At this I find myself somewhat puzzled. For while she may have been a trial to those in her immediate circle, she was actually rather good company if you were able to peel yourself away relatively easily. Even the blast of a bomb must, once you have reached a certain distance, provide nothing more dangerous than a lick of heat and a sense of danger escaped.

But this is the thing to do, I learn, in the world of AA: to apologise to anyone who might have got mixed up, one way or another, in your past scrapes. What does one do, though, when at the receiving end of such an apology? There was that line from an early Wodehouse story I quoted a few weeks back: the right sort of person doesn't need an apology, and the wrong sort take a mean advantage of them. I stammer something about none being necessary, but there is no getting out of this: I am to be apologised to, for that is part of the process of recovery. To brush this aside would not help.

I also start thinking about what would happen if I went down that road and had to start apologizing to everyone who was part of my alcoholic past. It would certainly take up an enormous proportion of my time, and involve saying "sorry" to pretty much everyone I'd met since I was about fifteen years old. I gather from sober friends that giving up alcohol not only increases the mental bandwidth but gives you a great deal more time to Do Things, and if I was going to go clean then I'd like to spend the extra free time learning how to play the piano properly. Not saying sorry to half the population of London.

Still, I wonder whether even without that obligation I would have the fortitude to stop drinking. The wife once tried to stage an intervention for me six years ago but I got wind of it beforehand and sent a withering email to all the parties concerned explaining why I considered this a waste of their time. For one thing, it was the party season, and how you get through that without a snifter is beyond me.

❦

So I am enjoying a pot of Assam, and a scone heaped with jam and clotted cream, on the terrace of the tea-rooms at Hidcote Manor Garden, Glos., and, as so many men in similar situations do, idly, and with no serious intent whatsoever, I'm checking out the talent. It's a Monday afternoon, so we have a mainly senior set of visitors around us. It occurs to me, with a mild shock, that apart from the Beloved, her twin sister, and her paramour, I am by some measure the youngest person here, if you don't count the staff. (The man at reception was older than me, though, and had a manner about him that strongly reminded me of Pickles, the louche long-haired posho who used to prop up the bar of the Coach and Horses and deliver withering verdicts on your personality in exchange for the odd drink. Could they be the same person? The reception-ist at Hidcote is being far nicer, but still has a way of talking that makes you feel as though you are sitting in the cheap seats and have been caught picking your nose. The Americans buying tickets are positively writhing in pleasure.)

This new-found youthful feeling is rather pleasing, if a little unsettling. The only time I could ever imagine being the youngest person in a place would be if I stood in a graveyard, and even then it would be touch and go. And yet here I am. Relatively young. But not, of course, as young as the B. and her sis, even though today they are officially a year older, as today is their birthday. Quite a few years – enough to insert a young person of voting age – separate the B. and I, but circumstances have contrived to make her seem as though she has come from an earlier stage of British history. Growing up in a household which never bothered to watch any TV, she and her sisters learned to make their own entertainment. I always suspected that the notion of doing without telly and "making your own entertainment" was bogus and intended to make people my age feel guilty about watching the Wacky Races, but it turns out it wasn't bogus at all, and when I'm with the B. it can feel like I've been catapulted back to the 1930s. Not only can they all play about five musical instruments each, some of them pretty arcane ones too, they are expert and inspired at making up games, and on the train to Banbury, where we are to be met, my book is confiscated and I am commanded to give the B. my full attention.

The first game is Hangman, by way of easing me into the whole concept of mutual conviviality. There is a small boy sitting next to us who starts taking an interest, and offers "DANGER" as a suggestion to the word I am thinking of, but when the B. works out that the word's first letter is a W and its fourth is a K, she confiscates the piece of paper and we move on.

"Guess which one of the colours in *Joseph and the Amazing Technicolor Dreamcoat* I'm thinking of," she says. "How will I know you're not fibbing?" I ask, although this is the least of my worries, as I have not seen the musical since my children's primary school forced an audience of stunned and disbelieving parents to endure a loose performance of this work about ten years ago, and not all of us were giving it our full attention. She scribbles a word down on a piece of paper and hides it, and after about twenty minutes in which I name every gaudy colour I can think of, and several clues, I correctly give the answer "ruby".

But then we have a pub lunch, and pétanque, and then off to the National Trust's Hidcote Manor. "Are you Trust members?" asks the man who looks like Pickles. "No," says the B.'s sister, "but our mum's on the cover of your leaflet," and fuck my old boots, but there she is, along with the B.'s older sister and her husband, busy admiring some lupins. I have landed, it would seem, bang in the middle of the most English family in the world. Being technically only one-quarter English myself, I find this extraordinarily thrilling.

We enjoy a delightfully rancorous and vengeful few games of croquet on the massive lawn (to play the game croquet properly it is important to suspend every generous and sporting impulse you have). I retire to smoke a crafty Jazz Cigarette under a massive pine and watch the others race around in improvised croquet-related games while the sun blazes down. The wood pigeons coo in the trees; we virtually have the place to ourselves.

After a while I beckon the B. over and whisper in her ear. "Sorry to bother you," I murmur, "but isn't Heaven meant to be rather like this?"

⁂

A friend of mine announces on Facebook that the other day the cashier at the bank shoved over a slip of paper which indicated that he was £96,900 in credit. "Just for a few seconds I had a glimpse into what it must be like to have £96,900 in your current account. Unequivocally marvellous sums it up. "The purest ecstasy," he wrote. I wonder. Naturally the mistake was rectified very quickly and the true figure, he went on to tell us, was actually exactly £100,000 less than that, so I can see why his heart might have leapt, but casual acquaintance with the wealthy has taught me that the they are never satisfied with the amount they have, and every so often some wizened creep like Bernie Ecclestone will let slip in an interview that all this money-gathering is simply a joyless exercise in ringing up some other plutocrat and saying "as of today, I now have more money than you," thus making said plutocrat choke on his platinum-plated cornflakes and try to reverse the situation by immiserating a further tranche of the world's population. This is how it works, and we've known this since Basil of Caesaria in the 4th Century AD said: "If each one would take that which is sufficient for his needs, leaving what is superfluous to those in distress, no one would be rich, no one poor . . . The rich man is a thief."

Which is not, of course, invariably the case. The other day I was at a sweltering barbecue lunch where one of the guests informed me, during the course of our conversation, that he was doing a little bit of wealth creation of his own: he was not only having his own children educated privately, but also lining the pockets of an estate agent by buying – "for a song" – a four-bedroom ex-council property so that said children could, when they reached their estate, have somewhere to live. The song he mentioned had a chorus which went "four hundred thousand pounds", which actually sounds like rather a lot to me. I mean not even an imaginary £96,900 is going to cover that.

The interesting thing about this information is that it was conveyed to me in terms which strongly suggested that I was meant to applaud. As the man does not know me very well he is not expected to know that I wear an invisible t-shirt whose slogans, which are visible in the right light, say "I loathe the rich" and "abolish private education NOW", but surely the gathering scowl on my face should have tipped him off.

I wandered off morosely and thought about my own children's future. The eldest has recently finished her A levels and is awaiting the results. Being far cleverer than I was at her age, she should be a shoo-in for any university she chooses, but Cambridge have already said "no way" which strikes me as a bit silly of them, for they let me in, for some reason. Now I come to think of it, it may have been the strong suspicion that my daughter is related to me that may have put them off in the first place. The dog may return to his vomit as the fool to his folly, but Cambridge U. isn't that foolish. There also seems to be a regression to earlier times, by which I mean the 1930s, going on in the higher education system, so that the privately-educated continue to stuff the top universities. Well, maybe there'll be a world war in a decade, and twenty years after that a social revolution comparable to the 1960s, but by then I'll be 80 and, even if alive, in no real position to enjoy it.

The only thing that seems to be getting better is the cricket. For six years now I have been unable to watch it on the telly, and so have had to resort to listening to it on the radio. This is actually no hardship and the tension towards the end of the first Ashes test still managed to communicate itself over Radio 4 Long Wave quite effectively. As the Australians inched towards what had once seemed like an impossible fourth-innings target I found myself feeling sicker and weaker and more comprehensively frazzled. There are still some people out there who think Test cricket is a dull affair but they know not whereof they speak. I, and anyone else who was listening, was a nervous wreck by the end, and I have still not recovered the full use of my legs. It also means that, what with the nice weather we're having, it looks as though we're going to have a real summer. I have just voted in the *Guardian*'s "is it too hot?" poll and am delighted to say that so far the "no" vote is almost twice the "yes" vote. The only problem with the sunshine is it brings the insufferable wealthy out, like wasps. A friend tells me he has been unable to sleep in this hot weather. Then another friend tells me the same thing. Then I read in a paper that there is widespread sleeplessness going on. A nation tosses and turns under its low-tog duvets, counting sheep to no avail.

I knew the misery of insomnia, especially in hot weather; until the age of fifteen, once the temperature rose above a certain point at night, sleep became impossible. I experienced every second of every summer night from 1969 to 1978. The earliest summers were the worst for my parents had invested in the soundtrack LP of the Musical *Hair*, rather against the grain of their characters and tastes, it must be said, and every time they had people round they would put this on when they thought I had gone to sleep, and I would lie staring at the ceiling wondering how many more times I could listen to "The Age of Aquarius" without going mad. (Actually, I rather liked the song, and have a soft spot for it even now. But it is funnier to say it drove me crazy.) The sleepless nights stopped abruptly in 1978 when I discovered alcohol. Or, to put it more accurately, discovered the poise and bearing which would, despite my lack of stature and being only 15, somehow reassure bar staff into thinking I was actually three years older. Ever since then I have, self-medicated, slept the sleep of the just, whatever the weather.

I also like the hot weather, for I am a child of the sun; my forebears came from warmer climes. The Beloved, on the other hand, is pure English, and like Manny, the character played by Bill Bailey in *Black Books*, succumbs to Dave Syndrome once the temperature hits 88 degrees Fahrenheit. (You don't want to know.)

So I am tucking myself in the other night, my ticket for the land of Nod presented and stamped, when a burglar alarm goes off over the road. It is a loud burglar alarm, pitched high, and designed by experts to be distressingly audible for about half a mile around. Thanks to the inverse square law, though, from where I am it is bloody loud. I try shutting the window but this shuts off the breeze, and I look at the Beloved's sleeping form and wonder whether this will make her succumb to Dave Syndrome in the middle of the night. (You really don't want to know.) I think of Martin Amis's example of the typically rubbish opening you get in entries to short story competitions: "The heat was stiffling." [sic]

Feeling that it is better to be deafened than stifled, I open the window again and assess the situation. It is not wholly devoid of interest, for the alarm has gone off on a building I have not noticed before. How I can have failed to notice an entire building a stone's feeble throw from my window when I have been living here for six years is a puzzle itself. The alarm seems to be the manifestation of the anxieties or violation of a very anonymous office building whose architectural style suggests the mid to late 1960s, or around the time *Hair* opened at the Shaftesbury Theatre in London. It is utterly characterless. Square, fronted by frosted glass, I must have passed it a thousand times and I have never known it was there until now. On either side the street is 1850 vintage, so this cuckoo's existence suggests the Luftwaffe gouged it out in the war. To pass the time I look up www.bombsight.org, the extraordinary site which tells you how many bombs fell where during the Blitz, but we can't blame the Hun for this one, it turns out; we can blame a council or a firm of architects for this blight.

And the noise goes on. I wonder what it is the alarm is protecting. Even if the offices within are in use during the day, who would be interested in carting off a photocopier and few bulky office computers? What else would be there? State secrets? If so, the place would be crawling with Men in Black, but the guardians of our safety are maintaining a stout indifference. Nor is there any sign of forced or unforced entry; the offices are dark and empty, a non-place. It is as if the alarm went off in response to the office's own inner crisis, a sudden existential awareness of its own lack of importance within a vast and uncaring universe. The alarm is simply saying "I'm here! I'm here!"

Several hours later, the alarm stops. I think there is a difference between the insomnia that one suffers in a quiet night, and that which one suffers when there's a racket going on. The dawn is breaking. I check that the room temperature is still below 88°, hum a few bars of "The Age of Aquarius", and finally drift off.

I am trying to think of the last time I took a holiday. A proper holiday: two weeks in a warm and sunny place, which means abroad. Somewhere with, at the very least, a reputation for good weather and drinkable local wine. And I'd like it to be in Italy, please. Anyway: last holiday? Not sure. I have a hunch it was Spain, which was a bit of a hair-raising experience at first when I discovered, at Luton airport upon being frisked, that the pouch of tobacco I'd groped for in a dark room before the pre-dawn drive to the airport turned out not to be tobacco at all. Which was especially tiresome as I had resolved earlier not to take any risks with that kind of thing when travelling internationally ever again. I was escorted to an interrogation room and invited the customs agents to look out of the window and look at my wife, above whose head could be seen the kind of gathering atmospheric disturbance associated with extreme meteorological events. There may have even been the odd flash of lightning.

"See that woman over there?" I said. "I'm far, far more scared of what she's going to do to me than anything you could." I had the pleasure of seeing the officers, one experienced, one young and keen as Tabasco, peering through the door's small window. It was a charming cameo seen from behind; seen from outside it must have looked rather comic. After a few seconds' observation, they turned around. The older one sighed. "Go on holiday," he said, scribbling on a piece of paper on a pad and tearing it off. "Take this chit. When you come back go through the 'something to declare' channel and present it." The farce of what happened on my re-entry into the country need not detain us here, but I can tell you that I got to say "what's wrong with me? I can't even get arrested in this town," without using the phrase figuratively.

That would have been, oh, ten years ago, I think. After that we stayed in the country for our hols because of the knock-on financial effects of having three children. Then we separated, and the financial knock-on effects of that are unbelievable, so apart from the odd snatched long weekend staying at a friend's place in either Paris or Rome, I just sit around in the sun. Last year it rained all summer long so I sat in the rain instead. It wasn't the same. But to tell you the truth, it's not just lack of funds that keeps me from travelling: it's an inability to organise a holiday. I've never done it. Parents, girlfriends and wives seem to have a knack that I simply do not possess. It's at times like these that I start thinking they should give air miles to people who can't afford to buy plane tickets, rather than hand them out to people who fly all the sodding time.

I have recently discovered that the inability to successfully execute plans to leave the country can be inherited. My daughter has had similar problems and so due to a scheduling error on her and others' parts, she is obliged to stay with me and the Beloved in the Hovel for a couple of weeks. It is all rather unusual. Normally I only have the children for two days at a stretch on alternate weekends so being a full-time parent for the first time in six years is a little weird. That said, the daughter isn't a child any more: she's eighteen, although looks rather elfin. But it means I can't tell her when her bedtime is any more.

That said, we do get on rather well. Have done ever since her mother screamed "she's you! She's YOU!" at me after an incident of five-year-old insubordination or insolence. She also seems to have adopted a similar attitude to the various cushions on the divan of pleasure. One evening I gently remonstrated her on not applying to my alma mater when making her university choices. I think they like that kind of thing, deep down.

"I don't want to follow in your footsteps, dad," she said. I gestured silently at the roll-up in her hand, the full glass of red wine in her other one, and then, as an afterthought, my wristwatch, which was telling anyone who wanted to look that it was well after midnight. To give her credit, she saw my point.

Having a mini-me around the place the whole time does make me wonder a bit about heritable traits, though. Did I stay in bed that late when I was her age? Yes, if not later. But was I as fluent a talker as she is? No: I was shy. And now she tells me she's arranged a combination of trains and planes to get her to her holiday destination. I could never have done that. Can't do it now.

꧁

It was, in the end, nothing less than a continuous pleasure having the daughter to stay for a fortnight. She's gone now, and is missed; she's off to stay for a while in a household in France which is, a generation up, infested with hippies. Real hippies, the kind who were just the right age to inhale the full blowback of flower-power in the mid-sixties. They're pushing their own sixties now, and you can spot them a mile off, which is handy if you want to distance yourself. Remember the TV ad for a bank some years ago which featured a woman in a headscarf going on about the feng shui? That was her, i.e. the chief hippie, or as close enough to make no difference. I stayed there once myself and made a present of some delicious local saucisson and cheese.

"Sorry," she said as I was putting them in the fridge, "but I'm getting back in touch with my Jewish roots and would rather you didn't put the meat and the dairy products on the same shelf." She is also very partial to wandering around the place completely starkers. This can come as a surprise at first but I suppose it is always well to have a *memento mori* around the place, like Sebastian Flyte with his skull inscribed with the legend "et in Arcadia ego". I, too, was, or am, in paradise. The ambiguity in tense is crucial.

Anyway, my daughter came to stay at just the right time,

i.e. at that awkward period at the end of the month when the Lezard economy enters its austerity phase. For those who think I exaggerate when I claim poverty, the last ten days of July were spent working out how to live off fourteen pounds, and for the first time in my life I started thinking about going to a pay-day loan company. I find something rather distasteful and dishonest about them, which probably doesn't come as news to you, and when I heard that if you borrow £100 off the most famous one and don't pay it back for five years, you end up with a debt greater than that of the United States. I haven't done the maths but I suspect it's true. In the end I kept the ship afloat by borrowing small sums, here and there, off (a) the Beloved, who gave me a funny look, and (b) my friend Toby, to whom I had only turned because I had already put the bite on (c) my daughter. I think it represents A New Low when you're reduced to that, no? Toby always does his best to help me save face when he gives me my pay-day loans, which he always does in his local, either handing the money to me as discreetly as a drug dealer handing over his wares in a public place, or else, if scrutiny is unavoidable, pretending that it is money he owes me. This is very chivalrous of him, but I think it is important not to dissemble in front of one's own children, and so peeled off a twenty then and there to hand to my daughter, who had come with me.

"There," I said. "Let that be a lesson to you."

But in the end, people paid me, and the sun came out, and this month I have resolved not to let things get like that again. Which is why it was probably unwise to treat myself, last sunny Thursday, to a plate of calamari and a carafe of house white at the Casa Becci. The problem with austerity being that its relief can lead one into bad habits again. But what is this life if you can't sit in the sunshine with some fried seafood, a chilled bottle and a copy of this magazine to read at leisure?

It is also well to recall civilised modes of existence. The other day I found that my sometime flatmate, this very magazine's distinguished and gifted correspondent, Laurie Penny, had received a death threat on Twitter.* It is all too easy, for men at least, to dismiss these as the tiresome yelps of the mindless savage, but the message giving a specific time at which the firebomb in or near your house is going to go off can be the last straw if you get nothing but abuse every time you write an article. It then occurred to me that had this kind of thing been all the rage a year or so ago, then Laurie's house would have been my house too, and there may well have been children of mine staying in it as well. It is at this point that contemplation of the kind of scum who get their kicks out of this kind of thing becomes more than academic. I might have gently teased the hippies a few paragraphs above, but really, what on earth is so funny about peace, love, and understanding?

❧

Once again, towards the end of the month, money starts getting tight, but the weather is lovely and holiday-type things must be done, so what to do? The Wallace Collection, that's good free fun for a start. It is, for some reason, an incredibly sexy place, and not just because it has that amusing Fragonard showing a young man looking up a girl on a swing's skirt.

---

* It is sad to think that I considered this worthy of note, when I think where we are now. Political arguments without death threats now seem as dated as periwigs, or codpieces.

Everything there is voluptuous somehow, and Howard Jacobson chose well when he made it the scene of a lover's tryst in his novel *The Act of Love*. That takes care of one afternoon. Loafing around Regent's Park with some bread, cheese, and a chilled bottle takes care of another; but the third afternoon is the best, because someone has paid me unexpectedly early, and although I could hardly call myself in rude financial health, I can at least top up the Oyster card and go somewhere on public transport. I'm only going to Hampstead Heath – my fellow columnist, Mr Self, regards pretty much everywhere on the mainland as within walking distance, which I think is rather splendid, but I am not going to inflict a three-mile walk to the Heath on the Beloved, especially as we are going to be walking around a lot when we get there. Also, as she is not a native Londoner, she has never seen the Heath before, and I am rather keen on introducing her to it.

The Heath looms large in the childhood of anyone who grew up, as I did, anywhere near it. I don't think there was ever a time when I was not aware of it, of its improbable vastness in the middle of the city. And the older I get, the more amazing I consider it. As readers of this magazine are doubtless acutely aware, these are terrible times, with our freedoms under threat from all sides – from freedom of association to the meanest use of the word "free": that is, free from cost. You can still, thank goodness, just bowl up to Heath and walk straight in. (I gather you now have to pay to use the swimming ponds, which is academic for me, as the days in which I would reveal my body, clad only in swimming trunks, to the world have now passed.) So one beaming Thursday we do just that, along with a couple of buddies who know the Heath at least as well as I do, and it is marvellous. We do see some lycra-wearing people walking up, and then down, and then up, and then down again, our chosen hill using those extremely silly walking poles, but they, too, have their liberty, so we confine ourselves to mild mockery and scorn while we eat our picnic.

Eventually our friends peel off, and the B and I are alone, so I show her through paths I remember from my childhood to the tree you can climb inside, and then on, using only my nose to guide me, to the Spaniard's Inn for a pint. I note with approval the blue plaque on the house next to it, which reminds us the social reformers Henrietta and Samuel Barnett, Christian Socialist reformers who did much to make Hampstead such a pleasant place, and to lift the poor out of squalor.

It is on the way back to the Hovel, via Flask Walk, that I notice the Bentley parked outside one of the impossibly adorable houses in the higgledy-piggledy streets between the Heath and Heath Street. It's not so much the Bentley itself – after all, London is now seething with them – it's the number plate: I H8 TAX. You geddit? Now, while the relationship between the taxman and me is not in itself a simple and straightforward one, it is a matter of my own incompetence rather than outright objection to the principle . So I am not, I must confess, very amused to see this number plate. It is not hard to come to some ungenerous conclusions about the charming man – it will be a man – who thinks this is a terrific joke.

I think back to the plaque for the Barnetts on their old home by the Spaniards, and speculate about the kind of people who now buy such properties. I imagine a London 100 years hence, and the plaques that will decorate the walls of Hampstead. "——, hedge fund manager, lived here from 2012–2040". "So-and-so, arms dealer, lived here off the blood of countless thousands between 2000 and 2020". You get the idea. We are now living in an age that would seem to consider the very idea of positive social reform as a quaint mug's game. London is now a playground for the rich, and they have had enough of being within smelling distance of the poor. I am also aware that the body responsible for Hampstead Heath is the shadowy City of London Corporation, and I wonder how long it will be before they monetize it.

☙

I am not over-fond of this time of year. Summer's lease hath all too short a stay. Date, I mean. Why do I always get that wrong? Anyway, it's now autumn. The windows that have been left open are now shut to stop the draughts, the summer plumage – linen, basically, and those cheapo desert boots you buy from shoe shops on the Uxbridge Road for £20 which last two summers max – is replaced by the winter version, and the Proms end.

This is particularly sad this year, as it is the first time since 1999 that Roger Wright, head of Radio 3 and the Proms, hasn't invited me along to his box to eat his smoked salmon sarnies and drink his wine. Maybe he has wearied of me. I thought he used to be amused by my having to climb over him for a pee during the long, long wall of sound that is Debussy's *Pelléas et Mélisande*, or making feeble passes at Jenny Agutter, or gawping at Simon Heffer's profile. How does he get jowls like that? He's only three years older than I am. Heffer, not Wright. Wright is older than either of us but has the ageless good looks of a Donatello *putto*. I sat and waited for his call all summer long but it never came, and when I heard "Jerusalem" bouncing off the walls all the way from Hyde Park I had a tear in my eye. So that's it, then, I thought. I know I'm not important any longer – I used to be radio critic for the *Independent on Sunday*, but they decided I was surplus to requirements about six years ago – but what about "Auld Lang Syne"? They sang that too, as if to wash their mouths out after "Jerusalem" and "Rule Britannia", and that nearly floored me. (Incidentally, I gather the *Independent on Sunday* has now decided all its critics are surplus to requirements, and has given the entire arts desk the heave-ho. You will write and tell them they're being silly arseholes, won't you? They had some fine writers on those pages.) Oh well; nothing lasts forever, and at least this year we had a summer to speak of, unlike last year's wash-out.

I used to like September, though. I was never particularly fond of school but at least you got to learn some stuff and there was always a good chance that I'd have some new masters who had yet to nurse any grudges against me. The start of the university year was even better, for leaving the family home meant the thrilling prospect of going somewhere where there were locks on the lavatory doors.

But that was when life was still a process leading to sunny uplands. Each year was going to be better than the last one: you'd know a bit more, be earning a bit more, and certainly be having more sex. After all how, I would ask myself in my late teens, could I be having any less? That's not something I'm worried about now, thank goodness, but as for the rest . . . well, anyone out there feeling happier, richer and more confident about the future than they were last year? I thought that, at the very least, this government had reached the maximum point of stupidity and malice a supposedly enlightened Western democracy was capable of, but now I read that the DWP are to start calling people in if they think they're not earning enough money and telling them to work more. Am I missing something, or is this not their most brutal move against the poor yet? Other solutions, say, raising the minimum wage, seem not to have occurred to them, or are only suggested in Cabinet for humorous purposes. Not only is one's own life going downhill at an increasingly uncomfortable rate, but the whole country is, too. The nights draw in, the clouds roll over. It's all very well battening down the hatches but what if one has no battens with which to batten them? The eldest child is going off to university and by the end of her course will almost certainly be in debt to the tune of £27,000, which worries me even more than the fact that at least one member of the Philosophy faculty not only thinks Descartes was a medieval philosopher, but pronounces his name "day car" to boot. (See p. 42) And the last time I mentioned that, I got accused of the most outrageous snobbery; I'm bracing myself for that again.

But it turns out that I cannot even take solace from such fragments of learning as I still retain. I take my melancholy and do what everyone does with it these days: air it on Facebook. "Summer's lease hath all too short a stay," I write laconically, hoping to impress everyone with the lightness of my learning, the deftness of my command of allusion to fit the mood of the time.

"Date," everyone writes back. "It's 'date', you idiot."

I suppose it all started when, at school, I learned about the Second Law of Thermodynamics. There you are, bumbling along in your safe little world, blandly assured that things will go on getting better, that everything will become more prosperous and ordered, and then, wham, you see that simple little equation, $\Delta > 0$, absorb the implications of the fact that heat cannot pass from a colder to a warmer body, and not only do you understand that eventually the universe will die in a uniform chill of something not much cosier than Absolute Zero, or something roughly around minus seven hundred degrees Centigrade, but you also understand how hard it is to keep your room tidy.

Since then I have fought only the most tentative and desperate rearguard actions against entropy. "You can't fart against thunder," as my great-uncle Cecil used to say when faced with a superior hand at poker (he wrote the Crockford's Poker Rulebook, calculating the odds of all possible hands with exact precision; look it up if you don't believe me), and things don't come much more unbiddable than the heat-death of the universe.

Women, though, in my experience, do not see it this way. And in case you think that's sexist, I should add that most men don't see it my way either. Men, though, are more slobby. There are women who are messier than me, but they are so spectacularly messy that they get featured on television. But the key words here, as far as I am concerned, are "in my experience", and last week, after a few months of Putting Up With Things, the Beloved decided to take a rare day off work, roll her sleeves up, and get cracking against the entropy. So that I can help her with this, instead of just lying in bed deeply sensing the futility of all human endeavour to a slightly intenser pitch than I did yesterday, she invents a game called "Keep or Chuck?", complete with theme tune. ("Keep

or chuck? Keep or chuck? K-k-k-k-k-k-k-k-keep or chuck?"
Roughly to the tune of the old TV *Spiderman* series.) The
game – and it really is quite clever of her to realise that to get
me to help, a game must be made of it, no one else has worked
that out before – is played to a strict time limit of ten minutes
at a stretch, and the object is to make as many decisions about
what to keep, or chuck, within that time. No overt reward is
given for chucking, as opposed to keeping, something, but a
little something in the game master's demeanour suggests that
chucking manky redundant things will be rewarded later, and
keeping manky redundant things will not so much.

So: title music, please. I am obliged. And . . . bathroom
cabinet first. (NB Bear in mind I have only been living in
the Hovel for six years.) Nyrelex for Chesty Coughs (expiry
date 1998): chuck. Night Nurse (now virtually crystallised,
best before 1997): chuck. Peppermint foot lotion "of the most
extraordinary consistency": chuck. Brush-on Facial Hair
Remover: chuck. Haemorrhoid Cream, b.b. 2004: chuck.
Clarins Honey Tinted Moisturiser (no best before date, but
only the letters "ARIN" of "Clarins" remain visible): chuck.
Rinstead sugar-free pastilles (b.b. 2005): chuck. "Soothing
and cooling" moist haemorrhoid tissues (b.b. 2004): chuck.
(I begin to sense a pattern here, and feel a pang of pity for
whoever lived here before me.) Eucril Tooth Powder – or, as
the Beloved calls it, "Eucril Tooth Powder???? What the fuck's
that???" – keep: I bought it myself. I then have to explain
it. Explaining Eucril Tooth Powder to pretty much anyone
under 50 is harder than you might think. Mitchum roll-on
deodorant ("so strong you can even skip a day"): Keep, the
name and slogan are hilarious. No, on second thoughts, chuck.
It predates me. (Later inspection shows that it has actually

been kept.) Ibis Mosquito Re-impregnation Kit, no date: keep. Unless climate change gallops along even faster than in the most pessimistic scientist's nightmares, I won't be needing this in the Hovel, but how cool is a Re-Impregnation Kit? Even cooler than an Impregnation Kit, surely.

And so on. Within the ten minutes allotted to "Keep Or Chuck" the Beloved has managed to show me an enormous array of redundant cosmetic/medical/unidentifiable products, which despite having been kept in a cabinet for years have not so much accrued a layer of dust as actually grown beards, and I wonder, not for the first time, what kink it is in my psyche that prevents me, or people like me, from performing this perfectly simple and reasonable act. It is possible that the childhood loss of a loved family member made me reluctant to throw things away, i.e. it's a reaction against rejection, death being the greatest rejection of all; but then again I know people with similar events in their backgrounds and they're not untidy at all. Search me. Or not. You don't know what you'll find.

❧

Ping! A text from, of all people, the Guvnor. For latecomers to this column, the Guvnor used to be the landlord of the pub down the road. Patrolling the tables with mild menace, he would occasionally startle favoured customers with asides of quite extraordinary obscenity, the product of a mind that was as quick as it was obscene. Although barely lettered, he was sharper than you and almost certainly much, much wealthier. Every so often if you were having lunch there and he took pity on you, he would join you and start bringing over bottles of wine from far nearer the bottom of the list than the top. You would stagger out of the place at about 5.30, barely able to see. He once had a porn film shot on the premises, only this being a British porno, with the *mise en scène* revolving endlessly around the visit of a couple of supposedly oversexed female Health and Safety inspectors, I ended up learning far more about the separation of meat and dairy products on kitchen shelves – absolutely no innuendo intended – than I did about sex. (He triumphantly produced the DVD towards the end of an extended luncheon I'd been having with the Moose, and the latter, a man of delicate sensibilities, nearly fainted.) If he wasn't doing that he was using me as a guinea pig for job-lots of dodgy herbal "Viagra" he'd taken consignment of, a job I only did once for him, on the grounds that the stuff nearly killed me. (It worked, in a way, and the story appears in *Bitter Experience Has Taught Me*, my first attempt at milking these columns for all they're worth.)

Since then he got exiled from the pub by his wife, who had wearied of his ways, and he became elusive. The last time I saw him was when he came to the launch of my book about the Olympics which none of you bastards have bought, accompanied by a Russian blonde ex-model about six inches taller than him, who had the air of a woman upon whom it would be unwise to try any oompus-boompus (as Bertie Wooster once described one of his aunts). He looked well-dressed, sleek, and happy. After that, about a year ago, I heard nothing. I imagined a period of forced exile, or a spell in one of the more comfortable correctional establishments. He popped up again at the pub a few months ago, but after that, when I asked the staff after him, I was told he was never coming back, ever, and I got the impression that it would be a good idea not to press the matter. Anyway, here he is again, and he wants to buy me lunch, and discuss matters of some import with me, so why not? So I arrive a couple of minutes early at the Social Eating House in Poland Street (Food, Atmosphere, Value for money, all 8/10, average price for two £120, *Guardian Magazine* review, 25/7/13), go to the bar upstairs and fail to enjoy a disgustingly sweet attempt at a Martini served by a boy with the stupidest beard I've ever seen, and you see plenty these days, and in walks the Guvnor, wearing, as well as more conventional clothes, bright blue brogues with brothel creeper soles (which, I later learn, cost £540 the pair).

It turns out that the Guvnor has been suffering from *ennui* and has been relieving the tedium by idly scanning the pages of a website devoted to single Ukrainian ladies. One of them has taken the fancy that he is some kind of intellectual and has been dropping in references to Proust and Boris Vian. Boris Vian, for Christ's sake. The Guvnor, whose idea of a library is two copies of *Razzle*, has been having to get busy with Wikipedia but thinks it might be wise to ask me for advice. He shows me her photograph.

"Looks like Kate Moss, doesn't she?" he says.

"Guv, that *is* Kate Moss."

He shows me another picture of her.

"Ok, maybe not. But you've got to admit there's something fishy going on here. I mean, you say there are 28,000 women on this website. They can't all look like that." The somme-lier arrives and although the Guvnor does not bother with a French pronunciation, the look in his eyes tells the wine-man that he is not to be trifled with. I used to feel, when in the Guvnor's company, that I was in a rude, postmodern episode of *Minder*. Right now, I feel like I'm in a Martin Amis novel.

But he is soft-hearted, as you'd expect, and at some point during the next bottle he starts showing me pictures of his kittens. (His last cats were called, brilliantly, Sid and Nancy.) The restaurant, completely full when we entered, empties. It is now about five o'clock. The manager suggests we repair to the bar upstairs. The Guvnor laughs him off, the manager backs away. You don't argue with people wearing shoes like that. They're capable of anything.

⚜

As I might have mentioned before, among the nice things that have been happening lately is the fact that I have, thanks to relatives who are the right age, and friends of the Beloved, been getting invited to lots of weddings lately. At my age, there is nothing bad about a wedding. Before I got married, going to the weddings of my contemporaries had something of the vibe of bomb disposal about it, or potential contagion: I wondered if my then-girlfriend would let all the celebrations cause her to lose her mind and insist on a wedding of her own. To me. Which wedding would be the one that would set off the unstoppable cascade of emotions? This far down the line, I can't remember which one it was, so I just hold them all equally to blame.

These days, all a wedding means to me is, happily, an excuse to dress up (three-piece suit for autumn/winter, lightly crumpled linen for spring/summer, thus making effective use of the two suits I possess, or are wearable) and get stuffed and hammered at someone else's expense. But the latest one fills me with a certain trepidation, for it is a military wedding, and one of the Beloved's friends is marrying a Flight Lieutenant.

At this point I can imagine what you're thinking. "Ah, that conchie Lezard is going to express his misgivings about the armed forces, and his guilt at having anything to do with the oppressive military-industrial complex and the forces of Babylon, etc." At which point I will have to gently disabuse you, and say that I am afraid the problem lies entirely in the opposite direction.

I remember vividly the fat-bottomed historian Andrew Roberts* once calling me a conchie (note to younger generation: "conchie" is contemptuously short for "conscientious objector", a position only barely tolerated, at the very best, during the last two world wars), live on air, saying that I would not have fought in the Second World War. The comeback that instantly sprang to mind was too incendiary to say ("my dear chap, I'm sure that you would not have hesitated to volunteer; only I am not sure for which side"), so all I could do was seethe. I most certainly would not have sat that war out. Being a leftie arty intellectual, part English, Polish, American, French and Jewish, I would have been wanted dead by Hitler six or seven times over, and I am very glad indeed that when I learned German it was because I wanted to, and not because it was compulsory. Not, of course, that I would have been able to learn it compulsorily; for, as my private school

* Legal note: I gather that since this exchange, Andrew Roberts has undertaken some kind of slimming regime and his rear end is no longer so adipose. But believe me, at the time these remarks were made, it was the size of Wales. Also, his credibility as a historian has been somewhat dented by the fact that he is the only person to have a kind word to say about Jacob Rees-Mogg's staggeringly silly book, *The Victorians*. So he is a lickspittle as well as a hypocrite. I have also heard some stories, from some of those who have been at the receiving end of it, about his seduction technique, and they are not edifying. As for Jacob Rees-Mogg, not even during my most fevered deliriums did I ever imagine that such a poison in the body politic would ever achieve such prominence as he has.

peers were keen on reminding me, I was "good enough for the ovens".

So when I get up close to the military, I am very mindful of the fact that their predecessors put their lives on the line for the likes of me, and I'm very happy indeed with the fact that members of my family did what they could, too. (My gambling-mad great-uncle Lizzie, parachuted behind enemy lines to see what he could learn from his old croupier pals, became known as "the man who broke his back at Monte Carlo", and was tended to full recovery by the French Resistance. Another great-uncle actually was a conscientious objector, but did his bit by volunteering to be a pathfinder: that is, flying, unarmed, ahead of a bomber formation in order to guide it to target. That takes some balls. Amazingly, he survived.) Things are made worse by the fact that this is going to be a proper RAF wedding, ceremony at St Clement Danes, reception at the Honourable Artillery Company, the works. Even the groom's father is an army chaplain. So I am very worried that I am going to get drunk, and start gushing, or worse. "Try and stay sober, Lezard," I say to myself as I try to remember how you tie a tie.

Oh well. Even before alcohol touches my lips, I am unmanned. RAF St Clement Danes (as it is officially called) bursts with history; the Guard of Honour forms an arch of swords for bride and groom to walk through; the bells, whose mechanism, whether by accident or design, seems to replicate the sounds of far-off explosions, play "Oranges and Lemons"; and every single person on the top deck of every single bus that passes swivels their heads to gawp at the scene. A lump forms in my throat and I seem to have something in my eye. The Beloved sees me, excited as a seven-year-old.

"You're a crap pacifist," she says.

⚜

When your luck runs out, it runs out all at once. I muse on this as I enter the third hour of my wait in A&E. The day before I had banged my little toe against the doorframe so hard that it was still too sensitive to touch a day later, and the configuration of the pain strongly suggested that a bone might have been broken. I suppose that there's nothing much they can do with a broken little toe, except tell you not to use it, which I think I could work out all by myself, so what I was really after in St Mary's was information, and validation of my own suffering. Which, after the rather painful journey to the hospital – it's a fifteen-minute stroll from the Hovel, but a rather longer hobble – was fairly acute.

Still, what the hell is this, my waiting here with a possibly broken toe (I did it while rushing to get the clothes out of the machine, which makes me one of the few people in the modern age to have hurt themselves while doing the laundry) when there are people around me visibly suffering? As I write, my friend Leyla Sanai is contemplating the amputation of her leg thanks to her scleroderma, and bearing her sufferings with a fortitude which is beyond comprehension. There is a young Spanish man sitting next to me who appears to have something terrible going on with his arm.

"Joan," calls a nurse from a consulting room. He looks up, and there is a silence. Of all the people in this room, none is prepared to answer to the name "Joan".

"Joan Estevez," says the nurse. The young Spaniard lifts his head. "Juan," he says.

"It says 'Joan' here," replies the nurse, in tones which suggest that the name 'Juan' which this young man seems to be claiming as his own is an imposture and an affectation. Eventually, though, as no one else seems to be claiming the surname "Estevez", she lets him go into the room.

The quarter hours go by. A nurse had offered me a couple of co-codamol on turning up, and I had accepted more out of politeness than need; in rest, the toe was quite docile, but she had charmed me by calling me "sweet pea" and I had a hunch that a couple of these on an empty stomach would have a rather soothing effect. They do, but I recognise another pain bubbling up: that of the end of a brief interlude of domestic happiness.

The Beloved, you see, has been offered a job in Gothenburg for something approaching twice the salary she is bringing in here. The offer was made some time ago and she has been putting off making a decision for as long as she can. I have been to Gothenburg and wouldn't go back there if you paid me, but she is for some reason enamoured of the country and the language; so it's rather as if someone had offered me a job in . . . oh, I don't know, Verona. Is that right? In my campaign to dissuade her from going, I have been doing a spot of research, both on the internet and the internot (i.e., books), and have come up with some killer facts about this country, for which I am beginning to nurture a dislike, as you would a rival in love.

"There are twelve people in Sweden," I tell her, only slightly massaging the facts to suit my purpose. "In the summer, three of them are eaten alive by giant mutant mosquitoes. In the autumn feral moose, pissed out of their minds on decaying windfalls, account for about four more. Those that remain blow their brains out in winter, which lasts for nine months. You can only buy alcohol from a small corrugated-iron shed in Malmö, and when you do your name is put on a criminal register, right next to the paedophiles and heroin traffickers. A bottle of beer costs 6,000 kroner and tastes of moose piss, for the very good reason that that is what they make it from."

I reinforce my point by demonstrating that when you type the words "bad things about Sweden" into Google you get 54,700,000 results (try it).* But it's a jump up in terms of her career, and if I was the one to hold her back by having a crying fit, I'd feel guilty for the rest of my life, so I know that all I can do is try to ignore my own very strong feelings for once, and think of what is best for her. Hence, perhaps, my concentration on my toe.

Which, as it turns out, is not broken (but a week later, is still painful and impossible to touch). It took four hours to learn that; as long as a return flight to Gothenburg, I reflect.

At time of writing I do not know whether the *Doctor Who* 50th Anniversary Special will be any good, but it had better be, because I've just had to lash out £174 inc. VAT on a new aerial – the last one got nicked – to be able to watch it. The children have, understandably, wearied of sitting round a computer monitor to watch the show, especially when there is a ropey internet connection and we have plenty of time to contemplate the plot holes while watching the little red circle

* I tried this again in 2019. It's now 403,000,000. But I suspect not all these results are about bad things about Sweden.

go round and round. Now it can just wash over us, as Stephen Moffat intended.

But one aspect of the whole 50th Anniversary of *Doctor Who* upsets me, and that is the word "50th". It is, I suppose, a privilege to have been born in the year that people are finally beginning to recognise as one of the most auspicious in the West's history, but I can't help noticing that it's all a bit . . . fiftyish. That's half a century. Footage from the 1960s looks as though it was filmed underwater, on a zoetrope, whatever that is. It was a time of full employment. I can still add up in Old Money. I made the bad mistake of alluding to the Old Money to the Beloved, who was born ten years after decimalisation, and I won't be doing that again in a hurry. Incidentally, while checking on the date at the Royal Mint website, my heart sank even further at its opening sentence: "For those of us under fifty . . ." Shouldn't that be "you"? I was sitting on the tube the other day and listening to a young camply gay man talking about his last night out to a couple of female friends. He was talking so loud it was impossible not to overhear, and besides, I'd forgotten to bring a book, so I thought I might learn something about the human condition. Every day's a school day. He described, in some detail, an evening that ended in the not-so-small hours watching a man singing in a band. "It was hilarious," said the young man opposite. "He was like so *old*, he must have been like *fifty*, and I had tears streaming down my face, I was laughing so much," and he made little waterfalls past his eyes with fluttering fingers to demonstrate.

The rest of the journey was rather spoiled for me, and even though it was only three stops to King's Cross it felt like – ha! – fifty. I contemplated winking at him and saying softly, "fifty isn't that old, you naughty boy," as I left, but thought better of it, and carried on to Hampstead, where I was going to spend the afternoon being shown round the newly-restored Kenwood House. There, at least, I'd be seeing things that were older than I was, although this thought was undermined when introduced to the curator in charge of the restoration, a rather attractive woman, who noticed the label of my jumper sticking out, and tucked it back in. Hell's bells, I think to myself, now I need curating. (Not that this good woman caused offence: I quite like it when that happens, and as my jumpers tend towards unruliness, it happens quite a lot.)

So I gawp at Gainsborough's portrait, all eight feet of it, of Mary, Countess Howe, and marvel at the way that there is some beauty which is so powerful that it transmits its signal undiminished through the centuries. (A spot of mental arithmetic informs me that she is the same age in the portrait as the Beloved is now.) But the one that really holds my attention, the one that gives me an unmistakable case of Stendhal Syndrome, to the point where I feel my legs might actually give way, is Rembrandt's *Self-Portrait With Two Circles*. I knew it was in the collection and was looking forward to seeing it, and I like to think that I'm tougher than I look, but this still took my breath from me. That incredible expression of indominability. The confidence and power of execution. I then recall that at the time of composition, Rembrandt was broke and had had to sell the plot of land his sister was buried in to keep himself in paint and canvas. Rembrandt's poverty bothers me even more than Mozart's at times. To think you can be one of the greatest talents the world has ever seen, one of about twenty people out of multiple billions who have changed the way we experience the world, and to die in poverty . . .

Eventually, after the most extraordinary visit – upstairs, in the Suffolk Collection, are 400-year-old portraits so preserved they look like they were painted last week – I cheer myself up by having a pint with my old friend John Moore in the Holly Bush. He asks if it is true that the Beloved is off to Sweden. Yes, I say. "Ha!" he laughs. "You'll never get laid again!"

※

Well, that's that, then. I've booked a ticket to Gothenburg in February. The generosity of parents over Christmas has ensured that I can cover the £100 return fare. I have been to Gothenburg before so I know what I'm letting myself in for, and the most amusing incident of the whole week I and the wife were there for was when we got stuck behind a Norwegian coach trying to do a U-turn in a parking lot. Our Swedish driver – it was arranged by a newspaper, so we were being given the Works by the Gothenburg tourist board – launched into a string of expletive-laden remarks about the fucking Norwegians, and then, after a pause, she sheepishly apologised, saying that the Swedes sometimes have a bit of a problem with Norwegians, whom they consider to be rough vulgarians with too much money (they seem to have nicked most of Sweden's coastline, and therefore all of its oil, and swan about the place like Scandinavian versions of Harry Enfield's Loadsamoney, doing the kind of things that Swedes can only dream of, e.g. buying a bottle of wine without taking out a mortgage).

The rest of the week was dull beyond any possible belief, and the only actually interesting thing that happened did so at a hotel thirty kilometres out of Gothenburg and was unrepeatable in a family newspaper, even though it's a bloody good story (and also, as it happens, involved Norwegians). It was and still is the only time I've not even started, let alone failed to complete, a newspaper assignment. And this is the place I am going to be seeing quite a bit of over the next three years, if all goes well. I think you have to be really rather fond of someone, to put it mildly, if you're prepared to go to Gothenburg for them on an even semi-regular basis. I believe they have the cheek to call the city "Little London", ostensibly on the grounds that 18th- and 19th-century British industrialists had a great influence on the place (although I have a dim memory of being told that these pioneers were actually Scottish), but also because they think that they're really creative and whacky and interesting, and that there is still one bar that can serve beer without having to serve food, too. "It's just on a much smaller scale," says one blogger, quoted in a piece in *Metro* which I have been looking at in order to get clued up on the wonders of the city, which for all I know might have changed beyond recognition since I was last there, but that "on a much smaller scale" rather sounds the death knell, doesn't it? And besides, London isn't that bloody great anyway, not any more, not now that the super-rich are infesting the decent bits of it like maggots.

I might seem to be ungenerous, but this is actually part of a proven strategy of thinking the worst about a place before I go there in order to be pleasantly surprised. Proven, but not infallibly so. Many is the place I have had a hunch would be ghastly and has turned out to be so, Stevenage for instance, but then this is a phenomenon familiar to all. I am prepared to be pleasantly surprised by Gothenburg, although given that I will, unless I start doing some serious saving, be seeing the place with the pin-sharp vision of the completely sober, which rarely puts me in a benign and forgiving mood. (My oldest friends all know that it is best to avoid me before six o'clock.)

One thing that really is worrying me is that in Sweden it is considered extremely rude not to take your shoes off when you visit someone's home. I suppose this is fair enough, given the fact that the weather is so appalling over there, but I hate, absolutely hate, taking my shoes off in someone else's home. Who do they think they are? The curators of a shrine, or place of worship? "We were thinking of taking our shoes off inside," said one host to me not that long ago, anxiously and hopefully looking down at my Loakes Chelseas, of which I am inordinately proud and fond. "I wasn't," I said with what I hoped was a disarming smile, and the matter was closed, for which I am grateful; had my host known about the state of my socks and my feet he would have been grateful, too. And yet this is the place to which the Beloved is committed. I think she has already decided that it might not be best for us to visit any of her colleagues; then again, the Swedes have a reputation for not being the most spontaneous and happy-go-lucky of people, so she'd probably have to wait about six years before being given an invitation. Of course, she might run into some Norwegians, and then anything could happen. They might even let us keep our shoes on!

Here's a funny thing: my bedroom has started smelling again. Not a terribly bad smell, but musty and slightly sweet, as if there were apples decaying under the bed. As I have not eaten an apple since the autumn I have to rule out that possibility. This is what makes it so disturbing, like Freud's notion of the uncanny: a thing that smells of decaying apples, and yet is not decaying apples. But up until only recently, my room not only smelled of nothing much, when it did smell of anything it smelt of something nice.

After a while it dawns on me that I have smelled this before: it is the smell of loneliness. It leads me to the remarkable conclusion that women not only smell nice in themselves, they make other places smell nice too – just by being in them. Remove them from the premises and the smell of entropy creeps back again.

As regular readers of this column will wearily know, it was not my decision to remove the Woman of the Hovel. My apologies, incidentally, to Mr Laurence Pollock of Cranfield, Bedfordshire, who wrote in last week under the impression that I was hired by this magazine to write about "books and ideas". I was not. I was hired to write – giving anecdotal evidence where necessary – about how a life in one's middle years can go wrong, the idea being to comfort those similarly afflicted or let those people unafflicted know what such a life may be like. Sometimes, I even throw in a joke or two.

Anyway, after an interregnum of really quite extraordinary contentment, I can assure you that not only does such a life suck, it sucks hind tit, as they say in Canada. As if things weren't bad enough, the eldest daughter has gone off to spend four months of her gap year being a chalet girl at an Alpine resort. She is going to earn the fantastic sum of £90 per week, which is really going to make a dent in her student loan. And for that she is going to be cooking for up to fourteen people at a time. She's happy because she gets to ski all she wants, but I think that really means is "ski as much as she can, which won't be very much, after cooking breakfast and dinner for up to fourteen people who may, just possibly may, I mean it is by no means inevitable, but then again it is not entirely beyond all boundaries of credibility, be a bunch of twats." I mean normally of course, the conversation in ski lodges tends to be of the highest calibre, revolving around an unusually stimulating selection of both books and ideas – one would get all the boring skiing out of the way simply in order to enjoy the conversation of one's fellow skiers – but every so often one met someone with too much money and too few brains and/or manners, and in the end it got to the point, as far as I was concerned, was that one of the few wholly good things about being broke and separated from the family is that I didn't have to go fucking skiing again.

And, moreover, one frets for one's children, and just because I tend to see them mainly only on alternate weekends, I don't fret any the less, and the news of Michael Schumacher's skiing accident didn't actually make me much more delighted about my daughter's choice of holiday employment. Personally, I think she should be reading Kant. (That way she could renew her acquaintance with the Categorical Imperative and ask herself what the world would be like if everyone went off to be a chalet girl for £90 a week, a sum which I have to keep looking at again and again to believe in it.)

Well, what's done is done. And there are other problems at home. There is unwellness in the family about which I suspect the family would prefer me to remain silent, but it is worrying and depressing, I assure you. The Beloved sends me a text from Gothenburg so heartbreaking that I spend a sleepless night wondering whether I should fly out there far earlier than intended.

Not for the first time, I reflect on Boethius's wheel of fortune, which can have you the toppermost of the poppermost at one moment, and down among the garbage the next. I wouldn't say I'm there yet – there are billions worse off than I am.

It's just that sometimes one gets the impression that the threads binding the rope that holds you on are unravelling and snapping, and it is a long way down and the safety net seems to be getting smaller and smaller. Nigel Molesworth's head-master would bray on about how each life must contain both triumph and disaster, fair weather and foul: "but he do not give the exakt proportions." How true. And also: why apples?

There is a new terror to travelling on the bus, or at least the 113: the video cameras which observe and relay pictures of the passengers. There's a screen handily placed just above the stairs, so while you wait on them as the bus inches through the clot of traffic that always builds up at the lights just before St John's Wood tube station, you are offered several vistas, shown in rotation, of your fellow "customers" (as London Transport sometimes whimsically calls us) looking bored, or dopey, or fretful, as is the case. People really don't look their best on these cameras, but even knowing this, I was unprepared for the shock I got when I caught a glimpse on the screen of a little old man waiting to get off and realised it was me.

Do not be deceived by the image that adorns this column: should you wish for a more accurate one, I suggest you find a bottle of Tipp-ex and paint the hair white. *Tempus fugit* and all that, but these days it seems as though it's running for its life. And yet every so often it loops round the back and meets you coming the other way, as occurred when my mother announced that she had made a dentist's appointment for me the other day. I don't know about you, but I think 50 is too old to be going to the dentist with your mother, so I feigned illness and cancelled in the morning. Also, it was raining. It seems to be doing a lot of that at the moment.

But, left to my own devices as I am at the moment, as I might have mentioned, I am given to introspection, very much of the unwelcome what-am-I-doing-with-my-life variety. I'm stuck, still, in a kind of limbo, without a real job, without any money until next Thursday, without a place I can call my own, without a girlfriend in the same country, without all sorts of things really, and one thought experiment that keeps cropping up unbidden revolves around what would happen when, should I choose to marry again, a putative mother-in-law peers down her lorgnette at me and asks, witheringly, "and what precisely are your *prospects*, Mr Lezard?"

So I am much cheered when my old friend the Moose comes round. (He has not, I suspect, really come to see me: he has come to see another old friend of mine, Amel, who has nipped over from Paris for a couple of days.) He also has no money, although that is because the machine ate his bank card. He does have an American Express card, which, as we discover, and as I had always suspected, is one of the most useless bits of plastic that can burden this unhappy planet, for it is not accepted by any restaurant within walking distance except the punitively expensive Royal China on Baker Street.

As I toy with my boiled rice I prick up my ears as the Moose tells us of an interesting wrinkle a writer friend of his has come up with in Paris. Basically, he signs rich Americans up for walking tours around his neighbourhood, and asks them to pay 250 – is it Euros, or dollars? It matters little – for the privilege. That's *each*. He takes them here and there coming up with any old rubbish about the area – it's near the Odéon, so the details are not exactly obscure – and then, as the Moose puts it, condescends to let them buy him an enormous dinner at the fanciest restaurant he knows. He is, we are assured, very fat, and very well-off, as a result.

This gets me thinking. One of the few pleasant things about my situation is the fact that I live fairly near Baker Street. And it has not escaped my attention that there has been a revival of interest in its most famous resident. Slowly, the rusting cogs of my brain start creaking into action. "Hmm," I say aloud. "I wonder . . ."

I think you begin to get the idea. Although it sounds rather like hard work, the idea of shepherding ten to fifteen wealthy Americans back and forth from the Hovel to Sherlock Mews at 250 smackers a head and telling them that that was where Sir Arthur got Holmes's first name from (I have no idea whether this is true, or whether the name Sherlock Mews postdates the detective; maybe a reader can enlighten) has its attractions.

Of course, like many schemes that are dreamed up on licensed premises, this may prove to be pie in the sky. But, as I go online and contemplate the area of desolation that, once again, is my bank account, I think maybe now is the time to get off my arse and actually do something for once. And then I would be able to look Lady Strebe-Greebling, or whoever, squarely in the pince-nez and say, "Madam, I am an entrepreneur."

Well, if there's one consolation, it's rediscovering the joys of Letting Oneself Go a Bit. One is not, after all, on the pull. Why, for instance, shower every day? No one else is going to be smelling me for a while. And showering in a cold house is a drag. With the heating off during the day, the thing to do is stay in bed until it comes on at six or so, which by an amazing coincidence is also wine o'clock. Meanwhile everything gathers itself around the body. I've mentioned this before: the Scholar's Mistress, that accumulation of books and periodicals beside one on the bed that eventually assumes the mass of another human being. Mine is now actually the entire length of the bed and becoming three-tiered. If I listed every book and issue of the *TLS* in it I could fill the rest of this column and probably have some left over for next week's, but that would be lazy of me and boring for you. Suffice it to say that the right-hand side of my bed is a testament to the enduring worth, power and consolation of the word as printed on paper. And the longer one stays in bed reading a book the less time you spend on the internet wasting your time doing "what kind of cheese are you?" quizzes on Buzzfeed, strangely compelling though they are.

Meanwhile the smell of apples has gone from the room. The bad news is that it has been replaced by some kind of nasty fug which might partly be the result of having the window shut for the last two months because of the rain. (The rain is beginning to drive me a little crazy.) The combination of stifled air and damp creeping in from the outside cannot be healthy, and moreover I am beginning to worry that if it rains any more Londoners may well evolve gills before too long. To avoid this I am staying indoors as much as possible. Which would be fine except the kitchen has now started smelling. This is very definitely a decaying-corpse smell, but whether it is of some rogue piece of food that has fallen between or behind the interstices of any one of the elements of the loosely-fitted kitchen, or one of Mousie's compañeros who has bitten the dust, I cannot say. I have just put a half a lemon which was nestling in a glass and growing a splendid coat of grey-green mould on its skin into the rubbish, so it may have been that. We shall see. The problem, or shall we say one of the problems, is that all this seems to be turning me into a bit of a nut, or an agoraphobe. The only trips I have made outside since my friend Amel went back to Paris have been either to Majestic Wine for supplies or to the hospital to visit my father. These visits are not as depressing as they need be for he retains his marbles and conversations with him are always amusing, but a hospital is a hospital, and moreover – for it is only a mile and a half up the road – I am consumed by guilt that I am not going there enough. Actually, at time of writing he has been discharged, so until I run out of food completely I have no excuse to go anywhere at all. How I am going to cope with getting to Heathrow, and then to Gothenburg, in this state is beyond me. It's a strange feeling, leaving orbit as it were. Earthly life, with its people leading normal lives, seems to be receding into the distance. When, I wonder, was the last time I did a laundry? I remember that the late genius Peter Cook recorded a series of duologues with that still-living genius, Chris Morris, under the umbrella title "Why Bother?", and I have to say that this is becoming something of a mantra for me. Cook ended his life sadly, it is glibly said, passing the time in the evenings by calling up

Clive Bull's late-night phone-in show on LBC in the persona of a melancholy, love-sick Norwegian fisherman called Sven, stranded for the time being in Swiss Cottage (note, here, the recurrence of the Scandinavian motif). This doesn't sound very sad to me, and the idea of the great Peter Cook giving his talent out anonymously and for free in a final act of generosity is one I find enormously touching. And there is kindness all around. The last time I went to Majestic I couldn't find my normal selection on the shelf; when I went to the counter to ask meekly what was going on and what on earth I was going to do now, it turned out they'd already packed it, and it was waiting for me already. How I summoned the self-control not to burst into tears is beyond me.

So in the end I made it to Gothenburg but I was so ill by the time I got there that all I could face to eat was soup. I was in the grip of a hurricane-force cold which would have legitimately had me calling in sick if I had had an office job; four weeks of mooching about the place feeling sorry for myself and hardly eating had finally taken their toll. Strangely, Sweden is not apparently a country that is particularly big on soup, if the shelves of the local supermarket were anything to go by. Even Tesco Express will have a tasty selection but in this neck of the woods the best-looking was something in a tin called "meat soup" made by an entrepreneur who was called Gustav Bong and who flourished around the turn of the twentieth Century. The Beloved looked at it doubtfully but it had a picture of a silver tureen and I was about to die so I feebly called for it to be placed in the shopping basket.

(Which, incidentally, is on wheels and is pulled along by its handle; when I was well enough to do so, I would amuse myself by pretending it was a dog, whistling and saying "here boy". I like to preserve the British reputation for eccentricity whenever I travel.)

The soup, on closer inspection, was perfectly acceptable, being composed chiefly of salt and water – the manufacturers, imaginatively using the scanty resources available to them, wished us a hearty "BONG appetit!" after the cooking instructions (they suggested, as well as heating it up, adding some herbs to make it taste of something). I came to learn a few things, some of them disturbing, about Swedish cooking. The B has a horror of fish so that rules out at least half of it, but there is plenty more to stir the appetite, especially if you are fond of variations on pork and potatoes. But it is not all like that. Take *Flygande Jakob*, which translates exactly as "Flying Jacob", a dish that the website scandinavianfood.about. com describes as a "classic Swedish casserole" but whose recipe was first unleashed in a cookery magazine called *Alt Om Mat* in 1976, the chief ingredients being chicken, bananas, peanuts, bacon, and whipped cream. "Allt Om Mat" is the Swedish for "you've been had" and I began to see the deep wisdom behind the Muppets making their crazed chef a Swede.

As it turns out, the Swedes have incredibly sweet teeth, and can be seen promenading around town every Saturday with a bag the size of a rucksack filled with sweets – the kind you'd get from a pick-and-mix in a service station. Apparently they used to do this every day until the dentists stopped seeing the funny side and made them promise to do this only on Saturdays. You think I'm making this all up, don't you? They're also very fond of their cinnamon buns, which even

I have to admit are rather yummy, and the miracle is that I didn't see a single overweight person while I was there. Not that I saw too many people. For a start, as I said earlier, there are only about twelve people in Sweden, and also I was mostly confined to my sickbed, being nursed by the B, with lashings of Gustav Bong's finest to keep me going. I had a fat new biography of William Burroughs to occupy me when she was at work. I didn't know, or had forgotten, that Burroughs had been to Sweden; Malmö, to be precise, which was in those days, in Burroughs's testimony , "one of the great centers for the distribution and dispersement of anti-Semitic propaganda." (Things are better now, I promise.*)

As for the country and her neighbours as a whole, Burroughs was not impressed: "Scandinavia exceeds my most ghastly imaginations," he wrote to Allen Ginsberg, which is quite something from the man who dreamed up the talking asshole and much worse, but I suspect some of his disdain may have been down to the draconian licensing laws in operation, which were even worse than they are there today, and that's saying something. You were only allowed two drinks of an evening – which had to be served with food (typically a couple of curling sandwiches, for legality's sake) – and whenever you entered a restaurant (there were no bars), a doorman would smell your breath to see if you'd been drinking already. It occurred to me that this might have been the origin of the Flying Jacob: a dish which was so patently disgusting that no one in full possession of their faculties would be able to eat it; a satirical dish, anti-cuisine. And yet for some reason the Swedes took to their hearts this concoction that William Burroughs himself could never have summoned from his darkest

* They've got worse again.

162

fantasies. I take my hat off to them. A nation that can eat a Flying Jacob is capable of anything.

❧

A new series of *Outnumbered* on the BBC. For those who do not know, this is a sharply-written (with, I believe, a little wiggle-room for improvisation from all the characters) sitcom about a very average family – we're squarely in the middle of the middle class here – starring Hugh Dennis, the voice of exasperated, left-leaning middle England – as the paterfamilias of a family with three children in it. This first aired around the time I got told I was surplus to requirements as a permanent fixture in the family home, although it was decided that I was useful for picking up the youngest from school, fixing the bits of the car that weren't beyond my capacity to fix, and supplying an enormous sum of money every month for the sake of the children's well-being. So the TV show and I peeled away from each other, so to speak, at the very instance of its first airing.

It was, for a time, too painful to watch. How Hugh Dennis's character – a harrassed teacher at a secondary comprehensive – managed to put up with his incredibly annoying, passive-aggressive wife (superbly played by Claire Skinner) escaped me; how he allowed his children – also all superbly played – to get like that was a bit less of a mystery; and how they both managed to afford their home was, and remains, a mystery for which, like the Giant Rat of Sumatra, the world is obviously not yet prepared. But the chief pain resided in the simple fact of the *mise en scène*: here was a family, and here was a couple, that had managed to stay together. They could do it; why couldn't we? It wasn't like I'd wanted to go.

This is always going to be in the back of my mind when I watch it, but the pain has receded somewhat. Time, or habit, or a combination of both, is a great analgesic, and also I have been given enough of it to understand that Hugh Dennis and Claire Skinner are not in real life married to each other, and so have no real reason not to wish the other one irrevocably absent.*

But still. It's in the accuracy of its portrayal of family life that it has been deservedly praised, and I watch it in the way that you might watch a parallel universe unfolding in front of you, for half an hour a week. This, I think, is what my future, or my present – for Dennis and Skinner's ages are pretty much the same as mine and the Estranged Wife's, and their children the same ages as ours, roughly – would be like, had I behaved considerably better, and my wife shown considerably more patience.

I have to say, I am beginning to wonder about the desirability of the whole domestic thing. True, Dennis plays someone who has had, at some point before the first series began, his balls chopped off, but teaching can do that to people as much as marriage; yet he suffers under privations that the last six and a half years have been strange to me. (The whole "having a job" thing has been strange to me since about 1990.) Only this could account for a real-life marriage in which there are no seething, poisonous and crackling silences, or weeping arguments, or hissed accusations along the lines

---

* Oh, I was so cynical. Or naïve? Or, somehow, both? In July 2018, it was revealed that they actually were in a relationship. I hope they still are. Life imitating art and all that. In a good way.

of "another one of your lies", etc. (how loudly can you hiss? Try it some time).

Then again, I'm not wild with the way things are at the moment. In the Hovel, things are a little too lonely. This is not a matter of personnel about one: the replacement lodger that has been called for would only bring my loneliness into sharper relief. That said, things at home would be a little too crowded, even with the eldest daughter now away from home until she packs up her things for university (she never got out of bed until about four anyway, can't imagine where she gets that kind of behaviour from). One wants things a little bit more like this over there, and a little bit more like there over here.

Still, one craves contact. An old friend whom I have not seen in years gets in touch via Facebook and asks to see pictures of the children. Women like seeing pictures of children, even when they're not they're own, it's a well-known fact. I have no recent ones and ask the EW for some, and their coolness (every picture in which they're all together at once looks like a publicity photo for a really good band, and this isn't just paternal pride speaking) makes me miss them all the more. Then again, maybe if I saw them every day I wouldn't notice that kind of thing, and just see them as three Enemies of Promise who have outgrown their prams. But it's nice that they're all considerably better-behaved and even more considerably less anxious-making than the kids in *Outnumbered*. Should Claire kick Hugh Dennis out?

Although the bidet in the downstairs loo has not worked since,

I would guess, the dying days of the Callaghan administration, it is an ill wind that blows no one any good and, as I believe I have had occasion to mention here before, it now serves as a handy receptacle for reading matter should you wish to improve your mind. In what some may consider a serious bid to get into "Pseud's Corner" for the first time in what feels like ages, this tends to be of a highbrow nature. PN *Review*, the *LRB* and *TLS*, a copy of Rilke's *Letters to a Young Poet*, Pessoa's *Book of Disquiet* and Kevin Jackson's book on Ruskin. True, there are some copies of *Viz* for the young at heart, and for a long time I found Bob Wilson's *Ultimate Collection of Peculiar Sporting Lingo* a much better and more fascinating read than I had, snobbishly, suspected it was going to be when I opened the jiffy bag containing it.

But the former Arsenal and England goalie's book has gone missing and so find instead a 1991 edition of E. M. Cioran's *Anathemas and Admirations*. This is always good for a chuckle. E. M. Cioran, in case the name is unfamiliar, was a Romanian exile living in Paris of such a bitter and gloomy nature that when he needed cheering up even more than he usually did, he would go and visit his pal Samuel Beckett. Apparently Beckett grew to dislike these visits, and the final one ended with Beckett throwing him out of his flat, saying "for feck's sake, Emil, lighten up, you miserable bastard. Things aren't as bad as all that." (I suspect I am embellishing the facts rather a lot here, so if you're writing an academic work on either Beckett or Cioran, it might be best if you do not quote anything from this piece as a primary source.)

Still, Cioran's maxims are always bracing. "On a gangrened planet, we should abstain from making plans, but we make them still, optimism being, as we know, a dying man's reflex."

That's the stuff to give the troops, and as one rises from stool one feels a braver and less deceived person for it. That, at least, is the intention. You could also have learned why a googly is called a Bosie in Australia, if some swine hadn't taken Bob Wilson's book with them. Visitors to the Hovel are now stuck with Cioran, Pessoa and the rest. This needn't be a bad thing. What was that about plans again? (And don't you love that "gangrened"? So much nastier, don't you think, than "gangrenous". You hear the green of corruption in it.) I have abandoned making plans ever since I used up the 2008 diary given to me by the Finn. This has resulted in countless missed parties and invitations – but then this, in turn, has resulted in people assuming I'm dead and so I now no longer miss parties because I'm not invited to them in the first place. However I am going to have to plan to clean up the living room within the next couple of weeks because it turns out that the woman who ran screaming from the place when she was shown round it last month has decided that, after all, it might be best not to be so fussy.

I sympathise with her. Most people, when they see the Hovel for the first time, see it, as Martin Amis said of Western tourists visiting India, through the mists of their own rejection, and I remember being distinctly unimpressed when I first saw my new home. But all new homes are sad in some way, especially when the circumstances of leaving the previous one have been traumatic. A shared home is doubly sad if you are not sharing it with anyone you love. But the new lodger will only be here for six months at the most; if she is not put off by weirdo Romanian philosophers in the bidet ("one can imagine everything, predict everything, save how low one can sink"), sixteen thousand books in the living

167

room (which I am under instructions to deal with; another plan I have to make), and a funny smell in the kitchen which is not the sweet, cloying smell of rotting fruit, like the last time there was a funny smell in the kitchen, but now something like an enormous loaf of bread that has gone mouldy which may well need the services of Rentokil. I look around me at the piles of books and jiffy bags in the living room. It will take, I estimate, a full day of hard work to sort them out, so I had better start putting the task off right now. But wait! It's Bob Wilson's *Ultimate Collection of Peculiar Sporting Lingo*! I think Cioran and Pessoa and the tidying can wait. I want to know why West Bromwich Albion are known as "the Baggies".

⚜

I went to a fancy restaurant in Soho the other night. Someone else was paying, of course – I can't remember the last time I went to a fancy restaurant and paid at least my own share of the bill. The person who was paying was actually a publisher, and moreover it was paying for about twenty people to dine at Bocca di Lupo, which gets good reviews but is stratospherically out of my financial league. But its co-proprietor did sack his Italian wine merchant when the latter called the Italian integration minister, Cecile Kyenge, "a dirty black monkey", so it has good karma.

Anyway, it was nice to be invited. "Dinner with a publisher?" asks my old comrade Matthew De Abaitua. "Give my regards to 1997." And there is something retro about it: the private dining room, the familiar faces, the way the waiters fill up my glass at the merest lift of my eyebrow. I leave earlier than the others, for I am tired – I'd been raising my eyebrow often – but I think the walk back to the Hovel will do me good. It's only about a mile and a half, and besides, it is one of those days when one is acutely conscious of a lightness about the Oyster card. As I walk down Brewer Street, a woman comes up to me and asks if I have a cigarette.

It soon became clear that the woman was not only interested in me as a kind of walking tobacconist. Asking me for a cigarette turned out to be near the upper limits of her English, but through emphatic gesture and the use of the word "alleyway" – one of those words which you don't often use in everyday life but with certain professions comes with the territory – I began to get the idea.

At the time, because I was full of drink, I was more amused than embarrassed. It is also not easy, rolling a cigarette for someone wile they are grinding their crotch against yours; I thought it best not to rummage in my pockets for a filter. My amusement revolved around the thought that at least Soho had not yet been sanitised beyond reproach. Howard Jacobson once wrote a very good piece about the importance of keeping Soho's squalid parts. When he was young, Soho provided the answers to these questions: "what's it like to do everything you shouldn't . . . what's it like to be in the hands of someone who knows more than you do and cares less; what's it like to let flesh rule you without consideration for your parents, your girlfriend or your homework . . . but why go on? You know what I wanted to find out. What's it ALL like?"

For me at least, these are questions that I no longer feel any pressing need to ask, and so I tried to steer the subject elsewhere and gently disabuse her of the notion that pestering me was worth her while. I asked where she was from (Poland, she said; I mentioned my Polish ancestry but she didn't take the conversational bait; also, I think she was from somewhere else); I told her I had a lovely girlfriend waiting for me at home; I started telling her I only had a tenner in my pocket to last me till the end of the week, which I probably now inadvertently owed her anyway, but then decided that she wouldn't believe me even if she could understand me. I gave her the cigarette, disentangled myself, lit it for her, and parted with an old-world-courtesy nod of the head and my best wishes. (I had been to a screening of *The Grand Budapest Hotel* the evening before – a film I recommend unreservedly, by the way – and was still feeling somewhat under the sway of a world of genteel, *MittelEuropäische politesse*.)

In the morning, of course, I wasn't quite so amused. I didn't like the idea of someone with only the most basic of street smarts and opportunities trying to get inside the pants of the likes of me in order to keep body and soul together. (That she was dressed no more provocatively than if she'd been doing the School Run was also vaguely unsettling.) I don't want to clean Soho up – my feelings on the subject of prostitution are roughly those of St Aquinas (in brief: a blocked sewer poisons the water supply) – but it is sobering to rub up, so to speak, against the truly down and out.

※

It is 8.30 in the morning. Never good. An out-of-town number, no name attached; could go either way, but probably not the way I'd like. The voice on the other end, businesslike, but with a charmlessness that borders on menace, asks me, without so much as a query about my health, let alone an apology for calling me so early, to confirm my name, address, and presumably a whole load of other questions.

"Hang on a moment," I say. "Before I tell you who I am, would you mind telling me who you are?" He names a company name unfamiliar to me.

"I'm afraid I am none the wiser," I say. "Could you tell me the nature of your business?" (Although I am beginning to form a shrewd idea as to what this might be.) He repeats the name, slightly less charmingly than before, and adds that this company has already sent me many letters, none of which I have acknowledged.

"In that case," I say, "we are at an impasse." I really haven't seen any of these letters, and say so. "I refuse to deal with someone of whom I have no knowledge, and you refuse to identify yourself and tell me what your company does. We are stalled." He then, with a voice that makes me think of a bailiff in a bad mood, and a bailiff, moreover, who has gone down to the kitchen in the dark with the idea of getting a snack to cheer himself up but has instead trodden on an upturned drawing-pin in his bare feet, suggests I look his company up.

We part on mutually suspicious terms. I think I know roughly what I will find if I look up his company name, because I did not come down in the last shower, but at the moment my mind is on higher things: I have to go to Birmingham City University shortly, in order to talk for about an hour and a half on what constitutes the rest of my income stream, apart from this column you are holding in your hands at this very moment. That is, book reviewing.

I am deeply familiar with my own lack of delight and competence in addressing an audience; I begin to sweat uncontrollably, which is a ludicrous phrase as one can't actually tweak one's sweating rate once it starts, but in my case it really does get visibly out of control, and this makes me lose the thread of what I'm saying, which makes me sweat, etc. But I was asked to do this last October by the writer Ian Marchant, whom I have never met but whose books I have not only praised but bespeak a geniality and worldview that would be a pleasure to encounter in person; there's a couple of long 'uns in it for me plus travel expenses, and, crucially, it's five months away, which is like never.

Around this time last month I woke up in the night with a jolt and remembered this gig, then decided that the date had probably been and gone, that everyone had forgotten all about it and that it had all blown over. This is my default way of dealing with things. Sometimes it works, sometimes it doesn't. Then a couple of days later I got an email from an ac.uk address asking me if I was still on. I sighed inwardly and said yes.

Why do I do this? Long ago I realised that to fill up forty minutes with continuous, scripted speech would involve writing somewhere between four and a half and five thousand words, which takes rather the gloss off the money I'll be earning, and bitter experience has taught me that it is unwise to go into the room with half a page of notes and a vague hope that one will be able to wing it. So I decided I'd spin things out by reading them George Orwell's horribly timeless but very funny piece "Confessions of a Book Reviewer" ("in a cold but stuffy bed-sitting room littered with cigarette ends and half-empty cups of tea, a man in a moth-eaten dressing-grown sits at a rickety table," etc.) and then . . . well, wing it.

In the end it was pretty much as I expected. I was feeling sick all the way up ("if he has recently had a lucky streak he will be suffering from a hangover") and toyed with the idea of pulling the communication cord; instead I wrote a couple of pages of notes in a crabbed hand. Which turned out, of course, to be illegible, and I sweat like a pig while talking but calm down and do much better when answering questions from the keen and intelligent audience; but one good thing has come out of it all: on the train back, I realise that I have completely forgotten the name of the company that called this morning. But I have a horrible feeling they'll be calling again.

⁂

I have come over all exhausted by all the talk in the budget – and before and after – about "hardworking families". Darlings, I feel like telling the Tory party, tell me about it. Every second of my day is filled with the most frenetic and exhausting activity, from the moment I wake up at 10.30 in the morning to the moment I go back to bed with a cup of tea ten minutes later. It is the mid-morning dreams that are most tiring: one horrible recent one had me racing Toby Young on a motorbike whose handlebars had fallen off.

It is the demonisation of those who would rather not work that hard that is particularly distressing. I was raised on the cartoons of Andy Capp, the layabout who would only ever leave his sofa for the pub or betting shop; musing, one day, that he might consider a job as a cartoonist, his wife Flo acidly commented that this would only happen if he could find a pencil long enough to draw on the ceiling. Since then my life has been a long, hard struggle against work. The idea is not necessarily to shirk, but to save one's batteries in case one day one really needs to get cracking. And as it turned out, in 2012 I had to write a book in 17 days, which I did – a rate which placed me, if only for 17 days, among the Simenons and Balzacs of the world – but that kind of tired me out so I'm waiting for my mojo to return.

The idea, though, is, in the vaguest possible sense, perhaps to the point where I am committing an insult on the original concept, Zen-like. I want to enter a state of the most delicate, attenuated condition possible, and I would rather do this by spending my days in meditation rather than working myself to the bone. This is one of the reasons lunch today was a packet of Smith's scampi-flavoured fries and half a bag of Tangfastics. (Well, more like three-quarters of a bag, actually.) I am refining myself out of existence.

Of course, I don't want to be completely idle, but just as William of Ockham advised us not to multiply variables, I do not want to add unnecessarily to my burdens. The Beloved startled me by telling me that she recently acquired a desk with a button on it you can push so it raises itself so high that you have to stand up to work at it. They are called, un-imaginatively, standing desks, and as the Latvian website of one of the companies that produces these vile things claims: *"mes atrodamies sedus poza daudz ilgak, kato jebkad ir darijuši musu senci vel pat ne tik sena pagatne."* Well, put like that, I can see their appeal, but really? Are we sitting down more than our ancestors ever did? And do standing desks really in-crease productivity 10%, as their makers and proselytes claim? I dare say being whipped while a drum beats out time in the stern helped the longboats go that little bit faster, but surely a captain wants a happy ship as well as a nippy ship? I explain to the B that one of the reasons I became a writer was so that I could minimise the time and distance spent getting from bed to workplace; but even sitting down all day could get tiring, and with the invention of the laptop I discovered that I actually did not need even to leave bed. To quote Beckett's translation of Chamfort's maxim: "better on your arse than on your feet, on your back than either, dead than the lot."

But there you go, there are people whose dreams are a mystery to us, even if we love them with all our hearts. And how even those whose dreams we share can turn out strangely; my old friend Tom Hodgkinson, who resurrected *The Idler* and reminded a generation of Bertrand Russell's superb essay "In Praise of Idleness" now complains in his newsletters about "liberal lefties" and works like a dog. But there are hundreds of thousands - millions - of people who want to work, and a lot of them are being kept out of it by people insulting and badgering those who just want a quiet life; a sofa to lie on, and a pencil long enough for the ceiling.

⚜

Here's a joke for you. What goes Ow, thump, ow, thump, ow, thump? Answer: me, trying to get up the stairs, one step at a time. Not very funny, is it? Well, you can all go and piss in your hats, because I have the hump, and I don't care. You try going upstairs when even lying down in bed, unless you are very, very careful, is agony. The intriguing thing is that I have no idea how my leg, specifically the iliofemoral ligament, got this way. I just woke up with it like that. (It's the bit where the leg joins the pelvis, and does a lot of load-bearing.) It may be a punishment; it certainly feels like the cherry on the cake. This has been a shit week and this pain is not making things any better. It's an ordure that has been slowly building up rather than one that has descended en masse, which is one thing; an unforeseen side-effect of a long-distance relationship. There are people who prefer to sleep alone every night but I am not one of them and so the reluctance to go to bed has made me keep increasingly anti-social hours, to the point were I have actually gone all the way round the clock to reset matters, and this can have no good effect on either one's mental or physical health. The only consolation is that at least I have not been given the boot and that there is someone not related to me who cares very much whether I live or die. That she is 650 miles away as the Boeing flies doesn't help, though. Last week, even before my leg decided to become my penance, I suffered one of those illnesses that leaves one unable to do anything except lie under the covers shivering and aching everywhere and listening to Debussy; that lasted two days, and I began to wonder how my body would be found if I died in my sleep. I do not even have a pussy cat who would be able to feed on my corpse should the worst happen. But I recovered, or all of me did, with the exception of my upper left leg. However, I am left open to minor infections of the soul.

One of the things about being given the boot is that you are at least spared the accumulation of smaller irritations. You only have one, and it is all-consuming. You are too busy howling with your own grief to get depressed at Mr Grayling's decision to stop people sending prisoners books. You certainly don't make the mistake, as I did, of reading Alan Massie's excellent piece for the *Telegraph* on why this is a mean and nasty policy, and then going on to check out the comments below the line. Ok, I should hardly be surprised that these were composed by the kind of people who, as children, pulled the wings off butterflies and as adults think Nigel Farage

Talks a Lot of Sense. The subset of what we shall loosely call humanity who wrote to that newspaper even before the days of online abusive anonymity weren't exactly all sweetness, light and charity either. But this is a new order of vindictiveness manifesting itself here.

And there is plenty to be getting on with. That hump is keeping itself well-stocked with bile. A quick look at the *Sun* while enjoying a plate of egg and chips in the local caff was an even worse idea than usual: it contained a petition, which you could sign, if you could, and send to Downing Street, urging Mr Cameron to start fracking as soon as possible. The Labour lead in the polls is vanishing. Scotland will be leaving the Union. I can't say I blame them but I can't pretend I'm happy about it either. I can't get to the shops and there's nothing left to eat in the Hovel but pasta and a 10-day-old heel of wholemeal, unmouldy but dense and obdurate as granite. And I stink. I haven't had the energy to go upstairs even for a shower for the last three days. What I really need is a long hot soak in a bath, with mustard in it, but even if I made it up the stairs I don't see how I'd be able to get out of the bath once I'd sat down inside it. One good friend has lost her job and another is struggling in hers, through no fault of her own, to the point of tears. You know that delight in other people's troubles the Germans have a word for? After a while you don't get it any more. Other people's troubles start bothering you almost as much as your own. Oh, if only I were a *Telegraph* reader. But I'm not. Ow, thump. Ow, thump. Ow, thump.

And so there is a new occupant in the Hovel. It can't be

helped. The general consensus among my friends is that the poor woman must be either on the run from Interpol, or a homicidal lunatic who has inveigled her way in here under false pretences, but as far as I can see she is neither: she is simply a house-proud northern woman about my age.

You begin to see the problem right there, don't you? "House-proud". I am many things, well, one or two, but "house-proud" is not one of them. I am house-shamed. As I may have mentioned before, I was blessed at birth with the ability to make a room messy just by looking at it. If I want to render it uninhabitable I have to sit down in it for about five minutes. This is much more than a class thing: it is actually supernatural. Then again, you will not find me scrubbing the doorstep every Saturday morning, whether it needs it or not.

Anyway, I came down on her first morning to find an entire room where the kitchen had once been. Everything had been tidied away. Where, I know not. The kitchen, which last saw development around the time Clive Dunn's "Granddad" was number one,* has six drawers, three of which are unusable because the bottom has fallen out of them, and three of which are unusable because they are full. The cupboard space beneath them is an area bitterly contested between the saucepans, assorted unnameable bric-à-brac and Mousie, apart from the cupboard under the sink, where even Mousie will not go. So either this woman has access to Time Lord technology, or some things have gone, perhaps forever. William of Ockham, whom I have had occasion to mention before, told us not to multiply variables unnecessarily, so I will for the time being

---

* January, 1971. Clive Dunn was 51 when he recorded it. More or less my age at the time when I wrote these words originally.

assume Time Lord tech. Not only theoretically, but practically, I know that tidying up is possible: after months of looking around me with a sick feeling and putting it off for ages, I spent the hours of midnight to 2 a.m. tidying up the living room the night before her arrival; but who does it voluntarily? The kitchen I had, exhausted, left alone, apart from cleaning the bread board and doing the washing up, bar a few items of cutlery which were beneath contempt. I couldn't see where anything else could go.

Things got off to an inauspicious start the next day. I have, since living practically alone, let myself go a bit. It's a gradual process, like one's children growing up: you don't notice it so much on a day-to-day basis, but if you haven't seen someone else's kids for a year or so, it can be quite a shock. Likewise, I think I might present an alarming spectacle to someone who last saw me, and that only briefly, about two months ago, when I had made an effort to scrub myself up. I now have a straggly white beard, like a strange fungal growth, or a cobweb in a cellar. My toenails have sheared through the front of my slippers and scratch, claw-like, on the ground when I walk. My eyes are red-rimmed and sunken from a strange combination of both too much sleep and too little sleep. My expression is that of a man hunted by the furies and hag-ridden by nameless fears. I look, in short, like Howard Hughes without the money.

"You cleaned the inside of the teapot," I snarl.

Dimly, the last human part of me – think of the remnants of Sméagol still minutely present in Gollum – recognises that as welcomes to the Hovel go, this is somewhat lacking in graciousness. But one becomes attached to one's mess, especially if it is all one has. Still, the inside of the teapot is another matter. If, like me, you are miserably fussy about your tea (because that, too, is all one has), then you will know that you never clean the inside of the teapot, because doing so ruins the taste. And, as it turns out, the poor woman does not herself drink tea. "My husband never cleans the inside of the teapot," she says. "I always thought he was just being lazy." I conceive an immediate bond of sympathy for this man, wherever he is. I deliver a brief but impassioned lecture about the unwisdom of cleaning teapots, or indeed anything else that is My Precious, and claw my way back to bed. Jesus, the poor woman.

⚜

I am in a pub in the middle of town, taking my first sip of a whisky and soda, and it is all about to go horribly wrong. The Globe in Bow Street is one of those pubs that you now find all over central London near the major tourist attractions: gussied up and over-lit, faintly reminiscent of how it used to be but overlaid with a kind of corporate blandness so that no one going in there, from any nation on earth, need feel overwhelmed or in a place which is not like millions of similar places over the world. They serve fat chips with little tubs of mayonnaise and tomato sauce; the staff are young, foreign, and wear tight black shirts. It is popular with people spilling out, from either work or pleasure, of the Royal Opera House immediately opposite. You can tell that once upon a time, but not for about sixty years, it was a very nice place indeed.

The night is getting on. I want to go home, but the person I'm with* wants to do some catching up with others and quite

* This person was, of course, the woman hitherto referred to as the Beloved. It looked as though the Order of the Boot was going to be rescinded. Don't worry, it got scinded again.

understandably so, so when she gets up to get a round in and asks me what I want I say "just a small whisky and soda, please", as I was full from the beer I'd had wile waiting alone, with a book, at the originally agreed venue, the Lamb and Flag. And I take a sip of the whisky and notice there is something wrong with it, and I see a slice of lemon bobbing about.

The point of the whisky and soda is that it is one of the safe, easy and universal drinks: there is a gag in one of Douglas Adams's *Hitchhiker's Guide to the Glaxy* books which says that every civilisation in the universe has a drink whose name sounds exactly like either "gin and tonic" or "whisky and soda"; the kind, moreover, whose instructions of manufacture are entirely included within the name itself. And yet, here it is, with a lemon where it has no place to be.

On the scale of outrages which can be perpetrated against the self, it ranks extremely low, I have to admit. So what perhaps moves me to go to the bar and ask for a replacement is not just the unwelcome taste of the thing, but a desire for simplicity and purity to be protected. I wait for one of the little blackshirts behind the bar to notice me. I have distinguished myself from someone just standing at the bar with a drink by taking the lemon out and holding it between pinched finger and thumb, like a small, wet, severed ear.

"I'm afraid someone has put a lemon in my whisky and soda," I say. "Who served you, sir?" "No one served me," I say; "someone else got it for me."

I am beginning to get a bad feeling about this. That "sir" was one of those "sirs" that serves just as well as an insult. There is a bit of faffing about behind the bar as the drink is taken away from me, and my small *Gauleiter* returns to ask me who served me again, and I repeat my answer and there is some more faffing about, and when he comes back to ask me the question a third time, something in me snaps, for I am tired, I've already had more to drink than even I strictly want, and the last three months have been shit, this whole business of making a fuss about a lemon is getting me down, and to tell you the truth I am beginning to get very tired, in a big-picture kind of way, of life's boring party trick of giving you a bit of happiness and then taking it away again, and there is something ugly within me that needs to be let out, so I say, "I've told you, no one served me, I just want to know what a slice of fucking lemon is doing in my drink." I waggle the lemon in an offended manner. At which he plonks down a couple of two quid coins and tells me to leave his pub.

"His?" I ask myself, irrelevantly, as I go back to the table and say that, for the first time since I can remember, although it must have happened before in thirty-five years of pub-going, I have been thrown out of a pub, and the faces of the company are suddenly doused in embarrassment, and I realise very quickly that no one is going to be on my side for this one, and I wonder if my little Mussolini realises that, because of a simple slice of lemon, events are going to be set in motion which will have possibly momentous effects upon at least two unsuspecting lives.

It was leaving drinks for the Yank the other day at the Uxbridge Arms. For those who missed her earlier appearances in this column, I summarise: New Yorker, loud, funny, often moved to sarcasm ("oh really?" sounds very good with a Noo Yoik twang), fond of a drinkie, and for a few months a semi-traumatised resident of the Hovel. (It's like being a ring-bearer. However briefly you carried the burden, you are in an exclusive club, and can be taken to Elvenhome when you're about to pop your clogs by way of recompense. Or so I have been assured.)

All was going swimmingly, until I heard someone at a table not far from me – the Yank, being popular, had managed to pack out one of the pub's bars – make a joke, or shall we say an observation, that revolved around my being something of a name-dropper. This rather dented my enjoyment of the evening, for I like to think of myself as not so much a name-dropper as the sprinkler of a little minor-celebrity fairy-dust in order to put a little sparkle into other people's lives. It's probably a fault I picked up from my mother, who until she met my father used to be a very up-and-coming star on Broadway, and I would, every so often, in that charming way children have of loving to hear a favourite tale repeated, ask her to tell me again about the time Yul Brynner chased her around her dressing room in his underpants when they were both appearing in *The King and I*. (To tell the truth, I was never entirely convinced of the veracity of this anecdote until I saw on the family shelves a copy of Michael Chekhov's *To the Actor: On the Technique of Acting*, preface by Yul Brynner, and with a very large and bold inscription to my mother from the bald thespian himself, in handwriting that seemed itself, all these years down the line, to be still chasing her round the room, in its underpants.)

Also: I liked the way that this column's godfather, Jeffrey Bernard's "Low Life", would also drop the odd name from time to time; when Bernard mentioned the actor Tom Baker (and his very sensible idea that the NHS should be allowed to prescribe money as well as medicines) I thrilled to the knowledge that this man may have been a miserable alcoholic perpetually on the edge of destitution, but he knew Doctor Who. I never thought, "huh, poser."

As it is, the number of names I can drop isn't that very many, and as they're almost all writers I have come to know after twenty-odd years in the biz, they shouldn't really come as a complete surprise, and anyway, the man who made the remark about me should count himself extremely lucky to be at liberty to have made it on licensed premises two and a half miles from Wormwood Scrubs rather than imprisoned within it, for he has done far worse things than name-drop, and for once I do not exaggerate for comic effect in the slightest.* But the problem that name-dropping reveals of the character of the droppers is the false estimation they have of their own importance in the grand scheme of things. This is all part of the fun.

Which is all by way of long introduction to explaining the

---

* Here's some name-dropping for you, which I unaccountably didn't put into the column; perhaps because it looked too much like name-dropping. It happened on my 49th birthday party. My birthday parties at the Hovel actually took place at the Duke, and at closing time the deal was that we could grab whatever alcohol and glasses that we could and it was All Back to Mine. No other preparation apart from reserves of red wine were made. And so on that evening, the writer Polly Samson, who is of course married to the Pink Floyd guitarist Dave Gilmour, came back, with her husband, to the Hovel. Being perhaps more used to a life of physical ease than I am, although he is a very generous man and gives much of his money away, he expects there to be something to snack on at about 11.30 in the evening. So I found him staring forlornly into the fridge at around that time. The only thing in it, really, was the elderly, wooden heel of a piece of Camembert. "This reminds me of the squats we lived in before we made any money," he said. Then he ate it. The Beloved was indignant when she found out. "But it's Dave Gilmour," I said. But as the only musical form she is really interested in is Opera, she wasn't impressed.

184

excitement I felt the other day when I got a phone call from Ian Hislop's assistant, checking she had the right number for me, and could Ian call me soon? Now, I do know Mr Hislop well enough to go up to him at a party and say "hello, Ian" and not actually be met with a blank look, but we are not quite on calling-each-other-up terms. So my thoughts about what was up went in this order: 1. *Private Eye* has discovered The Awful Truth about me and Ian is telling me now might be a good time to flee the country. 2. Something awful has happened to Francis Wheen. And 3., which I decided in the end was the one that I liked the sound of most, was that he has seen what was in front of his eyes all along and wants me to appear on *Have I Got News For You*. In which case my long struggle against alcoholic destitution will be over and my burgeoning TV career will sort out any financial unpleasantnesses for the rest of my life. In the bath, as I waited for his call, I fine-tuned my screen persona and frame of topical reference. Would I, though, do an ad for butter, like John Lydon? I don't know. It would depend on the script.

Later on, I learn that all he'd wanted was Laurie Penny's email address. A small world crashed. But did I ever mention that I know Laurie Penny?

❧

Another one of those awkward moments at the bank. Once again, I find myself with too much month at the end of my money, and as the manager happens to be doing a stint at the till (which I find commendable, like an officer leading from the front), I ask him again about a modest extension to the overdraft limit. The last time I asked this a central computer turned me down, and the manager looked pained and confused as he gave me the news.

This time, though, he suggests a loan. This will pay off the loan I already have, as well as a few other things, and it will probably work out cheaper than my frankly rather scatty approach to personal finance. All is fine: the brain in a jar that is the bank's decision-maker vents a few bubbles that say I'm good to go, and panic is assuaged until the next time.

A couple of days later I get a call from a woman at the bank. She is coming into the local branch next Wednesday and could she interview me please? This I do not like the sound of. Somehow, I do not think she is going to be interviewing me for a job, or a profile in NatWest's staff magazine ("This Month: Our Most Feckless Customers Reveal Their Astonishing Secrets"). Still, the bank has gone out on a limb for me, and it is only round the corner, so it would be bad manners to say no, if not actually unwise.

The day comes and I only remember about the appointment ten minutes before it is due. As I have barely had time to potter around before the first cup of tea, I have neither showered nor shaved nor, I notice, put on any trousers. I wash my hair with one hand, shave with the other, and pull my trousers on with my teeth and manage to arrive two minutes early. Like James Bond – I've been reading a lot of James Bond lately – I check the bank for available exits should things turn sticky. There are two: the door I came in by, and the ground, which will at some point open up and swallow me to cover my embarrassment.

What I thought was going to be an excruciating investigation into my expenses turns out to be nothing of the sort: instead, a charming young woman is trying to sell me life insurance. "Life insurance": the words have become associated with fiddles and scams for so long that I am amazed no one has come up with a euphemism or alternative term. Then again, if I take out a life insurance policy, who will be zooming whom? I'm not exactly a safe bet. Going through my personal details before sending them off to the other brain in a jar that is the insurance department's arbiter will take between half an hour and an hour, she tells me, which puts me in a bit of a panic because (a) I don't like sitting in a small, closed room in a bank for that long with anyone, however charming, and (b) I am conscious of the fact that I only had time to shower my head, which is generally not the smelliest part of the body that hasn't showered for a day. The reason it's going to take so long, as it turns out, is because she is obliged to read every word that appears on the screen out to me – presumably in case I am one of those customers who says he can read and write, but actually can't. I assure her that I can read, quite quickly as it happens, and that we can zip things along quite quickly. She looks doubtful at first but soon we get into the swing of things.

"I've never gone through this so quickly before," she says at one point. "Twenty minutes, that's amazing." We also establish a rapport. This might come as a bit of a shock to you, but I am given to flippancy in the face of official questionnaires, and exercise this gift more than once in the face of what are otherwise rather impertinent questions. She is by turns amused – "I'd love to spend the whole day with you, just to see what you'd say next" is a very nicely two-edged compliment – and horrified: "how many units a week? That's impossible."

By the end of it, we determine that if I decide to forego cover for loss of an eyeball and benign brain tumours, we can have a decent sum on my death for a modest monthly outlay. And I have been, largely, honest with my answers. The brain, I gather, will take three months to make its decision, during which time I will get free cover. Sounds like a deal. She presses the button.

Her terminal does not actually make a waah-waah noise; but a red thing comes up on screen which tells us that I have been instantly refused life insurance. I think of a few funny things to say to lighten the mood, but, in the end, keep them to myself.

&

An email from M—— on the *Independent on Sunday*. M—— used to be my editor on that paper until I got a phone call from the Actual Editor, John Mullen, telling me he had "gone over the figures" and decided that, after ten years of living high on the hog as its radio critic, I had driven the paper to the very edge of bankruptcy and only replacing me with the guy who brought round the sandwiches was going to restore the paper's AAA credit rating. (Now that the paper's owned by a billionaire, I suppose the sandwiches are these days brought round on silver salvers by liveried flunkies, and that even the flunkies have flunkies to actually hand the sandwiches over. That's what it's like when you're owned by a billionaire, right?)

But I digress. I always liked M—— and never tainted him by association with the Mullen regime. What he wants is for me to do something for them for Father's Day about my children. For many years I wrote a column for another paper called "Slack Dad" in which I offered anti-parenting advice for its Family pages, the idea being that there were quite enough writers offering idealised advice to be getting on with, and that there was surely room for the kind of person who did not, upon holding his new-born infant, burst into tears and declare this the proudest day of his life? Note: I am being gender-specific here. Men who are proud of having done little more than ejaculated into someone nine months beforehand and have had zero influence so far on the resulting baby, have a funny idea of what pride means. And for what it's worth, my time in the delivery room during Mrs Lezard's first labour was spent just out of reach of her nails, which had been beginning to dig into my thigh painfully, reading the cricket reports from Australia and wondering if I could get away with calling the child "Darren" if it was a boy.*

Since then I have had time to see how the Slack Parenting approach has paid off. The experiment is nearing its close – or rather, the close of its first stage, when the children reach majority. They are evenly spaced in age, 15, 17, and 19, which may give the impression some kind of master plan was at work, but as far as I'm concerned, they are all Acts of God.

As it is, the children have been featuring more, rather than less, in my life recently. One of the things about depression, or the low-level version of it that I have, which might as well be called "melancholy", is that you don't go out and see anyone any more. But you can't, thank goodness, get out of seeing your children. So it turns out that they're the people I've been seeing the most of ever since the B went off to Sweden. The youngest didn't want to go on a holiday with the others

---

* For non-sporty people: there was a bowler in the England team called Darren Gough, who was one of the few players that supporters weren't in some way ashamed of.

so elected to stay with me in the Hovel. It was great, and I learned that *Star Trek II: the Wrath of Khan* is an even better film than I remember it being. The middle one pops round every week after classes round the corner and gives me sage advice on the unwisdom of using this column to settle scores or nurse grudges. And the eldest just turns up when she feels like it, because at least she knows when she comes here she will have someone to sit up chatting with until 2 am with a glass of wine or two to help the conversation. My, how tall the middle child is!

So the fact that my children actually want to see me, after years of my not even remotely bursting into tears of pride whenever I contemplated them, is one of nicest surprises that this existence has granted to me. It also represents a salve to the bitterness of the last few years. There are many cruelties involved in divorce, or separation, or whatever you want to call it or define it as: and the cruellest is only seeing your children every two weeks. It is a matter of deep grief and pain, to the point where I forcibly shrug the thought away the second it occurs to me, that the youngest is coming to an age when he will have been alive longer with me as a distant parent than as someone living in the same home as him. Then again, it is maybe this lack of continual presence that has contrived to present me, to their minds, as a desirable occasional alternative to the official family home. Perhaps; but at what a price.

Alles in die Welt lässt sich ertragen,/Nür nicht eine Reihe von schönen Tagen. Yes, I know I've used this before, on page 66, but it's still a good 'un. I remember being sort-of-impressed at the time, thinking, Yes, that's just the kind of clever-clever thing a poet would say, but give me a row of beautiful days and let's see how much I mind it, okay? I also suspected, uneasily, that there may well be some truth in there. A few years later I came across Francesca's lament in Canto V of the *Inferno*, the one beginning *"nessun maggior dolore . . ."*: nothing worse than recalling happy times when you're in the shit. (I give you the gist.) This amplifies the signal of Goethe's lines, but at the risk of losing their paradox.

All of which is by tortuous way of saying I had a bloody good time last week, and I was sad when it was over. The B arrived from Sweden on Thursday evening for my birthday a couple of days later, the weather in London was perfect, I had a nice dinner with her, my daughter who had turned up to deliver a card, and a couple of friends, no one mentioned Nigel Farage, then the B had to leave on Monday, and there was a rather poignant scene of us waving goodbye to each other, she only dimly visible through the heavily smoked glass of the Heathrow Express, and me being yelled at by not one but TWO platform personnel for standing too near the train. "Step back from the train, SIR!"

Whether it spoiled the mood or enhanced it I am still not sure, but I do remember thinking: I'm 51 years old, damn it, I know how close I can stand to a train by now. It certainly didn't stop the eyes from prickling a bit, and a few deep breaths being needed to be taken to steady the self, on the mile-and-a-half walk back to the Hovel. Well, one lives, and there are worse things. At least I don't have to go around lying on dating websites about my height and age and teeth and deep misgivings about almost every area of human activity in order to attract a mate. But this living alone business is getting to me. There was a piece a couple of weeks ago in this magazine by a woman who had one of those deeply unsettling falls when getting out of bed; luckily, her husband was there at the time and was able to help. I was deeply affected by this detail. If I had some kind of stroke or heart attack who'd know? You have to get taken to hospital rather quickly in these circumstances and even if I was in a condition to be able to use the phone there is a good chance it would be in its regular place, i.e. nestled somewhere comfy but inscrutable among the books or the bedclothes. It's the kind of thought that makes me go and make myself a nice cup of tea to distract and console myself. Then when I put on the radio while waiting for the kettle I find it's *You and Yours*, which is bad enough news already, but telling us about yet another study that says people who live alone die younger.

Time to pull myself together. I am prey to a certain degree of grass-is-greenery when it comes to certain concepts and situations, to the point that my own experience is distorted or sometimes flatly ignored, so that (for example) when I encounter the words "my wife" or "my husband", I get, in certain dark moods, a kind of choking sensation beneath the breastbone, for what I hear is "my helpmeet, my lover, my lifetime companion, and the wind beneath my wings" when actually, as I should really know full well, the words "my wife" and "my husband" don't necessarily mean any of these things at all. Let alone all of them all at once. So to cheer myself up I think of all the people in dreadful marriages. (One does hear about some shockers.) I make tea, (checking to see it's not time for *You and Yours* or *Moneybox Live*) and exercise the mind by wondering whether, if I shaved according to the principle of lawnmowing, one stroke up and one down, I'd end up with an interestingly striped face. And also reflect on the really mind-bending piece of information I learned the other day: Nigel Farage is younger than me. Unless, of course, he's lying.

⚘

Meanwhile, because I am a good person deep down really (unlike my Lord Rennard,* when I grope someone I apologise like a man for it afterwards, and don't hide behind weasel words like "inadvertently", "personal space" and "may have"; in fact, come to think of it, I don't grope people at all), I accompany someone shopping. And not just shopping, but shoe shopping.

My motto, when buying shoes, is "as rarely as possible". A shoe will actually have to be hanging, exploded, off my foot, and making flapping noises as I walk, before I buy another one. Even the desert boots I get from that shop on the Uxbridge Road for £20. The last ones I bought there are still going, just. I've had to spend £15 at £5 a pop at the local menders gluing the soles back on over the years, but I still think that's good value. Although for some reason, it's their laces that have exploded. I didn't realise shoelaces had intestines. Who'd have thought?

So here I am in Covent Garden's branch of ——, while my companion chooses a pair of flatties. I sit down on a

* Lord Rennard was a prominent figure in the Liberal Democrats. As his Wikipedia entry puts it: "In February 2013 Channel 4 News ran a report on Lord Rennard, alleging a history of sexual harassment during his time as an official of the party. Channel 4 stated that the alleged victims decided to comment publicly since Rennard had begun to again play an 'active role in the Party'.He strongly denied the allegations." As a friend of mine put it drily at the time: "that's funny, he doesn't look the type." Go on, google his face.

comfy bench, the only man in the shop apart from a postman who pops in and delivers and then goes away again, and contemplate the music being played, the staff. They are all . . . of a type. The music is the kind where the voices have been compressed or stretched to fit the synthesised tune. Not my cup of tea, but I can understand the appeal. The manager, her face a triumphant copper mask of the tanner's art, rules over all she surveys. At one point my companion shows me a pair of shoes she has just tried on.

"One's bigger than the other," I say. She goes off and tries the next size down. I am smiled at from time to time, faintly contemptuously, but with a touch of sympathy, by the staff, and the manager. Something in her look, or mine, brings her over. Perhaps it is because I am still holding the shoes.

"Look," I say. "One of these is bigger than the other." She takes them from me. "No it's not," she says. I weigh up my options, and the wisdom of standing up for the truth. Now, I quickly decide, is not the time to go all *eppur si muove* on her.

"You're the boss," I say. "I certainly am," she says.

Next, to the ——— in Holborn. It is a shop that sells running shoes. Call it the Foot Monster, or the Running Shack, or whatever you like. For some reason, I have forgotten its name. But I have not forgotten the names of some of the running shoes that stare at me from their shelves as I contemplate them from the (much less comfy) bench that I have parked myself on. Pegasus 31. Ghost 6. LunarGlide +5. What happened, I wonder, to Pegasuses nos 1-30, Ghosts 1-5, and LunarGlides +1-4? My companion comes over to me while an assistant, having asked her several questions about her running and her gait, and got her to have a go on the running machine in the store, which she is not used to, but there is a man who has been pounding away on it like a twat for the last half-hour who would make anyone feel like a novice, gets her shoes.

"I'm mesmerised by the names," I say. (You do realise, of course, that this is the first time I have been in such a shop, and I am boggled by the novelty of the experience.) She, with the keen eyesight of youth, has noticed an even better one, and she points silently to it: "Vomero". Vomero 9, to be precise. Silently, well, after a brief but loud snort of laughter, I applaud the mischievous genius of the mind that came up with that. Short of calling it "Blister 500", "Ankle-Buster 60", or "CardiacFailure 12" they couldn't have come up with anything better to capture the experience of running. Or perhaps the "ImGoingToDieRightNow 51".

The assistant returns. I point out that the terrain that my friend is going to be running on is actually quite hilly, and not on paved roads or tracks.

"Hmm, good point," says the assistant, stroking his chin, which is odd, because what I had been expecting him to say, after quick appraisal of my build, gait, and obvious bemusement, like someone from a 1960s episode of *Doctor Who* who has stumbled into the Tardis, was something along the lines of "what the fuck do you know about it, you silly tool?" I count this, I suddenly realise, as one of my life's quiet victories.

So here are today's lessons. Never turn down an invitation to go shoe-shopping, for every day is a school day, and yes, it's true: you can fool some people some of the time.

❧

There's been a photographer in the Hovel, because the Sindie wants to have pictures of the kids and me to illustrate the big

Fathers' Day piece I mentioned a couple of weeks ago. I had, earlier, written loftily to the children, in that way you sometimes do after a glass too many ("you may be part of the social media generation, which values exposure above all things, but you have, to your great credit, not bought into these values wholesale," etc. etc.), in case they decided they didn't want to be photographed or associated publicly with me in any way, but they were happy with the idea although perhaps privately beginning to wonder if their old man was losing his marbles. Assuming he had many marbles to begin with.

The cleaning lady had been the day before and I had simply not moved for twenty-four hours in order to minimise any damage I could do to the order of the place, but as visitors already know, the Hovel's system of accelerated entropy has gone too far now for a weekly two-hour blitz to do much more than the most limited damage control. People who have never visited the place before, I realise, can never really be prepared enough for the sight that awaits them. The photographer had been told roughly what to expect, but you could tell when he entered the living room that he was deeply moved. That's the great thing about photographers: they see the world in purely visual terms, not moral ones (although he did tell me a story about photographing [name redacted on legal advice] which confirmed that my suspicion that [name redacted] was a complete shit was right on the money).*

I once used to joke with the great photographer Roger Bamber that his job was easy, as it was over in $\frac{1}{250}$ of a second, and even sooner if it was a sunny day, which never failed to enrage him, but golly, they do have to work hard. Writers

---

* I wish I could remember who this story was about. Let's say it was Boris Johnson.

may moan about their lot but we don't have to lug a hundred kilos of kit around. Bottom line, all a writer really needs is a Ryman's notebook (a fiver, indistinguishable, three paces away, from a Moleskine costing four times the price) and a biro. We do not need a lighting rig that goes FLASH and one of those umbrellas lined with silver. (You can safely dismiss any writer as a fraud who says that they would be Utterly Lost without their Macbook.)

We all had a jolly time until at one point the photographer asked me to stand on a chair. The children had already had their turn but standing on chairs holds no terror for the young. After the age of about 25, though, it becomes one of those things that you decide you've wrung every last drop of pleasure from, and that chairs are, in the final analysis, for sitting on. You can put your feet on a chair if you're already sitting in another one but that's about it. This is a feeling that intensifies with the years. It's one of the reasons why it takes so long for men over a certain age to change a light bulb.

Doing this made me feel a bit light-headed, and it also gave me a new perspective on the living room, so I noticed the Fez hanging off the antlers and suggested putting it on. This has been in the family gathering dust since a parental trip to Morocco in the 1970s, so I pinched it shortly after Matt Smith, in his incarnation as the eleventh Doctor, rescued the headwear from the grip of the late Tommy Cooper. Once I put it on, though, the mood among the children curdled. Embarrassing one's offspring is easier than falling off a chair, but this time I wondered if I had gone too far. After all, as my eldest son has remarked, it is not just me in my own little world. (Although, speaking in strictly philosophical terms, that's exactly what it is.)

We repaired outside to the terrace for some fresh air and more photographs. The outside is less hovelly than the inside if you turn away from half of the plant-pots and the heap of wax which looks as though a candle has vomited underneath the table. It's at this point I notice the daughter is suffering: it is bright outside, and she had, how shall I put this, stayed up rather late the night before. The sunglasses indoors had not been an affectation.

The photographer packed up, we shook hands (we'd got on splendidly), and the children left. Except the daughter, who stayed on the sofa and didn't leave till the next day. She spent the time drinking tea and watching *Withnail and I*. I wonder what on earth it could have been that drew her to that particular film.

٭

As I write these words, England have declared on 575 for 9 and Joe Root, the Yorkshireman who only became old enough to vote on the second-last day of 2008, has scored an unbeaten double century at Lord's. I should have been there, but I have to file this column.

At which point I have a confession to make. I shall do so in a roundabout way. Imagine, if you will, the scene. It is Queen Charlotte's Hospital in Chiswick, many, many years ago, and an American woman is entering the final stages of labour. Outside, in the corridor, her husband clips the end off his third Partagás in a row and, pausing only to give a passing hospital porter a thrashing with his Malacca cane, considers his options should the resulting issue be a boy. He only has one firm idea: that he should be a member of Marylebone Cricket Club.

Cut to many, many years later. That child, now grown to full estate, his marriage and finances in ruins, living in circumstances only two phone calls away from complete destitution, awaits an envelope. It is March; he has, to save money, turned off the heating in the Hovel he lives in. Wrapped in several layers of ancient jumpers, moth-eaten scarves and threadbare overcoats, he reads an ancient copy of *Metro* by the feeble light of a guttering candle, which he also uses to heat up the tin of Heinz lentil soup that constitutes his daily meal. He would burn the piles of review copies of books that surround him in the grate if he were not living in a smoke-free zone of London. Downstairs, the letterbox clatters, and he runs down as fast as his joints, now nearly completely seized up by lumbago, will let him. His hands, warmed only partly by his fingerless gloves, tremble as he picks up the brown buff envelope from the floor. Most buff envelopes are harbingers of fear and doom, but not this one. He has already checked the franking mark, palpated it, and felt the telltale resistance in one corner. It's here! His last link to civilisation, to the life that was his birthright. His breath condenses in the freezing air as he sobs his gratitude. His new MCC membership card has arrived.

You know, you don't get a lot of sympathy in some circles when you let on you're an MCC member. I have a feeling that even coming up with the above, a slightly exaggerated version of the truth (MCC passes are actually mailed in April), isn't going to stop me from getting a certain amount of flak from sections of this magazine's readership. My politics may place me firmly on the left of the Labour party,* but confess to

---

* This was written before the days in which, to be considered on the left of the Labour Party, it really, really helped if you were at least a bit of an anti-Semite.

owning an egg-and-bacon tie and people start looking at you in a whole new light. Which is funny, because it's like a mirror image of what happens when you sit down in the smoking enclosure in front of the Pavilion at Lord's with a copy of the *Guardian* and the latest *New Statesman*.

"Goodness me," one of the adjacent members will say as he notices my reading matter. "Is that the old Staggers? I didn't realise it was still going." They may then ask if they can have a look. I always say yes. I watch as he flicks through its pages. A slight empurpling of the features may follow.

"Do you really read this?" "It gets worse," I say. "I write for it."

By the afternoon, after a few drinks have been taken, the mood tends to mellow, and once or twice I have even elicited a vague promise from my neighbour to give this magazine another go, because it's much more fun than it was in 1923, which was when he last saw a copy. But I do not care too much, because as I have got older, I seem to love the game more and more, and in particular the long form of the game, with its easy pace, its relative courtliness; the very sound of it, and the look of the whites against the green. Also, you can't see the sponsors' logos from where I sit; and, as I refuse to pay for Sky TV, and couldn't afford it even if I wanted to, this is the only way I can get to see live international cricket. For a yearly outlay considerably less than that of a satellite or cable subscription, I can stroll into Lord's for any game I like without buying a ticket. Last year, after a particularly glorious day, during which all cares, and there have been plenty of these, had disappeared, I found my eyes brimming with tears of happiness and gratitude. This is not an exaggeration.

"Do your colleagues ever give you stick for being an MCC member?" I was asked the other day.

"Sometimes," I say. They don't really, but I like saying this next bit: "And I tell them to go fuck themselves."

⁂

Ping! A text appears. It is Razors, my ex-housemate, who is flying over to England to settle some old scores, or, as he euphemistically puts it, "see his family for his birthday". That old chestnut.

I'd completely forgotten he was coming over, but it is always a delight to see him, so I put on my pinny and take up my feather duster and give the Hovel a going-over in his honour.

"Jesus Christ," he says when he sees the place, "it's looking even more disgustingly Hovelly than it did when I was here."

"Well, you've grown a beard," I say.

We sit on the terrace, talking of this and that. Razors has become a key player in what I shall loosely describe as the media in New York, and I keep trying to steer the subject towards him giving me a job, but he manages to evade my skilful parries. Finally, I remember that he has occasionally shown a fondness for alcohol in small doses, so I go to the drinks cabinet and take out the bottle of Harvey's Bristol Cream I keep for special occasions. There is about half of it left, which should be plenty. I pour us each a little glass, and hope that the poison of drink will mellow him.

Well, that's how it always starts with Razors. You'd think sherry had a reputation as a civilised drink; maybe they put something in it these days. One thimbleful turns into another, and before we know it that half-bottle is gone. Razors has turned from a cultivated chap appalled at the Met's decision not to simulcast John Adams's opera *The Death of Klinghoffer*, to a raging maniac wholly enslaved by booze.

"Shall we get another bottle?" he asks. I know what he can be like when he gets into this kind of mood, so I go to the corner shop and buy a bottle of Blossom Hill rosé (his favourite tipple). Well, what with one thing and another, and after a few adventures of which we have no memory, but which leave us with minor unexplained cuts and bruises on our hands, a court order, and, for my part, the sore-throat-like side-effects of a choked windpipe, we find ourselves shooting the breeze, back at the Hovel, the debris of countless bottles of wine beside and around us, and it is six o'clock in the morning. The Hovel's other resident – not the woman who scours the inside of teapots, the other one – comes down in his suit to go to work. Normally, he'd be going for his early morning run at this time, which would have been more than I could have taken. However, he is an affable man, and if he is appalled at seeing his housemate and a strange man with a beard drinking wine on the terrace at six in the morning, he is good at hiding it. What he doesn't know is how much worse it could have been. The last time Razors and I tied one on, we came to in the hold of a tramp steamer in the South China seas and learned we'd enlisted in the Merchant Marine for three years.

It's funny how one's faculties and stamina diminish with age. I once drank Hunter S Thompson pretty much under the table many years ago – I always harboured an uneasy suspicion that I may have been slightly culpable in the matter of his early and unwelcome demise – but these days I find that six in the morning is pretty much my cut-off point. Perhaps it is the early summer dawns that are so tiring.

Later on in the afternoon, when I have risen again and Razors has tried to push a full English breakfast down me, without a great deal of success, I get a call from the Estranged Wife reminding me of our forthcoming trip to ———tomorrow, to take the eldest boy to a university open day. By coincidence, it is the same place that I went to with the daughter a couple of years ago, and I made a bit of a scene with a philosophy lecturer who didn't know how to pronounce "Descartes". (See p. 42) Relations with the ex are civil to the point of pleasantness these days, as long as we stay off the subject of money, but she had told me to behave better this time. "We'll have to leave at eight a.m.," she said.

I contemplate the almost visible springs and coils from my shattered body clock lying about me, and remember that Razors wants to watch the England game in a pub that evening. I explain that 8 a.m. will be out of the question, that Razors is here, and I am basically dead. She understands, but does not perhaps fully sympathise. I muster all the dignity at my command, say "you're not the boss of me", and relapse into a coma.

Midsummer's Day was unusual. That's good: a usual day, these days, involves lying in bed all day wondering when I'm going to tidy the bedroom up enough so I can let the cleaning lady have a go at it without me dying of shame or her resigning in disgust. When you don't have a lady friend in situ you tend to let things slide a little bit, and your motto changes from

"Excelsior!" to "what's the sodding point?", only with a more passionate qualifier than "sodding".

I had long planned to go up to the Heath on Midsummer Night and frolic under the stars. The last time I had a proper Midsummer bacchanalia was when my fellow-columnist, Mr William Self, arranged for a bonfire party on the beach near Sizewell, just round the corner from where he was living at the time. This was all very nice but I'd had to stay up half the night on the evening before, condensing *The Tempest* into a fifteen-minute version because he wanted us to perform it. (It took a lot longer than I thought it would, but I like to think I turned out a pretty good version.)

This time all I was going to do was lie on my back or walk through the woods, with a friend or rather more than one friend, as I did not want to be mistaken for the kind of person who goes up to Hampstead Heath in the middle of the night for one purpose only. (I am reminded of the wonderful letter in *Viz* which complained that gay men, going to the Heath for an encounter, can have their spirits uplifted in the knowledge that there is a small but definite chance they'll run into George Michael; whereas there is no public space on earth where a heterosexual man can go in the expectation, however small, that he'll run into, say, Angelina Jolie.)

So I am to go with my old friend John Moore; a couple of his friends, both women, will be joining us later. En route to my rendezvous I drop in on my old friend C——, who presses upon me one of those cigarettes which, by a curious anomaly, are perfectly legal in Colorado but, thanks to the stupidity and ignorance of successive British governments since 1928, illegal here.

I have noticed on more than one occasion that it is only

when one is enjoying the effects of such a cigarette that Providence decides to throw you rather more than your allotted share of odd occurrences. If paranoia is said to be a side-effect, then that might be because you have something to be paranoid about. So when an enormous shaven-headed man accosted me on the northbound platform of the Northern Line at King's Cross, I at first wondered whether my time had come, and that the various people and organisations I owe money to had clubbed together and decided that assassination was the only way forward.

"Excuse me for bothering you," he said very politely, "but from the way you're dressed" – it was a warm day, and I was wearing my summer plumage of white linen – "you look as though you might know what's happened in the cricket."

As it happened, I did, and I was in the middle of an involved account of how exactly England had got to 318 for 6 against Sri Lanka, when someone else tapped me on the shoulder. Jesus Christ, I thought, this is it. Mr Shaven Head was just a diversion. But it turned out to be Noah, a friend of my daughter's, who had recently befriended me on Facebook. He once broke a string on my guitar while he was playing it (he's sickeningly talented) so I made him restring the whole thing; as it's a twelve-string semi-acoustic, this takes about three hours. Had he been stalking me so he could push me onto the tracks in revenge? No, he wanted to thank my daughter for having driven him and his film crew to Wales.

By the time I got to the pub I had more or less recovered from two random human encounters on the tube in fifteen seconds, but was still jittery. As I sipped my pint a young man in a football shirt asked if I would take a picture of him and his friends. As I held the camera up, he asked: "er . . . are you Nicholas Lezard?"

My usual impulse when asked this is to say "no", for reasons hinted at above, but instead I said "yes", cautiously. It turned out that he was a fan of this column; and he even had a copy of this magazine, open at this page, which he took out of his bag for me to sign. Which has more or less made my year, to be honest, but Philip, if you're reading this: you nearly gave me a fucking heart attack.

⁂

To the summer party of A Certain Publisher. For many years I owed them a book, and so I would turn up in the spirit of Levin - is it Levin? - from *Anna Karenina* who would make a point of going to places where he owed money, just to show he wasn't scared. I remember once, at another gathering, having someone say to me "I don't know how you have the nerve to show your face here," and, for some reason, I found this rather thrilling. Anyway, even though the actual organisers of the party have no reason to glare at me (I gather it is a glitch in the system that gets me invited every year), apart from the fact that the book they published was more of a *succès d'estime* than an actual success, there are plenty of people there of whom I would be wise to steer clear.

There are, for a start, the small but ever-growing band of writers of whose books I have written unkind reviews. There are not many of these, but as I have always suspected, and as personal experience has taught me, the recipient of a stinker will remember it until the end of time.

Then there are the editors. There are two kinds. One is the editor of the book you are meant to be writing. You have to deal with these, even though the conversation may be pained.

Here is the funny thing: the relationship with an editor can often be more fraught after you have written your book for him or her than it was while they were still drumming their fingers on the desk waiting for it. Also, the question you learn very quickly not to ask is the one with the word "sales" in it. As a more experienced writer friend of mine explained to me a while back, they will be the first to tell you if there is good news on that front. If they have not personally called you up to congratulate you, it is not because they have had a busy day and it has slipped their mind. It is because they have little to congratulate you for.

Editor Type 2 is, of course, the editor of the publication you write for. Here, the rule is simply to avoid at all costs, but when the publication concerned is a newspaper, that's easy, as they move in different circles, usually several miles above the earth in gold-plated stratocruisers, being smeared in caviar by oiled houris of their preferred gender. The editor the common or garden hack has to deal with – i.e. the one you file to and who sorts out your sloppy phrasing – is a more *disponible* human being, someone definitely a rung or two above you but nevertheless recognisably of the same species. They're fine. The problem is when working for publications the size of, say . . . oh, I don't know . . . let us call it *The Modern Politician*. The editor of such a publication actually is approachable; he or she may indeed have hired you himself. But you must under no circumstances talk to this person when you have taken drink, because you will make a tit of yourself, either by word or deed, and the memory of this will haunt your days and nights with dread and remorse for years to come. Luckily, *The Modern Politician's* chief rival, a right-wing publication called . . . um . . . *The Onlooker* was having its own party that night, and they were serving Pol Roger, the bastards, and they may well have invited the *Modern Politician's* editor along to that, so no harm done.

However, the other category of people to avoid is those whose correspondence I have failed to return, whose invitations I have forgotten about, and whom through any number of acts of thoughtless omission I have offended; and the numbers in this category are large beyond counting. First up is Craig Raine, who berates me for not having replied to his suggestion that I write a huge piece on Gabriel García Márquez, for what I suspect would be a nominal fee at best.

"Never heard of him," I say.

In the end, after dodging the extremely large number of people I need to avoid by talking to the accordionist from The Pogues for a very long time (and he's also very sharp and funny too, so that's good), I suddenly find myself talking to a Famous Person who, it turns out, is reading my book. She has brought her husband along, who is An Even More Famous Person,* and, moreover, one who, like her, I think deserves his fame, and I get a bit giddy and tip my glass of rosé over her in my excitement. Things go downhill a bit after that, and, as I trudge home reflecting on the degree to which I have, yet again, made a tit of myself, despite all efforts not to, I think of Samuel Beckett's wise words from – is it "First Love"? – "the mistake one makes is to speak to people."

A call from an 0845 number. I ignore it at first but it turns out

---

* These were, reading from left to right, David Mitchell and Victoria Coren. I once made her brother Giles cry.

that someone in Miami – Miami? – has cloned my card and been making merry with the cashpoints. A bit here, a bit there; it adds up. I find myself curiously unoutraged at this crime; the bank will accept my assurances that I have never been to Miami, the money will be reimbursed, and I feel a pang for the people who thought that my account was a goldmine.

So for the time being the account is frozen and the card unusable. I have just enough cash in my wallet, I calculate, for a couple of pints and a Chinese meal. With nothing on the Oyster, I will have to walk. But it is a lovely evening and I feel like an adventure so I stroll up through Regent's Park and Primrose Hill so that I can sit on the Heath and read my book for a while before meeting my friend John at the Flask. I feel I owe him a visit; he had called me up earlier in the week to go for a drink with him and Peter Jukes, who wrote that astonishingly good piece in this magazine about the Brooks/Coulson trial a couple of weeks ago, but I had been feeling low and under no illusions as to how good my company would be.

All goes well, apart from a moment when, prone in the long grass and scribbling notes in the book I am reviewing, I hear a dog running towards me from behind. This is it, I think. What a way to go. Being eaten by a dog on Hampstead Heath. I had, ever since John told me that he had once bumped into Paul McCartney walking his own dog, entertained a fantasy about running into him on the Heath; but somehow, as the dog, frenzied by my intoxicating, musky bouquet, starts licking me all over the head, I think the ex-Beatle would not let his dog get out of control like this.

But my real problems do not start there. They start on the walk back later; and they are self-generated. I find myself, in short, being assaulted by memories; assaulted much as I was by the dog on the Heath earlier, only with less slobbering and with my glasses remaining in place. We start at the junction of West End Lane and the Finchley Road. First, there is the top of the road on which Hampstead Cricket Club's ground lies.

Until I was about 13, every alternate summer Sunday was spent on the boundary, watching my father score plucky 10s against opposition that seemed to get inexorably younger than him. I once saw him get struck on the thigh by a ball, and then goggling, baffled, at the sight of him dancing around the pitch with smoke coming out of his trousers. The ball had hit the packet of Swan Vestas in his pocket, and these, being non-safety matches, lit themselves.* In the end no harm was done except from a few hernias caused by laughter; but it is the kind of experience that can mark a player, and he never really recovered his form after that.

Arkwright Road, opposite: by freakish coincidence the address *and* the surname of the second primary school teacher I fell in love with. Miss Arkwright: the name still makes my heart tremble. I was eight. Two years earlier, Miss Ashby-Pickford had broken my heart, but I was determined to move forward.

Then Frognal. (Sorry if this column is a bit London-centric, by the way. In my defence, it started out being called "Down and Out in London", and I still live here, so there it is.) There lived one of the two Lacanians I had a brief relationship with. All I will say here is that Lacanians believe love is "giving something you don't have to someone who doesn't want it".

Moving on.

* This also happened, I gather, to Arthur Conan Doyle, of all people.

Then there's the building that used to house a famous squat in the 1980s. I remember a time in the basement one evening. A couple of friends of friends are chasing the dragon.

"God, I love heroin," says one.

"Me too," says the other. I am offered some, which I can tell is actually awfully generous of them. But I decline. Years later, one of them, who has become a good friend, and also kicked the habit, dies of a heart attack, aged about 40. I still miss him. (When don't you miss people you like who died before you, I wonder? Only when you don't think about them.)

Then . . . ah, but I must be boring you. The thing is I am afflicted by memories, the way some people are afflicted by their dreams. John went on tour supporting the Ramones in the 80s and doesn't remember he even did so; only the ticket stub he recently found in a drawer reminded him. Then again, I lost almost all of 1982 to drink; all I remember is that I was very, very happy.

But the rest: it's all there. I even remember, as I pass the folded-accordion shape of Swiss Cottage Library, being a weird 12-year-old, studying books on medieval orthography, for the sheer giddy hell of it. (I had retreated from love by then, temporarily.)

So that's it. I'm staying in for a while now, in the friction-less present, accruing no more of these pesky memories if I can possibly help it, for the time being.

❧

Once again, we come to that time of year when the last Test match has been played, the first proper chill of autumn seeps into summer, and I celebrate, if that is the word, the anniversary of my moving into the Hovel. Seven years. Jesus. Not for the first time, I think about moving somewhere else, only now it is not so much in the way one wants to change an itchy jumper, but with the urgency of someone who smells smoke when there shouldn't be any. A new lodger will be joining me: a young woman called Daisy, who, as one of my children observed, looked more like someone called "Daisy" than anyone else who had ever been given that name. She dresses, by her own admission, in the style of a hippy and is studying music at SOAS. Oriental or African music? I asked. I wanted to prepare myself for whichever style of percussion instrument was going to haunt my evenings. Both, she said.

I think I could afford to live in Kettering, I realise after doing some research. There is always the possibility of moving to Gothenburg, but although there would be the presence there of someone whom I really want to be with, the Swedes have a very different approach to breakfast to mine. It involves yoghurt and muesli, and, if you're lucky, a couple of slices of cheese, strictly rationed (don't they know there isn't a war on?). Some establishments serve the muesli in decorative bowls, but as far as I'm concerned, tipping the contents of a bird-feeder into a heart-shaped ramekin does nothing to alter the essential nature of the food. I also fail to see how I could persuade every publisher in the country to start mailing the books they think I'd like to review to Sweden.

Things are looking grim, then, and so when the Estranged Wife calls to say she's coming round to help me sort out my pension, I do not have the strength to say no. A little word about pensions. As everyone in the country has worked out by now, these are things into which one pays a sum – generally around £100 a month – to a company which invests the money with all the expertise and cunning at its disposal, so that, when you retire, you will have a guaranteed income of 50p a year. Personally, I'm not planning on retiring, but sometimes the world has other ideas so it is wise to plan ahead. The problem is, as the EW understands all too well, I have the financial acumen of a bumblebee. And not one of those brainy, hard-nosed bumblebees who have been to business school and got an MBA, but the dreamy, vacant kind of bumblebee who cares for little more than buzzing from flower to flower in search of nectar for his little ones.

In my case, my pension pot has been managed with all the skill one might expect, and I am the kind of customer, or strictly speaking "mug", that a callous, neo-liberal grasping financial firm dreams of. I just give them the money and hope for the best. But the EW, who has a 50% stake in anything I own, has spotted that something is amiss in the way the sums are being invested, and has been nagging at me for something like four years now to Do Something about it.

Luckily, relations between us have reached the point where the proportion of laughter to recriminations has been reversed, and we get on well now, although I am aware that if anything is going to put a strain on things, it is going to be this. I once changed the master password to my account in a panic when I feared she was going to do something unilateral, but I had misjudged her. I now know it is safer for her to have the password because I invariably forget it anyway.

So, fortified with wine, we go down the rabbit hole and look at the eerie world of my personal long-term finance. A few columns of meaningless names and numbers pop up on screen. (Annoyingly, I had remembered the password.)

"I see our holdings in Venetian Tarmac seem to be

underperforming somewhat," I say. "Although not as badly as our shares in the Tartan Paint Consortium."

We stare glumly at the screen, then turn away and drink some more wine. When we bring ourselves to look again, we have been timed out, and I have to re-enter the password.

"Damn, it worked," I say.

In the end, we decide that we should swap some money around from one useless stock to another marginally less useless one. God, these things are, excuse my language but it is called for here, such a fucking con. I suggest, by way of a last feeble, desperate throw of the dice, taking the lot out and investing it in fine wine. And then, I do not add aloud, drinking myself to death with it.

⁂

I like to think that it takes a lot to unsettle me, but actually that's rubbish: it takes very little to turn my world upside down. The other month I wheezed up to the counter of the local fags and mags shop for my twice-weekly packet of Cutter's Choice,* the roll-up tobacco smoked by connoisseurs. There was something different about its packaging, I thought as I took it. I discovered soon enough: it had been wrapped in an extra layer of plastic. This plastic was in the distinctive, familiar design; but beneath it, the tobacco packet proper, as it were, had an entirely new one: a field of tobacco plants in rows, or more strictly speaking files, and behind them a row of misty hills. A bit shit, really, in other words, *qua* design, but

---

* This column I include for historical reasons. It was a more innocent time, before packets became gruesome parades of terrible afflictions, and before smokers were compelled to buy a sack of the stuff with every purchase. Now a packet lasts me for, oh, ages.

(a) it was nice of the company to prepare its customers for the redesign by phasing it in like that; and (b) it was still the same stuff inside. This is important. One afternoon, about a decade ago, when I'd decided this was the stuff for me, I rang up the 0800 Customer Services number on the back of the packet.

"I have a question," I said. "Why is your tobacco so good?"

I hasten to add that I was completely sober; but I was also completely bored. The person on the other end, who had clearly not been expecting this question, shunted me around a few departments until someone said something about the moisturising agents in the tobacco, or some such, and I thanked him and hung up, hardly able to believe I had done what I had just done. Anyway, boredom and smoking going together like cheese and crackers, I found myself scrutinising the new packet at some length. I noticed that the blend was established in 1856, or almost exactly 140 years before I had ever heard of it, that it is "rounded", whatever that means, and that this is their "smooth blend". This, like the "fresh" in "fresh-cut sandwiches" is entirely phatic, given that one has yet to see a tobacco company describe its product as rough or jagged, although I have smoked some Kenyan cigarettes that felt as though someone had thrown a lighted firecracker into my lungs. There is a lot more text going on now, perhaps in an attempt to forestall the kind of enquiry of mine which wasted half an hour of their time ten years ago. Before one opens the pack, we are invited: "if you would like to share your perfect rolling experience with us, email us at . . ." etc.

Hmm. I am trying to imagine my perfect rolling experience. I suppose high on the list would be the experience where the paper doesn't tear, the tobacco within doesn't conceal knots and tangles which make smoking the damn thing like trying to suck a marble through a straw, and, taking about the longer view, one which doesn't give you cancer, emphysema, or heart disease. That would be nice if it didn't do that, wouldn't it?

Opening the pack, you see more guff about "what makes the perfect roll?" – and the misty hills now have three shadowy figures in the front, none of them apparently smoking, or rolling. "Is it the anticipation, the mood, or the moment shared?" Search me, squire. We learn that the tobacco is grown in Zimbabwe, which is news to me, and there is a diagram like something out of *The Day Today* which tells us that the tobacco is, among other things, "rich and mature", which, I reflect, is more than I am. It is while I chuckle about that – the wheezy, gurgling kind of chuckle of the smoker – that I remember something I noticed on the back, and I check it again. There's a box just above the "UK DUTY PAID" rubric, echoing it in shape, but empty. And above that, the words: "this pack belongs to:" – and then, as if to scramble our minds completely, beneath it, the words, in small capitals, "for adult use only".

At which point I find myself utterly discomfited. For what use only? The packet of tobacco, you see, recalls in its dimensions the last thing I saw with a space to say whom "this belongs to:" – that is, a schoolchild's pencil case. For a dizzy moment I imagine myself writing, tongue sticking out of the corner of my mouth in concentration, with boldly stylised capitals, NICK L in biro in this box, fiercely defending it from the school bullies and other miscreants in break, or the dinner queue. "Look. It says here. It's MINE. In MY handwriting.Well, British American Tobacco may be many things, but they are not fools, so if they have accepted the advice of a marketing guru to do this then who am I to say they shouldn't have? There's only one fool here, and that, dear reader, is me.

※

An email arrives from a friend I haven't seen in a while. "I've been reading about that shithole you infest for so long now I'm minded to come and take a look at the gaff – you around at the moment?" I read this while lying on the bed, around lunchtime, in my underpants. Around me, the scholar's mistress has been putting on weight. Downstairs, the living room is a heap of old plates as well as the usual piles and piles of books. For the last week or so I have been the Hovel's sole occupant. The Woman Who Scoured The Teapot has finished her stint of working in London and returned to the family home; the man who crashes here from Monday to Thursday to save himself a commute has gone on holiday with his family. My children are on holiday. My girlfriend is in Sweden. My cat . . . I don't have a cat.

Esse est percipi, Berkeley tells us; to be is to be perceived. Well, no one's perceiving me at the moment. So do I exist? I have let things slide a little bit, and the prospect of someone rocking up to the front door – someone who I happen to know is a man of tidy habits – puts me into a bit of a flap. Also, I have two deadlines, including the one for this column. I cannot shower, shave, get dressed, tidy up and write the words I am contracted to do as well as entertain someone, however desirable it would be to see him.

Solitude has strange side-effects. The loneliness is a given. What's surprising is the way you don't want to see anyone despite being lonely: it is as if one is no longer confident in one's ability to project a persona. One is also acutely aware of the gulf that exists between the figure shambling around in his undercrackers all day long making endless cups of tea, and the suave, witty and dapper raconteur which is how you would like to think the world sees you. To clean oneself up and talk as if one were a self-assured and functioning member of society who can make other people laugh would, in some way, feel like an imposture; and so you become like the tree in the Berkleyan forest, that falls without anyone being around to confirm it.

Still, you can't become completely isolated, however convincing the philosophical case, so when I get a call from my friend Toby, who is normally, after six o'clock, as hard to shift from the Uxbridge Arms as a limpet is from its rock, doing me the signal honour of proposing a meeting in the Barley Mow, my own local, for a pint, I accept. He brings with him, as has become most welcome custom, a plastic bag full of the last dozen or so *New Scientists*. (I find it is a magazine best enjoyed when gorged upon, rather than bought weekly.) And in the first one I open when I get back to the Hovel, I read from their 19th October 2013 issue, a piece about Cotard's syndrome: whose symptoms present as the conviction that you are dead. Or, as one sufferer cited put it more carefully, the "strong feeling" she was dead. These may not have been her exact words but I do like the nuance.

I vaguely recall hearing about this at the time of publication, and thinking: this is a delusion? The train of thought that had slowly set off last October, when another paper had picked up on this, as the canny ones do with *New Scientist* pieces, juddered into motion again. Is it possible, I wonder, as someone who first tentatively thought these things after reading "The Waste Land", specifically the lines about the Dantescan crowds flowing over London Bridge, that it is not to realise that you are dead that is the true pathology?

The idea, after some days, still grips. It would account for a great deal I have been pondering on for the last seven years. In fact, as an explanation for what is going on, as the *TLS*'s review of *The Matrix* said at the time, it makes a great deal of sense. And I have to admit that, as an excuse for late delivery of copy, "I can't file right now, I'm dead" packs a certain punch, but I suppose you'd have to save it for special occasions. I am also reminded of the excellent joke in "The North London Book of the Dead": that when you die, you just move to another part of London; and what is it that I have done but move to another part of London? QED. The problem with most sufferers of Cotard's who are on the records is that they are distressed at their condition; this, I would venture, is where they're going wrong.

I think it was Arbuthnot who complained to Jonathan Swift that Edmund Curll's biographies added a new terror to death; I have discovered a new terror to life. I call it "walking down Paddington Street, W1". My friend the Moose once startled me memorably by asking me, in all seriousness, why I was not in continual mortal terror of a man leaping out of a doorway in the street and bashing my head in with an axe; I replied that, hitherto, the thought had not occurred to me, and thanks for that, I'm going to think of men leaping out of doorways with axes for the rest of my life now. As fears go, it is barely reasonable. So, I would have thought until a few weeks ago, was the fear of walking under a crane on a construction site. When, after all, have I ever seen one of those fall over? To which I can now say: not yet; but I now know that it is only a matter of time: like seeing your first death. You might not have witnessed one, and yet they still happen.

I found this out when having a drink at the ——— with P———, who has had many jobs, but is, usually, a crane operator. I refuse to identify the pub, and P———, whose name does not even begin with a P, for reasons which will become clear. P——— told me that there had been an accident with one of the cranes on a site he'd been working on; and then went on to tell me of all the reasons how and why a crane might fall over. The how is generally a combination of imbalance and local wind speed; the why a combination of human bravado and cost-cutting. This in turn is the fault of the construction companies; and it is thanks in turn to the combination of their immense wealth, and the funds which are siphoned off to certain political parties, that mean that we tend not to hear of these accidents at all.

I could listen all day to this kind of thing, especially when P——— gets down to the technical details of jibs and weights and cabs and whatnot. But he affirms that there is a sinister side to all this, and that things get Hushed Up By Dark Powers Of Which We Know Little.

So now Paddington Street, along which I regularly walk on the way to the supermarket, or to pick up my copy of this very magazine, or get my shoes resoled, or wave to John-Paul, the extremely great manager of that jewel among Italian family-owned restaurants, the Casa Becci, or top up my Oyster, or fail once again to square up to the Scary Fish Man at the Farmers' Market on Sundays, has, on opposite sides of the road, facing each other, two enormous tower cranes, one of them erecting yet more unaffordable flats, and the other one busy removing bits from the disgustingly ugly office block that naff film buffs will recognise instantly as the building in *Sliding Doors* which Gwyneth Paltrow enters to deliver sandwiches to her boyfriend's evil, scheming girlfriend, the splendidly-named (in real life) Jeanne Tripplehorne. (A parenthesis on the film *Sliding Doors*, if I may. This film, abject though it is and scoring a relatively meagre 6.8 on IMDB, is, nevertheless, one that I find hard to pass up on its tellingly regular appearances on the BBC iPlayer. Why is this? It is itself a dishonest, crassly manipulative film, whose male lead is even more weak and feckless than men are in real life, whose female villain, the aforementioned Jeanne Tripplehorn, is considerably sexier and more amusing than the ghastly Paltrow, whose character has all the depth, resonance and charm of a tampon advert, and considerably less point. I suppose it is a strange weakness on my part for the chick-flick weepie, a sign of my diminishing reserves of testosterone, and a warped identification with at least one of the characters that it is best not to dwell on. But anyway, *revenons à nos moutons*.) So I now walk, when I walk up or indeed down Paddington Street, no longer on the pavement, but in the middle of the road, my eyes raised skywards, for that is what my brain, deranged with fear about enormous concrete weights falling from their cradles and flattening me to a *pûrée*, has decided is the safest route. Don't tell me I'm worrying about nothing: there's a distressingly informative website called craneaccidents.com, and there are YouTube videos full of nothing but crane accident porn; the "crain fail compilation" from February 2014 alone runs for eight minutes and has had half a million hits.

And it is what these cranes are telling me about London that is most worrying. There are people who wax lyrical about cranes, and the erections these machines betoken: but all I can see are ruined vistas, the collapse of community, and death from above.

Well, there I was about to return, after four years, to the subject of the end of a relationship, but more tenderly, in the nice, non-painful sense of the word (although of course there's pain too), when news comes to me of a crime against a close friend of mine. The crime itself is so vile that I am not even going to specify what it is, so traumatised has she been by it. The interesting thing is that I, and quite a few friends of hers, know the name of the perpetrator; and, thanks to certain social media, what goes through his head; or, to put it another way, what comes out of it after events have been digested. Clue: it is about as pleasant as the stuff that comes out of you when food has been digested, with the significant difference that there has been no nourishment taken.

There's nothing like anxiety for others to take your mind off your own troubles. I had been following the story of Alice Gross's disappearance with particular dismay, for I know the parents well: when I lived in Shepherds Bush, they were neighbours with a daughter the same age as my eldest, and they were great friends; and I had first met the mother, it turned out, back in our university days. Being a stay-at-home father myself, I'd see them almost every day but then they moved out of the area, then I did, but they were and are lovely people and the best kind of parents, and it is horrific to thing of what they are going through. When Alice first went missing, the hope to cling to was that she would soon return; that hope is the only thing that can stop the imagination becoming a fire hose spewing out nightmares. And one feels the anguish more keenly when one knows the people involved. It brings those nightmares much closer to home; you can feel their wind against your cheek as they fly by you.

At time of writing, I don't know what has happened to Alice;* but I do know what has happened to my friend, and the thought that it will be a long time before she has a quiet night again fills me with rage. It is not my inner *Daily Mail* reader that is awakened: that happens when your bike gets stolen, or someone knocks your wing mirror off. What is awakened here is a creature of primal, righteous anger, not necessarily of violence, but a creature that will not be appeased until the perpetrator is forced to face his crimes, and writhe in shame under the disgust and outrage in which society will hold him.

I wonder if it is a related inner creature that prompted me to write, earlier this morning, on the day the House of Commons was due to vote on the matter, to Andy Slaughter MP – no longer my MP (I now live in a constituency represented by the usual bog-standard hedge-fund Tory, a man of blandly contemptible beliefs whom only retirement, or a psephological miracle, will dislodge),† but a man of post-Blairite

---

* We learned.. Her body was found in the River Brent; she had almost certainly been murdered by a previouly convicted murderer, Arnis Zalkains, who in turn hanged himself.

† Not so blandly contemptible, it turned out. Mark Field, for it was he who achieved notoriety for grabbing a (female) Greenpeace activist by the throat and frog-marching her out of an official dinner where she was making the most peaceful of protests. Someone also once told me he started the whole Cameron-fucked-a-pig's-head rumour, because he hated the man. Well, so do I, but perhaps for different reasons.

principle who has worked as hard as he could to stop Hammersmith and Charing Cross hospitals from being, effectively, closed down – asking him if he would consider the views of this old leftie that there was nothing wrong with air strikes against murderous ideologues in Syria and elsewhere. No reply as yet – he answers his correspondence, which counts for a lot in a MP – and whatever will be will be; but the hand-wringing on the left (largely) about Whether We Have Thought This Through is one of the brakes on our capacity to take action against evil that end up simply allowing more innocent people to die, be raped, or stripped of all freedoms save the freedom to subjugate oneself.

I think back to the last weekend, in Gothenburg, sitting on the terrace of the woman I once called the Beloved (and she will always, in a sense, be beloved by me, for she is lovely), listening to the conkers thud down onto the roof of the bike shed opposite. We picked them up and put them on her table. So many conkers. I thought of taking a few back: there is a blight on British chestnuts, and the only conkers I have seen them produce this year have been the size of Maltesers, if that; but in the end I thought customs might start questioning a grown man with his pockets full of them. When I got back she texted me to say that the little Swedish children we had seen playing in the courtyard while we drank our wine had sneaked up to her table and removed all of them, save one; a crime whose very triviality only added to the poignancy and sadness of our moods. I am sorry that there are no jokes here this week. It hasn't been one of the funny ones.

Ah well, here we go again. Time to dust off the old dating site self-description skills. "Man, 51, teeth stained from years of wine and tobacco. No intention of changing." Hmm, perhaps not. Although it has the virtue of truth, when was truth ever a virtue when it comes to selling anything, especially oneself? I think back to my copy-writing days. Johnson said that it was "large promise" that was the soul of an advertisement, and I dimly recall he sold a share in a brewery by saying that the buyer, if he did so, would have the opportunity to become wealthy beyond the dreams of avarice. So: "Man, 51, kind, supportive, likes nothing more than going to Ikea, looking after babies, and distributing his enormous personal fortune to deserving individuals and charities."

Yes, it's that time of life: the boot. The boot has been hovering near the posterior lately but it hasn't actually connected until now. Hasn't happened for four years nearly, mind; for me, post-marriage, that's the best run yet. And it has to be said that there is no rancour or bitterness, none of the howling outrage and humiliation that accompanied the last occasion. Boy, that was something else. I still shudder when I think of it. I suppose that's one reason I'm not actually suicidal this time: the heart has built up a lot of scar tissue.

But that doesn't mean it's not awful. The ex-Beloved and I will, I think, always be good friends, or rather more than that; it was distance that killed the relationship, distance in years and miles. One or the other we could have managed, I supposed; but not both. Also, I had a visit from my old housemate, Emanuelle – remember her? – even though I'd said I was miserable and she was not to come round. She didn't take no for an answer and it's good that she didn't, for even though she's in her mid-twenties she is no fool and besides can offer insights into a woman's thought processes that men can only see through a glass darkly, if at all. It appears that there are many women out there who consider men as "projects", raw material that is to be moulded into a desired shape, and that I had been proving resistant to such moulding. Hearing this notion, it struck me that I had indeed come across it before, in life as well as literature, once or twice. And, as my joke about personal adverts in sentence 4 above suggests, I yam even more what I yam than Popeye. I don't like to be told to do things; hell, I don't even like calling myself an anarchist, as I think the label is too restrictive.

It is, though, perhaps time to change. This would be something of a big deal. The parable of the frog and the scorpion springs to mind; the frog carrying the scorpion across the river, saying anxiously, "you won't sting me, will you? If you did, we'd both drown." The scorpion stings the frog, and as they're both going under, the frog asks "why?", and the scorpion shrugs and says: "that's what I do."

That said, I'm not all bad, and the only person I know who really hates me (we had a bruising encounter last Sunday, so it is fresh in my memory) is the Grumpy Oyster Man who still refuses to serve me at the Marylebone Farmer's Market after a year and a half, suggesting that maybe my initial assessment of his character wasn't that far off the mark after all. So he's back to being Cunty Oyster Man again. What have I got to lose? I don't even live in London any more. (The snitch who passed on this magazine to him, an act that started this unpleasantness in the first place, is perfectly at liberty to do so again, but bear in mind that there will come a time when he or she may well have to submit to a Higher Authority.)

"If I knew then what I know now . . ." was how one wistful

sentence began from one ex of mine which she did not need to complete. After a certain age, women, just like men, have no illusions any more; but before that age, men can fall victim to what I call New Kitchen Syndrome: that desire to rip out and replace, entirely, the room in the house where food is prepared and eaten. Men, though, think "what's wrong with this one? The toaster works."

So, as I said, here we go again. Why do I go through this? I have many friends who are alone. But that's not for me. I love being with one woman I can cook for, whom I can make laugh, with whom we can arm each other against the world, who will scratch the back of my neck. The last one will be a hard act to follow, to put it mildly. "Man, 51, hates rice pudding." No, perhaps not enough of the Johnsonian large promise there. "Man, 51, practically perfect in every way." No, hang on a bit, I've got it: "Man, 49 . . ."

⁂

A month or so, or more, ago, I would rather not be precise, someone, I had better not say who, came round to the Hovel to enjoy a glass or two of wine.

"I can't stay too long," he said. Why, I asked. "Well," he said, "I went out a couple of weeks ago or so and got absolutely smashed. I was so pissed I even fell over trying to get through the front door. Badly enough to have to use a make-shift walking stick for the next couple of days."

I tut-tutted, saying that this was hardly the behaviour expected of a devoted husband and father. This world may be a veil of tears, and we should be allowed to mitigate the pain in any way at our disposal, I disapprove of excessive drunkenness, or behaviour which vexes the reasonable; and in fact I can tell you exactly when the last time I got pickled in such a way as to be noticeable to the casual observer: it was on the 16th May, when I met up with the old British Telecom gang, and if that is not an excuse to pluck the gowans fine and hear the chimes of midnight, then I don't know what is. And all I did then was act a bit tiddly and goggle in temulent indecision at the snack bar's display on the platform of Sloane Square tube station.

To return to my friend. I also wondered, for there was something in the way that he had imparted this information that had rung a faint alarm bell, what this had to do with me.

"Surely," I said, your wife had something to say to you the morning after, if not that night?"

"No, it was fine," he said. "I'd told her I was going out with you."

The emphasis, one of those slight but subtle emphases that can so much change the meaning of a line of poetry, was, in case you were wondering, on the word "you". Not, although I grant it would have made the beginning of a much funnier and more complex anecdote, on the word "out".

"I beg your pardon?"

"Well, she was expecting the worst," he said. "Pretty much anything short of a call from a police station at 3 a.m. was going to be acceptable."

Hmm. It is one thing to have a reputation; it is another to have one that is undeserved. And it is a more complex thing to have a reputation which is undeserved and yet to which one would be hard-pressed to refute should this kind of thing ever come up in a court of law. After all, is not this very column in part predicated on the idea that not only do I behave myself in a fashion which is contrary to the prevailing medical advice, but boast about it without apology or excuse?

But it's not like that, not really. The censorious will always have the advantage over the do-what-thou-wilt. For example: everyone, even the dictionary, thinks "Epicurean" means "self-indulgent", or something along those lines, a calumny that has been around ever since the pious needed a stick with which to beat the atheist Epicurus, whose actual idea of a blow-out was a plate of olives and a few pieces of cheese. It was when he answered the question "do the gods listen to our prayers?" with the words, "I don't know, mate, I've got more important things to think about", that certain minds began to worry, and rumours began to be concocted; rumours still going strong over a millennium later. And as it happens, this evening I am meeting for dinner a man who has been on the wagon for nearly twenty years; and yet, such was his reputation, that it was only in the last five that people have begun to let the notion sink in that he isn't sinking a bottle of whisky every afternoon or, in John Peel's memorable phrase, rubbing heroin into the roots of his hair.

But it's so much easier to rely on hearsay rather than get yourself up to speed with the facts, isn't it? The other day someone on the Archers had a Martini (which is in itself an almost unbelievable event) and the phrase "shaken not stirred" was trotted out, thus perpetuating the entirely erroneous notion that that is how the cocktail should be prepared.

Meanwhile, all over London men who should know better are going on the lash and then claiming that they'd been with me, simply in order to remove all notions of their own agency or responsibility. Look, I like the idea that people think of me as a fun person whose personality is so strong that no one is able to put a hand over their glass when I am pouring. But I really do wish you'd stop doing this, lads. One day, someone's going to get hurt.

⚜

I appear to have, and not for the first time, taken to my bed for a week. It seems like the sensible thing to do when the life is loused up beyond repair and you're feeling ill on top of it all. Someone recently suggested crosswords and a spot of baking as a cure for depression and as I am assuming the intention was not to alleviate the gloom with a flash of rage she has been sacked.

Gosh, you really do get to find out who's on the ball emotionally and who isn't when you come clean about this kind of thing. The ones who say it's the weather are fairly vexing. The weather may well be a factor but if I listed all the other more proximate causes, then it would become quite clear it was only a minor one. And anyway, I kind of like autumnal weather. It used to betoken a new school or university year, the latter signifying escape; at home, it meant doing things like chopping up logs for the fire. I bet you can't quite imagine me chopping up firewood but I assure you I was quite the dab hand at it. It is also pretty much the most satisfying chore involving physical labour a man can perform. There's something magical about the way the log splits just so when the axe-blade hits it at the right point. Sometimes you feel you just have to tap it. Sadly, I remember one winter's day, around February or early March 2007 it would have been, when I realised that what with the way the marriage was going and everything, this would be the last time I'd be doing it there. It's not so easy chopping wood when there are tears in your eyes. Tends to compromise the technique.

230

But to return to the weather. I have been invited to Rome by my old friend Małgosia, whom I have not seen in ages. She says that the warm weather there persists until the end of November. I quite like the sound of that but I wonder whether seeing Małgosia again would be good for the nerves. Polish and beautiful but possessed of all the infectious but insightful craziness her proud race can muster (I hasten to add that, being half-Polish myself, I not only know whereof I speak, I can get away with speaking it too), she once, in Warsaw about twenty-odd years ago, looked at my hand for the purpose of reading my palm. She foresaw an early death, sometime in my mid-fifties was the suggestion, and when I asked if I would at least have led a fulfilled life said something in Polish which my friend Paweł later translated as meaning basically "sort of, but." I am supremely sceptical about stuff like horoscopes and palmistry and whatnot but there was something in the way she said it that gave me the heebie-jeebies. Then again, as I have mentioned before, I have Cotard's syndrome so am already dead, so what's the problem?

The problem is that I didn't know being dead was quite so exhausting. As I said, I have been bed-bound, pretty much by choice, for the last few days, and there's something about this that makes you question at a fundamental level whatever impulse it was that made you get out of bed in the first place. At the moment only hunger does that, and I can hold on for ages if I have to. (Making tea is another matter.) Even the arrival of wine o'clock hasn't been stirring the limbs, and the other day I found myself unable even to finish the first glass of the evening. Which suggests actual illness, and come to think of it, there does seem to have been some internal rearrangement going on among the organs. Is this what Ebola feels like?

Meanwhile, I am able to confer and take solace from those of my friends who know what it is to be hounded by the black dog. Of these I have a wide selection to choose from, for some reason, and I sometimes wonder if they ever talk about me and say "poor Nick, he really ought to be on medication, or in therapy, or possibly both." But they offer sympathy and counsel patience, for from time to time even the black dog gets bored and wanders off for a while. Unfortunately, as Robert Burton so astutely observed, he is less likely to do so when one is both solitary and idle, and I don't think drinking endless cups of tea and reading Agatha Christies in bed counts as industry.

Perhaps my sacked friend was right. Maybe baking is the answer. An obsession with baking seems to be the only thing that's uniting the nation at the moment, after all. But then again: I may be screwed up right now, but I'm not as screwed up as this wretched country. Rome it is. Money permitting.

⁂

A call from my mother. In days gone by I would routinely let her leave a message on voicemail and then let it marinade for a day or so before replying. I offer no justification for this heartless behaviour. It was just the way things were. Perhaps it was down to the fact that when I was growing up there was never a lock on the inside of the lavatory door; so one was never really able to relax in there, if you see what I mean, and one was always having to keep one's ears open. Did one betray one's presence and deter the unknowing intruder by pretending to have a cough, or by humming, say, "Rule Britannia" or "Maria" from West Side Story? Or did one just sit there fearful, trembling like a vole, hoping that whatever threat would pass if you just sat there quietly enough? It all rather tried the nerves, and whenever I went somewhere with a bog with a lock on the door and, moreover, unlike a school cubicle, a door which went all the way down to the floor, I would sit in there rather longer than usual, just for the pleasure of it. Friends' mothers would ask if I was unwell; never better, I would say.

Thirty-three years is maybe a long time for that particular aspect of my upbringing to have an effect on seeing the word "Mum" appear on my telephone screen, although the psychologists may beg to differ. I gather they make much of this kind of thing, and who can blame them? But sometimes the more psychologically boring explanation is the right one: one does not look forward to the phone call, because likely as not its opening gambit will be a mild but pained rebuke for not having answered the phone previously, or called up in the first place, even if the reason one did not call up in the first place was because one feared a mild but pained rebuke for not having called up in the first place. If you follow my reasoning. I can't be the only one.

This has changed for two reasons: having children of one's own, and also the need to keep up to speed with news of my father's health, which is not of the best, but at least he has his marbles – and also a very British notion of not wanting to upset anyone with bad news. My mother, being American, is less reserved.

But having the first child go to university does change the way you think about the filial bonds. For some reason it feels like more of a rupture than the gap year. (The daughter, bless her, did not do anything daft like swan around Laos for six months, catching things. She earned some money and learned how to cook for fourteen people at once. I suggested that when she claims her philosophy degree she start a themed restaurant called, perhaps, I Just Kant Get Enough, but she said A Good Plato Food would be better.)

When my parents dropped me off at university, I was like one of those cartoon characters who disappears from the frame leaving only a dust cloud and ricochet-like "piaowww!" noise. And it wasn't just because I couldn't wait to have a crap in guaranteed privacy. It was the time when I could rid myself of the vestiges of childhood. (By acting in a remarkably immature fashion for three solid years.) In those days, though, there were no mobiles; if you wanted to speak to your parents you had to (usually) queue for the payphone in a draughty corridor near the laundry room with a few ten pee bits in your hand; if you didn't want to speak to your parents, and frankly there was never really a reason to speak to them unless you needed money or wanted to say happy birthday to them (because you'd forgotten to post a card in time, or at all), you didn't. And the traffic was always one way: you had to call home; home couldn't get in touch with you barring dire emergency.

I shudder to think how often my mother would have called me up had the mobile existed then. And so I resist the urge to ring my daughter. (The Estranged Wife had complained about the newly-empty room in the house; I reminded her with perhaps unnecessary asperity that I already knew very well what it was like to be separated from my children for longer than you wanted.) An email here, a text there. And so, with no pressure to do so, she calls me up: either how to fake harissa, or my Secret Gravy Technique; sometimes even just for a chat. So now I answer the phone when my mother rings.

Finally. The last time she did so she was round the corner and took me to lunch. And you know what? It was really nice.

❧

I was recently the subject of a nasty letter in this magazine. I would have preferred not to dwell on it but the mind has a habit of clinging to its misery, so when a reader of this magazine says I am not funny, I take it to heart more than I should. In fact, I have spent the last week more or less completely in the foetal position, waiting for the pain to go away. After all, we columnists live for our readers; without them, we are nothing, ghosts that squeak on the wind and are gone.

That is, until someone showed me an issue of the magazine from about a month ago, and addressed my attention to the "Subscriber of the Week" page. As I said when this feature started, this added yet another terror to existence for the writer, for each of us who does not appear as a subscriber's favourite writer suffers another one of those small hammer blows to the soul, the kind that do not cripple at once, but accumulate, like dust in the lungs, or ice in the freezer, until at one point it all – life, everything, the fish fingers – seems no longer worth continuing with.

But on that week, one Lois Whitehead went the extra mile and said that not only was I her favourite writer, but she'd put me on the cover and, for all I know (I do not have a copy of the issue to hand) get stuck in a lift with me.* Although, sadly, things Can Never Be with Ms Whitehead (our contracts

* One of the other questions is: which political figure would you least like to be stuck in a lift with. Hence the lift business. Oh Lois, are you still there?

here explicitly forbid exploiting or traducing the sacred nature of the relationship between writer and reader), she may rest assured that there will forever be a place in my heart for her, for she softened the bitter winds of autumn (figuratively speaking; it's been lovely lately, hasn't it?) and with her kind words dried the very tears from my eyes. And a tip of the hat to Gajendra Singh this week, who also had a nice word to say about me. Don't worry. I know how these things go. For the next few weeks it'll be back to the usual invective, just to keep me honest.

But you really have to worry about some people. There are those who blame the rise of the internet and the below-the-line anonymous comment for the general decline in civility, but as far as I'm concerned there have always been people whose first instinct in any given situation is to play the tosser. As it happens, I will always respect the person who insults me but does not hide behind a pseudonym to do so; and there is something about being told your prose style and/or general drift of your argument sucks by someone hiding behind the name Bumblecat84 (or whatever) that makes such criticism lose some of its force and grip.

But my greatest respect, when it comes to rudeness, is for those who turn it into public spectacle for the rest of us to delight in. Reader, this happened in my local Waitrose a few weeks ago: a man in the checkout queue was trying to reach one of the sustainable hemp bags, but he was too far out to achieve any purchase. This means you can tell at least two things about him already: he means well, and is prone to act on benign impulse even if the best moment has passed. So he asked the woman standing right by the bags if she could possibly pass him one. This was delivered, as you can imagine, with all the self-deprecating embarrassment that the English middle-class male of A Certain Age (he was on the young side of middle age, I'd say) can muster; which is quite a lot. The woman, herself of a certain age, turned to him with an expression of contemptuous disdain. Also a certain weariness. "Excuse me," she said, "do I work for you?"

Sometimes things happen which make you suspect they have been arranged simply for one's own amusement, or that of an invisible audience. This was one of them. For a start, the woman possessed a North American accent. This made it all the more exquisite. There was the frisson of genteel xenophobia that it occasioned (anti-Americanism, which I find not only offensive but personally offensive, is the last prejudice standing tall among the *bien pensants*); the added weight to the words (hearing the "r" in "work" there really gave some punch to her remark); and, above all, the refusal to give a damn about the custom of the country; in fact, to tell the mild customs of the country that they can go screw themselves.

There was an awed silence in the Waitrose queue. The man and I locked eyes and raised our brows in a "what can you do?" fashion. But let's be honest. Rude North American Woman really made our day.

❧

I have to go out, but as I open the front door I see a ladder propped up bang in front of me. Like many rationalists who revere science and the rule of reason, I am deeply superstitious, all the more so for knowing that it is Very Silly. It is the very silliness that exercises its grip on me.

But there it is: it is bad luck to walk under a ladder, and

now I am paralysed by wondering if opening a door to find yourself already under the ladder can be said to constitute walking under it; and then trying to work out whether I am slightly to the left or right of its centre, so that if I sidle out in that direction, I can claim that I have not, strictly speaking, contravened the injunction by not having passed through its vertical axis. That's what "walking under a ladder" means, right? Right? Which is all very annoying, as I am cutting it a bit fine for the thing I have to go to, and do not have time to go back in, have a cup of tea, and hope that the workmen painting the bit above the front door will have finished and gone away again the next time I try to leave.

I muse a lot on fortune, though. Long-term readers of this column with unusually retentive memories may recall that I used to invoke Boethius's *Consolations of Philosophy*, in which he remarked, while in prison after having fallen spectacularly out of favour with Theodoric the Great, that life's all ups and downs, innit, although he put it rather more elegantly than that. We are all at the mercy of Fortune's Wheel, he said; consul one moment, awaiting execution and sharing your bread with rats the next.

My great good fortune, of having been born in an affluent country at an epoch in history where there are anaesthetics and medications that relieve asthma (once, gasping without an inhaler in the middle of a spidery house in the middle of nowhere in France, I found an old medical textbook which confidently asserted that asthma attacks were "never fatal"; had I been born even a century earlier, nothing on the broader scale of time, I would have been killed by medical ignorance) means that there is a certain resistance to the downward motion of the wheel; if you're born to a poor family in most parts of the globe (and, increasingly, this one), then your lowly position on the wheel isn't going to change very much.

So I'm not grumbling. But there is a certain contingency to all lives, and somehow it has to be acknowledged. I once thanked Providence that I had met a certain person; she replied that this sounded a little bit like thanking God. Maybe it is; but I tried to wriggle out of this one by saying that it is a neutral way of not taking things for granted, and "providence" means nothing more than a shorthand for "what has happened" or "the way things have turned out", although yes, I did capitalise the word in my head, just in case "providence" turns out, despite all the lack of unambiguous evidence, to be a matter of the Abrahamic God, or the Fates, or some Nordic crones with a thing for spinning wheels, who have a stake or an agency in what goes on. I like to cover my bets – for the precise reason that one never knows what might happen.

And meanwhile, I know that very bad things indeed can happen. Even if you have been born to become adult in 21st-century Britain. It may not feel like that at the moment, when you see the rise of Nigel Farage, or any of the other clowns who constitute the political scene at the moment; but there are terrible things out there, the imagination can become a firehose spewing out nightmares if you let it run away with itself, and even if touching wood, or thanking Providence, are obviously futile gestures which will have no bearing on anything, they at least represent, like the coin in the chugger's bucket, a token of consideration, the homage made to the sense that one ought to do something, however small, however feeble the gesture. And I am still aware, as indeed are the National Westminster Bank and all my other creditors, that I am too near the precipice to be able to walk with a carefree swagger through life.

After a while, I decide to sidle round the doorway as far to the right as possible, the people in the shop next door thinking that I, always clearly on the brink of madness, have finally sailed off the edge, and, breathing a sigh of relief at having outwitted the Norns, or whoever, I get run over by a number 13 bus on Gloucester Place. Well, all right, I don't actually: but it could have happened.

❧

This morning I received an email from someone. I won't say who but you don't have to be Sherlock Holmes to work it out. It was a model of brevity and concision. The two are not the same thing. You can be brief and not say much. But you can be concise and say plenty. This email consisted of two questions. The first question was a sum of money I had paid as part of what we may loosely describe as an ongoing programme, followed by a question mark. The second and final word was: "Seriously?"

I know, I know, is how I wanted to reply. I feel your pain. (And I would also like to publicly thank the person involved for not Going Off On One. All that needs to be said has been said; the message has got through.) At the time of writing I find, though, that I am owed a four-figure sum for work done at various points in the past, and when one is bumping along the bottom, or riding on the rims, or whichever metaphor for financial precariousness you care to use, this kind of thing can be catastrophic. I hasten to add it is not my regular employers who are at fault here. This is extra stuff, done in order to stave off the crisis that comes when the cost of living goes up and rates of pay stagnate. The problem is that doing more work can breed a false sense of security. "Oh great," the foolish freelancer says to him- or herself. "I've done more work! This means more money! I can now go to a restaurant/buy that coat in Sue Ryder I've had my eye on/stock up on malt whisky!" And you buy these things and then the accounts departments of the places you've done work for are sluggish, and before you know it, you are in deep crap, and you start replying to emails which end with the word "Seriously?" with phrases like "right now, the emphasis is on not getting evicted."

As for work itself, I am beginning to get sick and tired with the way that it is now becoming seen as an undisputed good in its own right; indeed the phrase "hard-working families" is now a shibboleth of both the Left and the Right. What a miserable world this is turning into. "Hard-working families"? Does this mean that not only parents but children, too, should be at work? Are we now meant to spend all the hours God sends doing stuff that we don't like? I happen to really like my work – that is, I bet I like my work more than the vast majority of the rest of the population likes theirs (unless you are "really passionate" about, say, accounting, or driving buses, or working a till) – and I would still prefer to spend my time mucking about. Meanwhile, a friend posts on Facebook, the water-cooler of the internet where writers gather to piss away the time, especially when deadlines loom. She alerts us to the page in a recent publisher's catalogue where we are given a summary of the career of, and latest novel by, one Nora Roberts, who apparently has sold, over a 30-year period, 27 books a minute. She is the third-biggest-selling author in the world, apparently, presumably after you-know-who and you-also-know-who.

I am not familiar with the work of Ms Roberts, and from the paraphrase given I am not sure I am ever likely to be. Even the publishers, who presumably have a vested interest in piquing the interest of those in the trade who read their catalogue, would seem to have fallen at this hurdle. Then again, they are not to blame for the material they have to work with. Ms Roberts's latest addition to the canon is the story of one Shelby Pomeroy, whose husband, having died in a freak accident, turns out to have been a cad, bounder and chateau-bottled shit of the first order. (Not the publisher's phrasing. Nor Ms Roberts's, I suspect.) Going back to her childhood home in Tennessee, along with her "gorgeous little daughter Callie", she is determined to get her life back together, along with the hope embodied "in the handsome form of carpenter Griffin Lott, a straight-dealing man who couldn't lie to her if he tried." Why can't I write this crap? I had a go. "Shelby Pomeroy looked sadly out of the window. She had been betrayed by the man she loved. Could she ever trust again? she wondered sadly." Is being able to churn this guff out with a straight face, indeed, to actually call a character "Griffin Lott" without having hysterics, all it takes to sell 27 books a minute, or 38,880 books a day? And get this: Nora Roberts has written "more than 200 novels". The phrasing suggests that even her publisher has lost count. I am going to have to raise, or lower, my game. Seriously.

In the middle of the journey of my life, well ok, maybe a little after the middle. I found myself in a windowless basement conference room in the European Commission in Brussels, listening to a man talking about the structure of the European Union, its efforts towards cultural exchange within itself and towards other parts of the world, and a few other subjects I am not actually able to relate, for as I look at my notes from that meeting I see they consist of: a castle with a tree growing beside it; a mountain range with dark clouds raining on them; a Santa in dark glasses smoking a large spliff; a house with smoke coming from its chimneys and a winding path leading to its front door; a cartoon rat with a fag in its mouth; innumerable random geometric doodles; and, firing its phasers at one of them, a rather competent small-scale rendition of the Starship Enterprise which had grown out of a couple of squiggles. It was that kind of meeting.

What, you may wonder, was I doing in Brussels? Later on, someone texted me the very same question. "I DON'T KNOW", I replied. But I did, sort of: I was bunking off.

Some months before I'd been invited to go to a shindig celebrating the European Prize for Literature, which I bet you've never heard of, and I hadn't either until I learned that if I turned up at the Eurostar terminal at 8.10 a.m. with a valid passport and a toothbrush, I could go to the fancy awards ceremony that very evening. Fine, I thought, I've never been to Brussels, this is all free; dinner, booze, a fancy awards ceremony followed by more booze, meet some other people, and the next day maybe say hello to my friend Ann, whose Facebook posts from Brussels, to where she had moved, showing pictures of interesting-looking beer in dimly-lit bars showed much promise. Also, there is the fact that I never get to go on these kind of jaunts. There seems to be some kind of unspoken agreement among the Illuminati who run the literary world that I will never be invited onto a panel, or to a literary festival that anyone has heard of, or to be paid medium-sized sums of money to dispense my wisdom on the subject of literary criticism, despite having done it for nearly thirty years, and counting, touch wood.

So although I would have preferred Venice, or Malta, or New York, to Brussels, I realised that beggars can't be choosers and that was why I turned up, despite my misgivings, at an ungodly time of day, warning everyone not to talk to me for another five hours at least if they wanted to get anything civil out of me.

The whole set-up had the potential for enormous embarrassment. I was the only writer, by which I mean the only person who wrote and did nothing else at all; the others were publishers or agents or translators or people from various administrative bodies. In other words, they were all socialised, whereas I have become a kind of hermit, able to interact with no more than two people at once; when I see a list of participants in some outing like this with my name on it, all I see are the *dramatis personae* at the beginning of an Agatha Christie novel. Which means that at least one of us was going to be killed, and at least one of us was going to be a murderer.

In the end, it looked as though if anyone was going to be killed, it was going to be me, for the dynamics of these things turn out not to be crime novels but school outings, and I found myself slipping naturally into the role of Bad Boy. After the first meeting I decided that if I wasn't going to be given food or alcohol during it, it wasn't for me, so I bunked off almost all of them (I recommend the Musée des Beaux Arts, where I saw lots of Bosches, to prepare me for the world to come). The trip's organiser and host fingered me pretty early on as a troublemaker and I found myself, after making a particularly sarcastic remark based on the shortcomings of Brussels's contemporary architecture on a social media website to which I thought he did not belong, being pointed at and called "Lezard" in a way which I had not been since I was in short trousers.* The thing is, I rather enjoyed myself. There were people there who were so manifestly decent that it was impossible not to make friends with them on the spot; the whole literary prize seemed like a good idea and had some good winners, and the only regret I had is that because I bunked off the talks, I didn't get the chance to shout a rude word at Nigel Farage, who was spotted outside the European Commission, when he was meant to be helping a UKIP candidate contest a by-election. Obviously, he must secretly love the place.

❦

An email arrives from a publicist, trying to stir my interest in a book. I cannot blame her. It is, after all, her job. "I hope you're well," she begins, "and having a great week." This gives me reason to pause, and go into a kind of reverie. Am I having a great week? I ask myself. And why a week? I suppose asking if I am having a great month too readily admits the answer "as it happens, no"; and ditto asking if I am having a great day. I suppose there is something wrong with the adjective "great", as well. When was the last great week I had? I must

* The sarcastic remark, accompanying a photo of one of Brussels's ugliest modern buildings, and there is stiff competition for this, was: "Brussels opens itself up like a flower." (It was also raining, which helped.) Jeremy O'Sullivan, for it was he, later gently explained to me the importance of not being mean about the European Union. As I said, these were more innocent days.

have had one. Maybe when I used to go on holiday, before childcare turned holidays into something else entirely. Yes, some time in the early 90s, in Tuscany, that was a great week, getting blotto on the local wine and grappa with the wife and our friends Nick and Ian. *Eheu fugaces, Postume, Postume,/ labuntur anni* . . . alas, the time flees, Postumus, and being righteous isn't going to stop you from getting old. So no, I am not having a great week. I have not, as all sorts of things keep reminding me, not had all that great a year, come to think of it, and when the time comes to bid farewell to 2014 I shall advise it not to let the door bang its arse on the way out. It is barely the end of November and I am shattered. A combination of too little sleep and not enough food has left me looking more or less like Gollum. My hair floats on my head in lank wisps, my eyes bulge and gleam greenly in the twilight, and I scuttle through Waitrose in a ragged loincloth, muttering to myself and looking for sausages. For it is Thanksgiving (long gone by the time you read this, especially if you're mooching off the online version), and I have rashly offered to cook dinner for my ailing parents, who are getting too old to stand around in a kitchen peeling spuds and basting turkeys for hours. Come to think of it, so am I. But I offered, and there it is. For Thanksgiving coincides, either approximately or exactly, depending on the year, with my father's birthday, and what with one thing and another, there is a rather strong possibility that this may be his last. It is not given to us to know the hour of our passing, but sometimes you can have a rough idea, and right now we are concentrating on keeping him going until the Ashes series of 2015. He once, around the turn of the millennium, expressed severe doubts that he would ever see the Ashes in an English team's hands again, and

I sympathised, and fretted; for, even more than I do, he feels that a world in which we have not in some way humiliated the Australians is one that is barely worth living in. But anyway: thanks to my mother being American, and my father having a birthday around now, this is all rather a big deal. (You may blame my mother, incidentally, on the autumnal Americanis-ation of this country. The first American to set foot on these shores since the Revolution, she would, in the early 1960s, put a jack-o'-lantern in the window for Hallowe'en. For the first few years baffled crowds would gather round the front of our house, one or two people occasionally floating the idea of burning her as a witch, but eventually they decided they liked the idea and look where we are now.)

But at the moment my mind is fixated on this damn turkey. Twenty minutes a pound and twenty over, but it has come to me in kilos and right now I do not have the bandwidth to do the mathematics. I also have two articles to write, including this one, before going up to East Finchley and taking command of a dinner for what was originally going to be six people but is now going to be ten. It has been suggested that I start cooking the bird now and then finish the job in the family home, but carrying a partly-roasted turkey on the underground is an ec-centricity too far, even for me. Why, oh why, I howl to myself and to the stars, did I ever learn to cook? My brother didn't learn how to cook mashed potato until he was forty ("I suppose I have to cook this first," he said, holding up a raw potato as if it was a grenade) and he is a wealthy and successful man. I suppose it has made me popular, to some degree, with women, but then with that comes a whole other raft of responsibility and complexity. But what I'd like right now is a week in bed. That would be a great week. That would be the greatest.

Three emails, hard on each others' heels. (I know this is the second week in a row I have used recent emails as the kick-off for a column, but you know what? They're among the few human interactions I have these days.) Number one asks me to accept a 20% pay cut for something. Number two is from a TV company, which is making a programme about "Bohemia", the concept rather than the historic country. They want to bend my ear, for reasons which do not entirely elude me. Number three is from another organisation, which is asking me to be on a panel for something related to the London Book Fair. They can pay my travel expenses, but nothing else.

The first email involves me having a little bit of a panic, and a cry, followed by a period of Pulling Myself Together and replying – mindful of the fact that a 100% pay cut is never going to be entirely out of the question, and too outraged a tone might be catastrophically counterproductive – that a 10% pay cut might be more acceptable, at this end.

Number Two email is easier to deal with, especially after email No. 1. I tell them that in my experience, being interviewed by a TV company involves having them pinch my ideas for nothing, unless you count an undistinguished cup of coffee something, and then not being on the telly. I take some satisfaction from doing this. (When in doubt, ask yourself: What would Beckett do? And as far as I know, he never appeared on telly.)

I feel a bit worse about the London Book Fair gig, but by this time my dander is up, and I feel full of piss and vinegar. Even though the person chairing the panel is someone for whom I not only have a lot of professional respect, but whose beauty maddens me like wine, I reply curtly that I do not work for free.

Then another email. It is from my accountants. As you might have suspected, for I have hinted at this for some time now, I hide from my accountants. To be charged a substantial three-figure sum to be told that I am fucked goes against what I consider to be the life well lived, and although they did go through my books some years ago and tell me that they had never seen someone so honest quite so fucked – and went through such rudimentary books as I had at a level of detail which means I would happily pay them to have done so, for they deserve to be paid, if I were not fucked – I am fucked, so can't quite pay them right at the moment; but anyway, there they are in my inbox, and very politely so considering the circumstances, if I may add.

One detail does not escape me, and that is HMRC's take on all this, which my accountants have thoughtfully passed on, and they, too have been patient, but it is along the lines of the wheels of justice grinding slow, but fine. And if I thought I was fucked before, at the end of the first paragraph of my accountants' email, that was nothing. Those were the good days. The years of plenty. When, in the relevant paragraph, I see the penalties alone, I go into a kind of fugue state, for they are amazing. But not unjustifiable, on their part. I can see their point of view. Maybe if I was not so fucked I would hire an accountant to bring it down a bit, but at the moment what I really need is the testimony of a mental health panel, and I do not have the time or non-fucked-upness to sort that kind of thing out. Which is itself a kind of testimony. After all, if my friend Professor BetterNotNameHimOrHer can, after years of trying to persuade the relevant people that HeOrShe has Attention Deficit Disorder, but somehow managed to get a teaching post at a very prestigious university, why can't I, with my piles of books, my inability even to ask for money I am even owed, and my generally disastrous circumstances?

The answer to email Number One comes back. They will accept my terms, which comes as a pleasant surprise. Number Two email is answered with an assurance that I will be paid a small three-figure sum for my time. This, too, is acceptable. Number Three email has not at the time of writing received an answer, but this is understandable, for I had been very curt, what with one thing and another, and had not made a jokey comment about how the chairperson's beauty maddened me like wine etc. But the wolves are gathering around the door, and, in true Bohemian style, my tiny hands, like Mimi's, are frozen. I was inoculated against TB at school but it'll be something else that gets me, I warrant.

⁂

The last thing I remember is having an arm around Neil Kinnock, giving him some tips about how he should help Ed Milliband win the next election. I also, for what it was worth, put in a good word for the nearest thing I have to a Labour MP, Hammersmith and Fulham's very own Andy Slaughter, who has, as far as I can see – and I've been keeping an eye on him – been doing a very good job. However, as I said, everything went a bit hazy after that. It had got a bit hazy before, to be perfectly honest, because I had drunk about six bottles of wine and several shot glasses of slivovitz. The wine was, although not entirely my fault, as I will explain in a minute, rather a matter of personal indulgence, as it so often is; but the slivovitz was in the line of duty, as it was being poured for us in order to toast the hard-working staff of the Gay Hussar. And they deserved these toasts, for the restaurant was completely packed out with members of the Goulash Co-operative (look it up), formed by the likes of Martin Rowson in order to buy out and therefore save the restaurant, which will otherwise be sold; turned into a Starbucks or something equally boring. For those who do not know the Gay Hussar (although I would imagine that this magazine's core readership has a pretty good idea), it is a restaurant that has been going for 60-odd years, nestling in the armpit of Soho Square and Greek Street, serving an unchanging menu of Hungarian food to a clientele largely composed of Old Labour politicians. The walls are adorned with caricatures of various luminaries; the downstairs dining room alone has some 60 of these, all drawn by Martin Rowson. I suspect the idea was to pay for his meal in kind; that's a lot of free dinners. Not that I am censorious. I, after all, was his guest; the people on his table had bowed out, and Martin, asking himself the question "whom do I know who would accept an invitation to a free lunch at almost the last possible minute?", came up with my name, for some reason.

It was, though, a happy choice. I have a fondness for Hungary and Hungarians, ever since I worked on a film in Budapest in the mid-80s (with, let me boast, Marcello Mastroianni, writing additional dialogue for him in English, a language he did not speak; the greatest gentleman Italy has ever produced, he treated me with a courtesy that few have ever treated me with since). I can count to ten in Hungarian still; I can read sentences aloud with such a good accent that few would realise I can't understand what I'm reading;

and have a few phrases still left to me, along with some ripe expletives which used to come in handy when the kids were young but I wanted to express frustration at some immediate outrage. Also, my politics are as red and peppery as the restaurant's goulash. It is telling, isn't it, that Tony Blair never ate there; its old-world atmosphere and menu would have repelled him; and he hatched his conspiracies in more intimate surroundings.* The Gay Hussar may have been a place for off-the-record conversations, but there is a kind of honesty in having a rendezvous in a place open to the public so that even if you're going to be in a private room, people will have seen you and your co-plotter entering around the same time.

In short, history has been made there, and it is a sign of the end of a certain kind of politics that they're thinking of giving up. I also blame the end of a certain kind of lunch. That is, a phenomenally alcoholic one which you don't pay for. Publishers and agents used to do them very well; now a combination of austerity and prissiness has produced a nation which sits at its desk, dyspeptically nibbling on a Pret sandwich while worrying about being fired. This was one of the grand lunches: between Martin, his agent, and the Moose (the other last-minute guest) we managed to get through a lake of wine and a large pondful of duck and smoked goose. And, because I have been gently steered towards writing something appropriate to the festive season, I shall pass on the thought that what with the bill of fare, tending as it does towards the robust, and the national colours of Hungary, and the, shall we say, heavily-oaked decor of the place, the Gay Hussar is the

* For my changing politics, or views on the Labour Party, see footnote on page 199.

kind of place that feels permanently Yule-ish; but in a good way. Let this not be its last year.

꧁

It's a weird period, the week between Boxing Day and the New Year. It's as if the whole country is wandering around in its pyjamas, muttering to itself. I hunkered down in the Hovel behind a barricade of wine bottles; it seemed like the wisest course of action. Company eventually came in the form of the daughter, who likes to use the Hovel as a launch-pad for her return to university. She also finds it a convivial place and seems to enjoy both my company and my ideas of how to entertain ourselves in the evening. (Her brothers, whom I hasten to add she loves, are not given to conversation once settled in front of their screens.) So the first part of Monday evening is spent eating pizza and watching *Withnail and I*. Normally I am strict about the matter of talking when a film is on, but we've seen *Withnail* so many times between us that occasionally we feel moved to comment when we have something we think is interesting to say about it.

There are, I gather, people who not only do not particularly like this film, but who think that it is a bit odd to have watched it around fifty times. (This is a conservative estimate.) To which I can only reply: would you put a limit on the number of times you would listen to a favourite piece of music? Moreover, although the film may have, to us, reached the condition of music, there are plenty of times in life when it seems directly relevant. One of them, which I keep quiet about, occurs early when Marwood (this is the name of the "I" character), as the result of a 60-hour speed binge, says "my thumbs have gone weird". I have not been on such a binge myself, and neither have my thumbs gone weird; but my groin has. The only way I can describe it is as if someone has left a very tiny mobile phone in the front of my undercrackers, and left it on "vibrate" mode, set to go off every three seconds or so. It is the kind of thing one hesitates to go to the doctor about. Not only is it painless, it is not entirely unpleasant. Then again, it is not normal; I certainly haven't read about this in the user's manual. I am, at the moment, due to illness in the family, and terminal illness at that, becoming rather sensitised to the shocks that flesh is heir to, and I wonder if this is the start of something nasty. Then again, the toes on my left foot have been ever so slightly numb for about ten years now. That hasn't got any better; but then again, it hasn't got any worse.

I suppose I am at the age that the downhill progress starts accelerating. I can see this happening right now on the machine I am using to write this piece. A Lenovo PC of some venerability, it is sort of held together by Sellotape and the keyboard makes a funny squeaking noise as I type. The built-in mouse has ceased to function, as has the fingerprint reader (a rather snazzy feature which particularly impressed my children when this computer was a new arrival). Somehow I managed to dig out an external mouse from the crap on my desk; only now the cursor seems to skip about after a few hours of use, and I will suddenly look to the screen – I've never learned to touch-type – and see that I have inserted several sentences into the first paragraph, where they do not belong.*

Which is all rather tiresome, but not unliveable with. After

* Four and a half years later, I'm still using it.

all, the alternative – to get something done about these things, rather than simply put up with them – does not appeal. One would involve a doctor either putting his or her hand down my pants, or telling me to stop wasting his or her time; and the other would involve either buying a new laptop, which is financially beyond me, or replacing its keyboard again. Having had both a new keyboard and a new screen, my laptop now resembles grandfather's axe, or Theseus's ship, thus raising the philosophical problem of whether something all of whose component parts have been replaced can still be said to be the same thing. Meanwhile, buzz, buzz, goes the groin again, as if a miniaturised submarine full of tiny doctors (including, wondrously, a microscopic Racquel Welch) had got jammed somewhere below the pubic bone. Everything else down there, I hasten to add, is in fine working order. Certainly in finer working order than I might reasonably expect from someone of my age, with my lifestyle. So one does not want to go to the doctor in case one is told that one of the body's key components needs replacing. Or that one needs an external mouse. Actually, that's a line of speculation I'm going to close off right now.

⚜

As a historical footnote, and to confirm the veracity of my account of the Hovel, here below is what Will Self wrote about my trying to cook dinner for him after the astonishingly boozy lunch at the Gay Hussar. Honestly, I was more drunk than I had been for many years; that Mr Self, sober for many years, did not comment on this means . . . something, I suppose.

I COULDN'T BELIEVE THE HOVEL WAS AS BAD AS NICK LEZARD MAKES OUT, SO I WENT TO SEE IT

by Will Self

From without in the chilly night, the Hovel – which is a maisonette above a shop – looked cosy; I could see lamplight and books ranged on shelves.

B EING A SENSITIVE soul (no, really), I was struck by my old mucker Nick Lezard's plaint about his Thanksgiving predicament in his column in the issue before last. If you'll recall, he said that his parents were too old to stand around in the kitchen cooking a turkey et cetera (the et cetera are the trimmings), then there was a palpable half-beat pause in the prose before he supplied an ironic afterthought: "Come to think of it, so am I." Hearkening to his catarrhal wheeze against this dual-generational dying of the light, and wanting to do a bit more for him than just chortling at his misfortune week after week, I arranged to descend on the Hovel with some care cigarettes: I've given up and am de-accessioning one of the finest tobacco stashes still in private hands. Anyway, I thought we might have a sort of freelancers' Christmas party together; usually I just stand by myself in the corner of my writing room, chug on a bottle of crap white wine while shouting at the wall, then masturbate under the desk. When I wake up a couple of hours later I swear I'll never do it again – but perhaps if I did it with poor Tiny Nick (or so I unreasoned), I might feel more wholesomely festive.

I had an ulterior motive as well: I can't be alone among regular readers of Nick's column in finding his portrayal of the Hovel slightly implausible; this, despite knowing him personally for twenty years and having witnessed his complete inadequacy in the face of the most routine household tasks (apart from cooking). Trust me, he is indeed completely boracic – the last pot he was pissing in has long since appeared in the window of Cash Converters by the Edgware Road – but the Gormenghast-inflected portrait of his gaff, complete with rats, filth, cobwebs and indigent ne'er-do-wells, has always struck me as a little de trop. I had to find out for myself whether it was really that bad, and perform a public service by either exploding the myth or confirming the reality. Anyway, the day before I was due to chip up, Nick emailed suggesting he feed me.

Such largesse! There were further exchanges about my high-class food intolerances before he settled on the idea of doing pork belly. Then, approximately three hours before I was due to arrive, he texted saying perhaps it would be better if I ate before I came. Narked – but still sensitive – I texted back asking if he was broke, but the reply came: "No more than usual, it's just that I've had a rather large and bibulous lunch at the Gay Hussar . . . however, there are leftovers available." This mollified me: despite his inability to put on his own underpants (the problem occurs when he's lifted the first leg up; forgetting he's done so, he'll often raise it a second time, fall heavily, and spend hours unconscious before he's discovered), Nick is a superb cook and his leftovers would be anyone else's culinary triumph.

From without in the chilly night, the Hovel – which is a maisonette above a shop – looked cosy; I could see lamplight and books ranged on shelves. Mein host appeared pretty chipper as well when he answered the door. He led me up tip-tilted stairs past a half-landing piled high with old wine boxes; on the scruffy carpet pile lay dust-devils the size of tumbleweeds, while the walls and doors were covered with bilious textured wallpaper of a kind I'd last seen in a B&B in Bideford circa 1974. In the kitchen there was a lot of lino, some of it on the floor, and a shelf of greasy jars and sticky bottles full of desiccated crap. Somewhere in there, I was convinced, would be a small canister of arrowroot that no one had ever opened. But the sink and cooker, though old, appeared serviceable – and there were good smells wafting from the oven. Nick took a pot of boiling rice off the hob; I held the strainer and we drained it together.

Then, just before he was about to dump the rice in the casserole with the lamb I reminded him again about my vampirism: "You're absolutely sure there's no garlic in that lamb?"

"Well," he conceded, "I probably used a clove or so when I was cooking it, but it'll have long since deliquesced by now."

"Um, Nick, that's still some garlic. And anyway, let's get real: no one cooks lamb with just one clove, now, do they?" He admitted that this was surpassing unlikely, and I – being, as I think I've remarked, sensitive to a fault – made light of it, saying: "That's all right, I'll just have some rice."

So we sat in the Hovel's front room at a table strewn with books and papers; Nick had a glass of wine, I had a plate of rice. It was pretty good rice, actually, and I savoured it as I looked about at the broken-backed furniture and the huge collection of valetudinarian "holiday" booze bottles some former flatmate had piled up in the nook by the book-filled fireplace. After supper I went upstairs for a piss. In the bathroom the bath had been turned into some sort of art installation: knock-kneed drying racks were arranged in it and draped with dog-eared fitted sheets. And I saw, lurking in the otherwise empty cabinet over the sink, a medieval box of Alka-Seltzer and thought: "I should be so lucky."

This book has been typeset by
SALT PUBLISHING LIMITED
using Neacademia, a font designed by Sergei Egorov
for the Rosetta Type Foundry in the Czech Republic. It
is manufactured using Holmen Book Cream 70gsm, a
Forest Stewardship Council™ certified paper from the
Hallsta Paper Mill in Sweden. It was printed and bound
by Clays Limited in Bungay, Suffolk, Great Britain.

CROMER
GREAT BRITAIN
MMXIX